Bay Ridge on the Chesapeake

Bay Ridge on the Chesapeake

AN ILLUSTRATED HISTORY

BY
JANE WILSON MCWILLIAMS AND CAROL CUSHARD PATTERSON

BRIGHTON EDITIONS

1986

Copyright © 1986 by Brighton Editions
All rights reserved
Printed in the United States of America

Brighton Editions
P.O. Box 3158, Annapolis, Maryland 21403

Library of Congress Catalog Card Number: 86-72096
ISBN 0-9617617-0-9
ISBN 0-9617617-1-7   (pbk.)

CONTENTS

Foreword   Edward C. Papenfuse — 9

Preface — 11

Introduction — 17

CHAPTER 1, *The Farm* — 23

CHAPTER 2, *The Victorian Resort* — 39

CHAPTER 3, *The Summer Colony* — 107

CHAPTER 4, *The Suburban Community* — 161

Sources — 194

Photograph and Illustration Credits — 196

Street Map of Bay Ridge — 202

Index — 203

*To our parents for the gift of Bay Ridge
and to our children who continue to cherish it*

FOREWORD

"Lover's Lane," between Bay Drive and Barry Avenue c. 1932

For many generations, families remained within a fairly small geographic area throughout their lives, and the background of each family was closely tied to the history of the home neighborhood. This history was absorbed from early childhood as traditions were passed down orally in the natural patterns of daily living. Individuals felt a sense of place and permanence. Today's families, responding to the requirements of employment and the general mobility of modern times, often settle far from the original community of childhood days. Frequent moves can produce a feeling of rootlessness that denies or mitigates against the comfort of familiarity and the sense of belonging. Knowing the history of a community provides this sense of belonging for the newcomer and permanent resident alike.

The recent enthusiastic interest in local histories probably stems in part from this need to touch base with permanence in a changing environment. But there is also the lure of nostalgia—local histories show us the way people lived years ago in what we may assume, however wrongly, to have been an easier time. They provide us with insight into our past and allow us to make comparisons between that past and our own lives today.

From the standpoint of the Chesapeake Bay, any insight into its past is helpful now, as we seek to reestablish the former health of this valuable estuary. Documentation of environmental changes, especially as shown in the Bay Ridge photographs, demands attention. Photographs also play an important role in supplying details, which help us to better understand the customs, interests, and mores of society at a given time, details too ordinary to warrant inclusion in history books.

Carol and Jane have compiled a history that superbly illustrates the merit of photographs to tell the story, to validate the story—not only of Bay Ridge, but of our common heritage. These photographs effortlessly present minute details of daily life when people sailed and fished in long dresses or suits and ties, crabbed in beach pajamas, swam in elaborately modest garb, and traveled in boats with paddle-wheels and smokestacks or in automobiles with side lanterns and running boards. The cycling act at the amusement park, the children's Maypole dance, the crowds of excursionists disembarking at the pier, all are scenes of the way things were but are no more. The Bay Ridge Collection (MdHR D 1710), established by Carol and Jane in preparation for this book, owes its success to the many people who shared their personal and family histories and who permitted their cherished photographs to be reproduced to become part of a more universal record.

The early prints, carefully posed and taken with cumbersome and elaborate equipment, were most often the work of local professional photographers such as George R. Buffham or very talented amateurs such as Margaret Taylor Randall or George W. Riley. Because of the pains taken by these early artists we are able today to step into scenes from the past at will. The later prints, often family snapshots from a hand-held camera, make up in immediacy for what they may lack in photographic quality and thereby capture, informally, the action of the moment. Carefully documented and catalogued, the more than four hundred photographs of the Bay Ridge Collection are a valuable addition to the Maryland State Archives.

—EDWARD C. PAPENFUSE
Archivist and Commissioner of Land
Patents for the State of Maryland

PREFACE

Black Walnut Creek c. 1932

This book is the result of a love affair with Bay Ridge that goes back to our childhoods in a long stream of pleasant memories—memories of summer sun shimmering on sparkling water, of our first small sailboats, of cozy winter Saturdays with friends, of holidays and parents and a neighbor's warm smile—memories of growing up. We first planned to write about Bay Ridge during lazy summer days almost twenty years ago as we watched our own children toddle happily at the edge of the Chesapeake Bay to begin a lifetime of similar memories, and we realized the continuity of that love handed down through the generations. Since then we have worked on the book, sometimes sporadically, at times diligently, but always with the encouragement of other Bay Ridge residents whose cheerful queries of "How's the book coming?" have reinforced our own sense of excitement in the project.

In 1969 and again in 1974 the Bay Ridge Civic Association printed our pamphlet, *A Short History of Bay Ridge*, the foundation on which this book was built. From there, the insatiable search for further details began. Like detectives we followed clues into the past, finding answers to our questions in state and county records, in historical societies and archives, in nineteenth-century newspapers, in ancient hand-drawn plats and maps, and in the wonderful photographs and memories of those who have shared their knowledge, reminiscences, and love of Bay Ridge with us.

Because the past is elusive and can be known only through what has survived, the materials we used, as well as the distinct periods of Bay Ridge history, have defined the shape of the book. Chapter 1, "The Farm," broadly reconstructs the two centuries during which the land was farmed under a number of distinguished landholders. It is based on information preserved in ancient land and tax records and early court cases. Chapter 2, "The Victorian Resort," is a detailed account of the turn-of-the-century decades when Bay Ridge flourished as a grand resort served by steamship and train. It is based primarily on accounts found in nineteenth- and early twentieth-century local newspapers and to some extent on interviews. Chapter 3, "The Summer Colony," describes the pleasures and "pioneer" hardships inherent in the development of Bay Ridge as a summer beach haven for city dwellers. It derives from local records, including the early minutes of the Bay Ridge Civic Association but, moving well into the period of living memory, relies most heavily on oral history and personal accounts. Chapter 4, "The Suburban Community," recounts the establishment of Bay Ridge as a year-around residence for more than three hundred families and the way the community has coped with, and enjoyed, the modern age. It is based on contemporary accounts found in the *Bay Ridge Newsletter,* Bay Ridge Civic Association minutes and records, oral history, and personal memory. The distinct changes in the book's style from one chapter to the next come as much from the shift in source material as from the shift in author, Jane having written Chapters 1 and 3 and Carol having written Chapters 2 and 4.

Some 225 illustrations depict the life-styles and events of each era. These include hand-written land records, illustrated plats, drawings, portraits, newspaper advertisements, and photographs from the days of the steamboat, train, and grand hotel, through the era of Tin Lizzies and flappers, and into the present with Little League teams and pleasure boaters. The illustrations permanently record the fact that people in Bay Ridge have always abundantly enjoyed the pleasures of beach, water, and natural setting, and that although styles in clothing, boats, cars, and homes may have changed, many human pastimes and traditional events have remained the same through the years.

This book is also about people living together cooperatively but as individualists, about traditions and customs handed down from generation to generation, about grass-roots ingenuity and faith in democratic processes. Through words and pictures we have tried to describe the tangible and intangible elements that make Bay Ridge the special place that it is.

Many people are a part of this book, people past and people present, people who have always been part of our lives and people recently met, all of whom are or have been in some interesting way connected with Bay Ridge. Without their interest and support this project would not have been possible. Our debt to individuals and institutions is both enormous and heartfelt.

Through our many years of work on this history, we have enjoyed the support of the Bay Ridge Civic Association. With the assistance of C. Stanley Hollander, former president, we were given access to the association's minutes and papers, a requisite source of information on the twentieth-century history of Bay Ridge. In our search for photographs, we received help from Laura F. Brown of the Steamship Historical Society of America Collection at the University of Baltimore; Mary Mannix and Jeff Goldman at the Maryland Historical Society, Baltimore; Paul Conner and his associates at the National Archives, Washington, D.C.; Alfreda L. Irwin at the Chautauqua Institution, Chautauqua, New York; Franklyn J. Carr and E. E. Edel of the Chessie System Railroads, Cleveland, Ohio; Averil Kadif, Wesley Wilson and Barbara Waybright of the Enoch Pratt Free Library, Baltimore; Mickie Clarke at the Chesapeake and Potomac Telephone Company archives, Baltimore; Brig. Gen. Bernard F. Feingold and 2nd Lt. Kenneth S. Bielecki of the Maryland National Guard, Baltimore; James Cheevers at the Nimitz Library, U.S. Naval Academy, Annapolis; Robert Worden, historian of St. Mary's Roman Catholic Church, Annapolis; as well as the staffs at the Library of Congress, Washington, D.C.; the Annapolis branch of the Anne Arundel County Library; the Baltimore *Sun*; the Annapolis *Capital*; the Circuit Court for Anne Arundel County, Annapolis; and the Smithsonian Institution, Washington, D.C.

We are indebted to Lt. Col. John E. Merriken, USA, ret., well-known railroad historian, for delightful talks, for an on-site inspection of the Bay Ridge and Annapolis Railroad bed, and for permission to quote from his articles and to reproduce his memorabilia and photographs of early railroads and trains. Colonel Merriken has often surprised us with interesting tidbits on Bay Ridge discovered in the course of his own research.

We are also indebted to Dr. Ronald Swerczek, assistant chief of the Diplomatic Branch of the National Archives for arranging the use of previously classified documents of the U.S. State Department; to Jane Anderson O'Meara and Gloryanne Baur Sandrey, who allowed us to quote at length from their written reminiscences; to Philip Cumyn of Montreal, Canada, who generously granted us permission to include photographs and quotations from the book written by his late wife, Anna Key Bartow Cumyn; to Patricia C. Guida for drawing tract maps of early patents and Polli Barker Rodriguez for preparing our base map and the overlay; to Ann Steckmeyer and Glenn Young for timely advice; and to the many individuals who shared their knowledge, memories, photographs, memorabilia, and enthusiasm about Bay Ridge.

Among those with whom we talked, often at great length, or who loaned us materials are Dorothea H. Alter, Charles Barker, William P. Barnhart, Nancy Bauer, Bonnie Stumpf Belch, Dot Bornhoeft, Victor R. Boswell, Charles J. Bove, Jr., Margie Bryce, Harvey R. Butt, Sr., Bill Campbell, Marilyn Carroll, the late Mabel Chappelle, L. Eugene Cronin, Inez Cushard, William G. Cushard, Jr., the late George Daw, Emerson E. Deale, Jr., Mary Tastet Deale, James Dollar, Horace J. Donnelly, Jr., Margaret Moss Dowsett, Clare Green Duckett, Adelaide M. Ervin, Frank D. Ervin, Margaret Collins Ervin, Catherine Faulds, Nick Ferri, Helen Gasch, Mattie Gates, Alice Gilbert, John T. Greeves, Carola Grubbs, Keith Harvey, William A. Hatchl, Raymond J. Hayden, Fred Hecklinger, C. Stanley Hollander, Richard A. Hollander, Ronnie Hollander, David C. Holly, Joseph W. Hopkins, Jr., Kathryn Hopkins, Judith C. Housley, Carol J. Hutchinson, Dorothy Huston, Caroline Ervin Josey, Rose Kass, Dorothea Kelly, Clarence F. Kettler, the late C.

Carroll Lee, Marie Leffingwell, the late Corneal J. Mack, C. John Mack, the late Helen Mack, Anthony J. Maggio, Thelma Iager Maloney, Ed Mason, Margaret Mason, Steve Mason, Ruth McLaine, Henry T. Meneely, Jr., Elizabeth Meneely, Rhea W. Meneely, Brian Merritt, Debbie Mueller, Sandy Brooks Newark, Ralph E. Ogle, Marcia McLaine Outerbridge, L. Noel Patterson, Jr., Ella Paulson, Margaret Paulson, Rolf Paulson, Jane Paynter, Garth Read, Marvin Reeser, Charlotte Rhines, Christopher Rhines, Jean Rhodes, Becky Riley, Rhonda Robins, Polli Barker Rodriguez, the late Mary Irene Roeth, Jean Russo, Renee Sander, James C. Schryver, Susan Senesi, Helen Shores, Eugene H. Sloane, Annie A. Riley Smith, Katherine Smith, Julian Stevens, the late Vesta Tombaugh, the late D. Ross Vansant, James S. Vansant, Elizabeth Vansant, Marion E. Warren, Mary Collins Widmayer, Benjamin B. Wills, Jr., Kathleen Wills, the late Eldeane Wilson, the late James B. Wilson, Mary Ann Hollander Wilson, Ruth Wittler-Rose, Margaret Worthington, Virginia Worthington, and Miriam Yerkes.

When we first decided to include photographs, Dr. Edward C. Papenfuse, Archivist of the State of Maryland, suggested that we establish a photographic collection in the Maryland State Archives to preserve these valuable visual records for future generations. With his support, we were able to draw on the excellent resources of the archives' photographic laboratory. With painstaking care, Paul Houston copied the photographs and memorabilia that we collected, and his sensitivity and skill often illuminated details hidden in faded or damaged photographs. Both at the Hall of Records and, later, from his private studio, Paul worked closely with us to ensure the quality and consistency of the photographic reproductions. Under the guidance and management of Susan Cummings, archivist in charge of Special Collections, and with the logistical support of Teresa Fountain, director of Photolab Services, over four hundred images have been placed in the Bay Ridge Collection. We are indebted to Mame Warren for the system of cataloging these images as well as for her advice on collection procedures and her enthusiastic encouragement. The entire staff of the Hall of Records has been unfailingly patient and helpful with both our research and the collection. Copies of all the photographs in this book, and many others that could not be included, are deposited in the Bay Ridge Collection in the Maryland State Archives at the Hall of Records. Additional photographs will be placed in the collection as they are received.

Joseph Browne, Lynne Browne, Alice Cronin, Eugene Cronin, Stanley Hollander, Phebe Jacobsen, Norwood Johnston, Marcia Outerbridge, and Noel Patterson read all or part of the manuscript and offered thoughtful and much-appreciated written suggestions.

When the time came to publish, we relied on a number of talented people who shared their skills and experience with us: Gerard A. Valerio, who first gave us valuable advice on the organization of materials; Ann Hofstra Grogg, who believed in the book and edited our manuscript; Nancy Bramucci, who rescued us from computer ignorance and keyboarded the typescript; and

Alex and Caroline Castro of Hollowpress, Baltimore, who, with creativity and enthusiasm, designed the book and supervised its publication.

Finally we want to thank our families. Their patience, interest, and good humor have made it possible for us to take the time to put this book together. Special credit and thanks go to Carol's husband, Noel, a fine amateur photographer, whose darkroom enabled us to meet last-minute deadlines.

We hope that this book will be read and enjoyed with as much pleasure as it was researched and written, and that it will strike a chord of nostalgia in a heart or two along the way.

Bay Ridge	JANE WILSON MCWILLIAMS
June 1986	CAROL CUSHARD PATTERSON

INTRODUCTION

Bay Ridge is a small residential community located in Maryland on the western shore of the Chesapeake Bay, approximately three miles southeast of Annapolis. It is within an hour's drive of Baltimore to the north and the nation's capital to the west. The community is situated at the end of the Annapolis Neck peninsula between the Severn and South rivers and is itself bounded by the Severn, the Chesapeake Bay, Lake Ogleton, and Black Walnut Creek.

In summer, prevailing winds blow from the southeast across the wide expanse of the bay, providing welcome relief in hot and humid weather. In winter, the Severn side is battered by cold northwest winds; and at any time of the year northeasters can howl in for three days or more, bringing chilling dampness and high tides.

The land at Bay Ridge is gently rolling, rising from sea level to a windswept bluff at Tolly Point. Low hills and valleys extend from the point to Lake Ogleton and Black Walnut Creek. On this land, the hardwood forest of the precolonial period gave way to cultivated fields of tobacco and corn. Later, those fields, no longer farmed, matured into today's random woods. Here spring bursts to life with native dogwood, wildflowers, and ancient fruit trees now gone wild. Honeysuckle, clematis, trumpet vine, wild rambling rose, bittersweet, mimosa, wild grape, and cherry are native to the area and coexist with the specimen plants of homesites. Blue hydrangeas and orange day lilies traditionally brighten summer yards, while pink, lavender, and white crepe myrtle signal summer's end.

Cottontail rabbits, black and gray squirrels, opossums, and raccoons persevere against encroachment by humans and domestic pets. A host of waterfowl—swans, ducks, herons, ospreys, and gulls—regard Bay Ridge as home on a seasonal or year-around basis. Although the bay's bounty has diminished in recent years, there are still bluefish, perch, crabs, and oysters to be found and enjoyed. Jellyfish, or sea nettles, continue to plague swimmers in years of little rainfall.

For more than three centuries the land's relationship with its inhabitants has paralleled the growth of the Chesapeake tidewater in general. Through the transitions from forest to farm to resort to summer haven to suburb, the history of Bay Ridge is similar to that of other waterfront communities of the upper Chesapeake Bay. And like these other communities, Bay Ridge has a distinct personality of its own. In addition to a common love of location, in addition to a continuity of customs, traditions, and memories, in addition to a certain "down home" warmth and friendliness, what then is the special, intangible quality which Bay Ridgers value so deeply?

It is not pride of uniform appearance, for the architecture of Bay Ridge is eclectic, ranging from "winterized" beach cottages to important architectural gems and including large Spanish stucco villas, modern colonials and Victorians, space-efficient split levels and ranchers, and natural wood homes of contemporary design. It is no longer the identification with a common background, for many of today's Bay Ridgers have come from other sections of the country, bringing with them a wide variety of experiences. It is not insistence upon a particular life-style, for if Bay Ridge residents are anything, they are individualistic. Not for them the regimentation of the controlled and carefully planned residential development; not for them the enforced mores of the socially self-conscious neighborhood. Young or old, wealthy or of modest circumstances, native or newcomer, gregarious or reclusive, Bay Ridgers have always freely enjoyed community life, each in his or her own particular way.

Perhaps this, then, is what makes Bay Ridge so special, for it is to preserve their individual freedoms that its residents work to preserve the community. Somehow, over the years, Bay Ridge has attracted people who understand the basic tenet of a democratic society: that freedom entails responsibility, whether that means long hours of volunteer service in a sixty-year-old civic association, representation at a local hearing, participation in a fund raiser or cleanup project, or simply cooperation in abiding by the zoning and Commons rules. The routine give-and-take of neighbors is repeated in the community-wide pattern of caring: caring for neighbors as individuals, caring for the community at large, caring for the land and the water and the life that has been shaped from past to present.

Bay Ridge on the Chesapeake

"Raking for oysters off Tally's Point reef," 1879

1. The Farm

The mildnesse of the ayre, the fertilitie of the soyle, and situation of the rivers are so propitious to the nature and use of man, as no place is more convenient for pleasure, profit, and mans sustenance, under that latitude or climat. . . . The waters, Isles, and shoales, are full of safe harbours for ships of warre or marchandize, for boats of all sorts, for transporation or fishing.

       Capt. John Smith, 1606

CHAPTER I

The Farm

JANE WILSON MCWILLIAMS

Capt. John Smith, traveling up and down the Chesapeake Bay in the first decade of the seventeenth century, was probably the first European to see the peninsula of land that would later be known as Bay Ridge. Before him, Indians had hunted on the land, leaving behind arrow points found by later residents. The first man to realize the land's potential for settlement was William Durand, leader of a group of religious dissenters, who fled Anglican Virginia with his family and servants in the winter of 1649. After receiving permission from Maryland's more tolerant government, he scouted the Chesapeake Bay for a place where he and his colleagues might settle. He chose a long, narrow river on the western side of the bay well away from the Catholic settlements at St. Mary's but across from Kent Island, which at that time had a fort and a fair number of inhabitants. In December 1649 Durand's fellow dissenters left Virginia to begin a new life in Maryland at a place they called Providence on the north shore of the mouth of the river they named Severn.

Using Providence on Greenbury Point as a base, these Virginians, already experienced in colonial settlement, ranged the shores of the bay and its rivers from the Patapsco south in search of suitable tracts for their plantations. Durand himself claimed the area that is now Bay Ridge, but never had it surveyed or patented and almost certainly never lived there.

The first recorded English resident of Bay Ridge was Thomas Tolly, who gave his name to the point where the Severn River joins the Chesapeake. Tolly, whose name is also spelled Tolley, Talley, or Tally in the records, arrived in Maryland in 1654 as an indentured servant. By 1657 he was living on or near the point, and in 1664, having fulfilled the obligations of his indenture, he was able to buy one hundred acres surrounding the point from Durand. The fact that Durand had not secured title to the land from Lord Baltimore caused problems for Tolly's children, but that first Thomas, "not mistrusting the title of the said Durand to the said Land, Did build Improve & quietly enjoy the same During his life." Thomas Tolly married, had a family, and became a reasonably successful planter. When he died early in 1670, his belongings included four beds, three books, a looking glass, brass kettle, skillets, and "Chaffendise," and two male servants of his own. His house had "inner" and "outward" rooms, and his stock included hogs, thirty-two head of cattle, and a riding horse with bridle and saddle. Dr. Jean Russo has estimated the value of Tolly's personal property at 24,326 pounds of tobacco, or about £114 sterling. According to her recent study of seventeenth-century Anne Arundel County residents, Tolly was in the middle wealth bracket for the county as a whole and well above the £75 sterling average estate value of his fellow Middle Neck Hundred residents.

Thomas Tolly's neighbor near the point was Samuel Withers, who had immigrated as a free man in 1653 and married Elizabeth, the daughter of William Durand. In 1657, for 2,000 pounds of tobacco, Durand sold Withers land adjoining Thomas Tolly. Withers had the good sense to have his land surveyed, and in 1663 he received a patent for 250 acres extending from Howell's Creek (now Lake Ogleton) to the bay and from Tolly's land to Saughier's Creek (now Black Walnut Creek). He named this tract Withers Durand, presumably in recognition of both his and his wife's families.

Samuel Withers rose quickly in politics, serving on the Parliamentary Commission that governed Maryland from 1654 until 1658, as justice of the Provincial and Anne Arundel County courts, and finally, in 1669, as a representative to the General Assembly. A merchant as well as planter, Withers patented more than 1,300 acres in Anne Arundel, Talbot, and Cecil counties and, when he died in 1671, owned personal property worth more than three times that of Tolly, including nine servants and twenty-four muskrat skins.

Most of the early settlers of Anne Arundel County had come as religious "Independents" or as Anglicans, but some later harkened to the teachings of Quaker missionary Elizabeth Harris, who visited the Severn in the late 1650s. William Durand, Samuel Withers, and Thomas Tolly and his wife were among those who became associated with the Society of Friends. For many years the owners of the peninsula were Quakers—industrious, educated, and highly principled.

After Thomas Tolly's death, his son Thomas, Jr., became suspicious of the title to his land and applied for permission to survey and patent it. His certificate of survey for 103 acres, which he called New Worcester, was filed in October 1679, but shortly thereafter Thomas, Jr., sold the land to Capt. Richard Hill. Thus it was Richard Hill who finally received the first official patent for Tolly's Point in 1684. The bounds of Hill's patent follow earlier descriptions; his new total of 140 acres was probably the result of a more accurate survey. The bounds of the Tolly's Point patent

Fig. 1. Modern drawing of the metes and bounds of the Withers Durand patent, 1663. William Durand's sale of land to Samuel Withers specified that its eastern boundary adjoined Thomas Tolly, but an error in the recorded patent put Tolly's land to the west.

Fig. 2. Modern drawing of the metes and bounds of the original Tolly's Point patent, 1684. Because ancient boundary descriptions referred to trees and waterways and gave only general directions for each line, they are almost impossible to plot accurately.

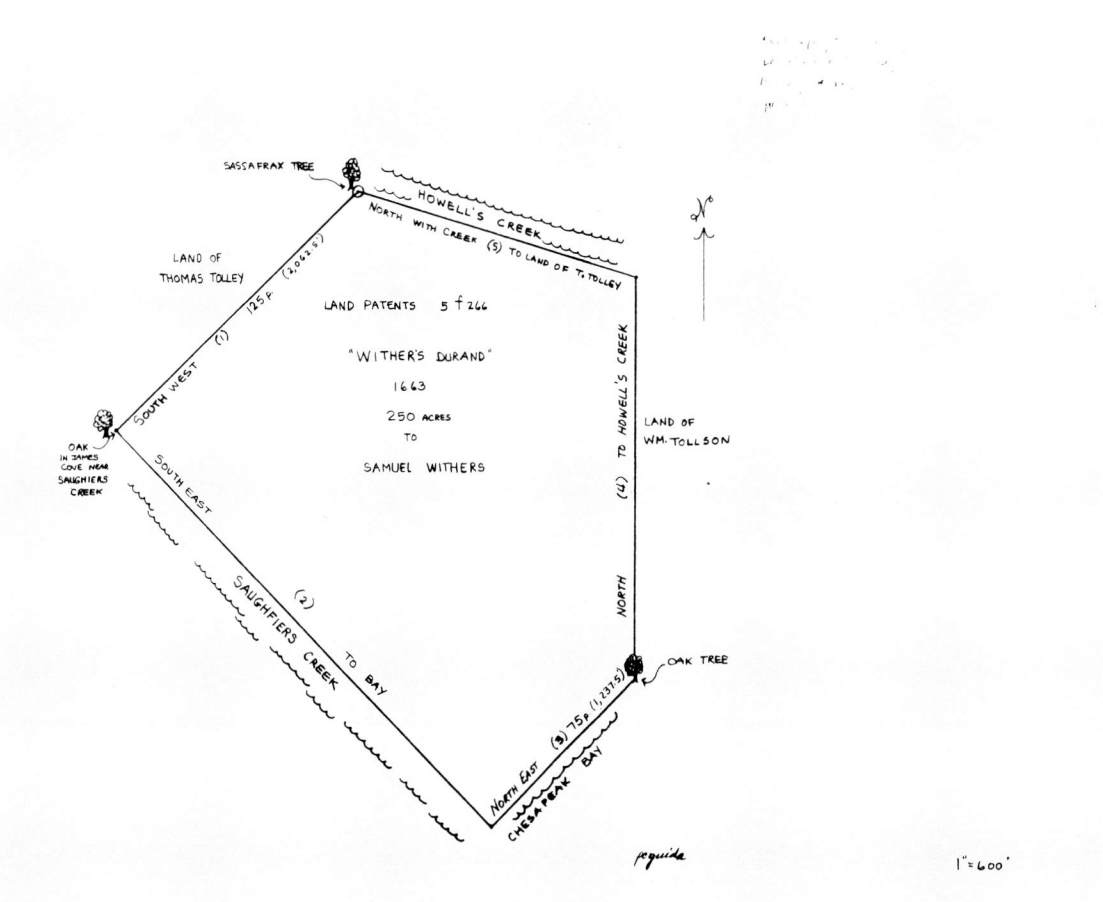

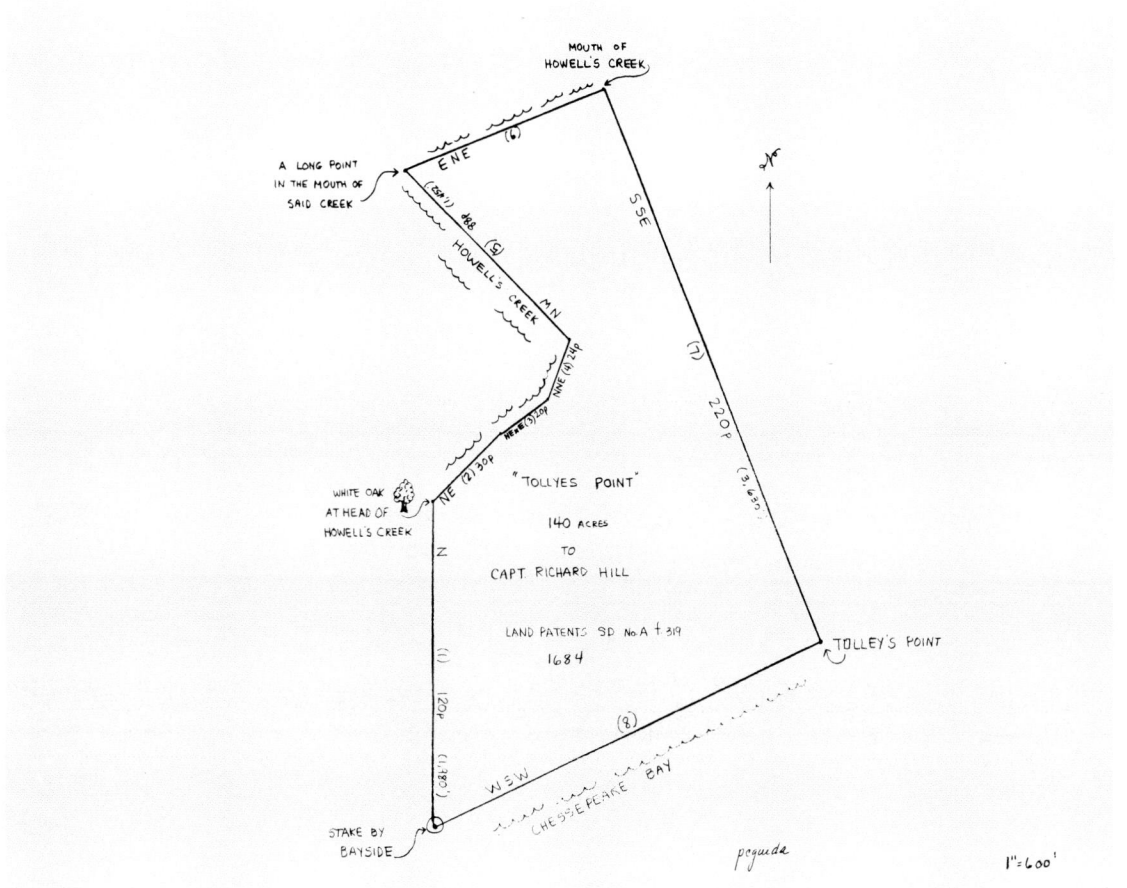

Given att our Citty of St Maries under the great seale of our said Province of Maryland this three & twentieth day of Aprill in the ninth Year of our Dominion
over our said Province &c Annoq Domini One thousand six hundred
Eighty four Wittnesse our selfe

~~~~~~~~~~~~

Capt Richd Hill
Pat: Conf 140 Ac.

Charles &c To all persons to whom these presents shall Come greeting
in our Lord God Everlasting Whereas Thomas Tolly late of Ann Arrundell County in our said Province of Maryland Deceased
the Second day of September One thousand six hundred Sixty four
bought & purchased of William Durand of the same County a small
tract or parcell of Land Contayning about One hundred Acres as
by a Certaine Writing of Bargain & Sale thereof Doth appear
Whereupon the said Thomas Tolly not mistrusting the title of the
said Durand to the said Land, Did build Improve & quietly enioy
the same Dureing his life And Thomas Talley sonne & heire of the
said Thomas Talley deced hath since the Death of his ffather quietly
enioyed the same and paid our Rents for the same & noe person
had molested or troubled him in the quiet Enioyment thereof
But the said Durands title not appearing upon Record the said
Thomas Tolly Junr was in great fear not Only of loosing his said
Land but alsoe all his Labour Cost and trouble in Improveing
& building upon the same unlesse Wee should relieve him there
in And thereupon he humbly supplicated & Obteyned our Speciall
Warrant to Resurvey the same And Whereas Capt Richard
Hill of Ann Arrundell County aforesaid hath Informed Us that
the said Tolly pursuant to Our said speciall Warrant Caused the
said Land to be resurveyed & laid out according to the tenor of
the said Warrant but before he Could returne the Certificate
to Us in Councill he Dyed haveing first made Sale of the said
land unto the said Hill as the said Hill made appear unto Us
Whereupon the said Hill humbly supplicated Us to grant him
a Pattent of Confirmation for the same to him & his heirs
and he haveing made Returne of the Certificate of Resurvey
aforesaid into Our Land Office and Wee Willing to make good
and Confirme his title to the same Wee Doe therefore hereby
Give grant & Confirme unto him the said Capt Richard Hill

Tolleys point

all that tract or parcell of land now Resurvey Called Tolleys point
lying in the said County on the West side of Chessopeake bay beginning
att a marked stake by the said Bay side & runing North One hundred
and twenty perches to a bounded White Oak standing att the head
of a Brooke Called howells Creek then Northeast thirty perches
then North east and by East twenty perches then North Northeast
twenty four perches then North West Eighty Eight perches to a long
point

began at a marked stake on the bay side (probably just south of present Upshur Avenue), stretched diagonally across the peninsula to the head of Howell's Creek (probably near where Lake Drive divides), and then followed the creek to the Severn, came around Tolly Point, and continued down the bayfront to the stake. In a 1736 deed for this property, the diagonal line across the land is described as a ditch, whether natural or man made is not noted, and in a later deed the line is marked by a row of cedar trees.

Thus, before the end of the seventeenth century the 387 acres of land that is now Bay Ridge had been divided into two patents, or land grants, from Maryland's proprietor. Together, Tolly's Point and Withers Durand encompassed the peninsula bounded by Howell's Creek, the Severn River, the Chesapeake Bay, and Saughier's Creek. The land was heavily wooded, with stands of oak, sassafras, poplar, and hickory. Even though situated in an ideal location, neither tract developed into a typical Chesapeake tidewater plantation with the traditional manor house and outbuildings, because almost all of their seventeenth- and eighteenth-century owners had their principal plantations elsewhere. For most of the colonial period and well into the nineteenth century, the land was occupied by the tenants or slaves of absentee landlords who, although wealthy and often highly placed men with an eye for good property, were none the less probably only occasional visitors to Bay Ridge.

Capt. Richard Hill was a prominent planter and merchant who held a variety of county and provincial offices from 1674 until his death. He represented Anne Arundel County in the General Assembly, was naval officer of Annapolis, chief justice of both the Provincial and Anne Arundel County courts, and an officer in the provincial militia. He married the widow of a respected Anne Arundel County Quaker and owned more than 1,700 acres of land as well as property in Annapolis, the new capital of Maryland. Hill probably did not live at Tolly's Point; it is more likely that he leased it, although no record of such a lease survives.

Fig. 3. The patent for Tolly's Point, granted to Richard Hill April 26, 1684, described the history of the land.

When Richard Hill died in 1700, Tolly's Point descended to his eldest son, Joseph, also a merchant and Maryland legislator, and from Joseph to his brother Henry. Henry resurveyed the land in 1728 to include the West Lake Drive peninsula and increase the tract to 159 acres. Eight years later, he sold it, with "all houses, edifices, and buildings," to "John Andrews of Anne Arundel County, Gent.," for £100 sterling.

Meanwhile Withers Durand and the rest of Samuel Withers's land had been transferred by will to Samuel Withers, Jr., who subsequently died in Talbot County in 1697, leaving a widow but no children. Withers Durand and the hundred-acre tract adjoining it on the west, James's Hill, were eventually left without tax-paying owners and, under provincial law, were thus available to anyone who wished to buy them again from the proprietor. In 1707 William Bladen took ownership of the two tracts and combined them into a new patent called Isabella's Farm.

A well-educated English lawyer, Bladen held several high provincial offices and owned thousands of acres of land in Maryland.

No doubt he patented Isabella's Farm as pure speculation, for he immediately sold it, in its original pieces: 250 acres, formerly Withers Durand, to Alice Moore, and 100 acres, formerly James's Hill, to Ezekial Gillis. James's Hill included most of the area now known as Annapolis Cove.

Alice Moore had initially been married to Samuel Withers, Jr., but married three times after his death. Her fourth and last husband was John Andrews, the same John Andrews who bought Tolly's Point in 1736. Since there were specifically mentioned houses and "edifices" on Withers Durand in the 1720s and 1730s, it is possible that Alice maintained her home there throughout her various marriages. John Andrews died in 1742 and Alice in late 1744, both with wills and both with relatives only in England. John left five slaves and some silver plate marked with arms and crest to Alice, but his land went to one of his sisters in London, who sold Tolly's Point to Joseph Hill in 1744. Alice devised her real estate to her brother in Long Ashton Parish, Somerset, if alive, or to two local friends if her brother was dead. As it happened, her brother predeceased her, and, although his sons claimed the land and attempted to sell it, the two local friends asserted their rights and split the 250 acres between them. Their heirs sold both 125-acre parcels to Joseph Hill in 1758 and 1759 respectively.

A descendant of Capt. Richard Hill, Joseph Hill owned plantations on both sides of South River. He did not live on either of the Bay Ridge tracts and probably leased them to tenants. At the time of Hill's death in 1761, his land on Annapolis Neck extended along the bay and rivers from Harness Creek to Spa Creek and included much of what is now Hillsmere, Arundel-on-the-Bay, Bay Ridge, Annapolis Roads, and Eastport. His young granddaughter, Henrietta Margaret Hill, was his primary heir and became the owner of more than 2,000 acres of county land.

Henrietta, who usually signed her name "Henry Margaret," married Benjamin Ogle in All Hallows Parish on September 13, 1770. She was nineteen, he twenty-one; their marriage would last almost thirty-nine years. They were perhaps the most illustrious owners of the Bay Ridge land; but, as had so often been the case, this was not their principal residence.

The only surviving son of Samuel Ogle, who had served for many years as governor of Maryland, Benjamin Ogle was educated in England. Shortly after his return to Maryland, he gained possession of his father's 2,177-acre estate, Belair, in Prince George's County. Belair and their Annapolis townhouse were home for the Ogles and their young family. Henry Margaret's land across Spa Creek was known as The Farm. There Ogle raised cattle and sheep and thoroughbred racehorses. Ogle may have had a special interest in part of his wife's land since he was the great-grandson of William Bladen, who had patented Isabella's Farm so many years before.

Although Benjamin Ogle had been a member of the Provincial Council until 1776, he subscribed to the patriot's Oath of Fidelity in 1778 and joined an Annapolis company of revolutionary militia. He was later elected governor of Maryland for three consecutive one-year terms, in 1798, 1799, and 1800.

In March 1776, during a standoff between Maryland's warship *Defence* and the British sloop of war *Otter*, the local militia manned Tolly Point to prevent a British invasion (although there is no evidence that one was planned). The following June, when HMS *Fowey* anchored off the point to take on board Robert Eden, Maryland's last provincial governor, and accepted some servants and a deserter against the orders of the revolutionary government, the militia again turned out along the shore and small armed local vessels patrolled the waters between Tolly, Greenbury, Hackett's, and Horn points.

There is no record of who stood on Tolly Point to witness Adm. Richard Howe's formidable fleet of 260 British transports as they sailed menacingly past the mouth of the Severn on the morning of August 21, 1777 on their way to land troops near Elkton for the invasion of Philadelphia. Surely someone was there, awed at first by the fearsome power of the British navy and then disgusted by the refuse that floated ashore. Locals complained that the beaches were littered with the rotting bodies of British horses that had died in transit.

The deprivations of war curtailed the exciting social life the Ogles had enjoyed in the first years of their marriage, so Henry Margaret was overwhelmed with enthusiasm when troops under General Lafayette camped on her land across Spa Creek in the spring of 1781. "The town is so dull it would be intolerable were it not for the officers. . . . The divine Marquis de la Fayette is in town, and is quite the thing," she wrote. "We abound in French officers, and some of them are very clever. . . . But the Marquis—so diffident, so polite, in short everything that is clever." When patriot troops embarked from Annapolis that September for Yorktown, Benjamin Ogle was less enthusiastic. Four sheep from his farm were killed and carried off by sailors without payment. Years later Ogle's son remembered that his father had been "much plagued" by intruders from ships in the bay.

After the war the Ogles resumed their social whirl, unfortunately beyond the extent of their finances. They sold almost half of Henry Margaret's land during this period, but retained the Eastport and Bay Ridge peninsulas. In 1790 Ogle had fifty slaves in Anne Arundel County and, according to a 1798 assessment, owned houses on both the Eastport peninsula and at Tolly's Point. On Tolly's Point there was a single story frame dwelling measuring 40 by 20 feet and a "negro quarter" 30 by 18 feet. The distinction between "dwelling" and "negro quarter" would seem to imply that the dwelling was occupied by a white family, either a tenant or, possibly, the Ogles themselves as a farm retreat. The latter is more likely at this time since they had conveyed Belair to their son in 1796. There were no buildings on Withers Durand in 1798.

In April 1808, Benjamin Ogle resurveyed Tolly's Point and Isabella's Farm into one tract of 470½ acres that he named Ogleton. The bounds ran from a point on "a Creek called The Cat Hole, otherwise called Howell's Creek," with the creek to the Severn, around Tolly Point, along the bay to Black Walnut Creek, up the northeastern shore of Black Walnut to a cove called James's Cove,

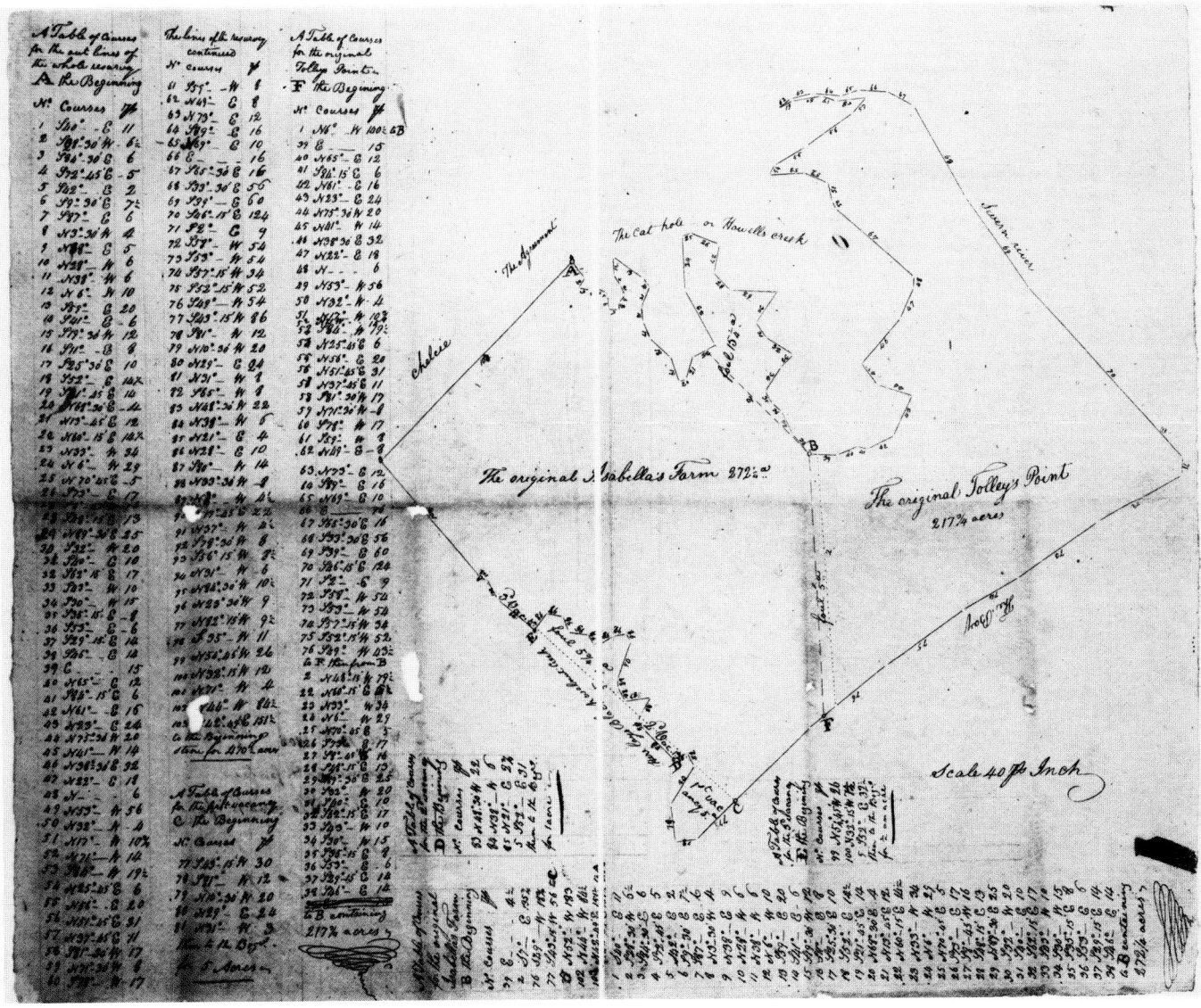

Fig. 4. Surveyor's plat of Ogleton, April 14, 1808, combining Tolly's Point and Isabella's Farm (originally Withers Durand and James's Hill). By this time land descriptions had become much more specific.

and across the land, adjoining Lewis Duvall's property, to the beginning. In several areas, especially along Black Walnut Creek, the surveyor found that the shoreline had changed since the last survey eighty years before.

The Ogles never patented Ogleton. Benjamin died on July 7, 1809, and the Annapolis *Maryland Gazette* of July 21, 1809 noted: "His remains, agreeable to his request, were privately interred the same evening on his farm near the city." Ogle could have been buried on either Horn Point or Ogleton; his grave has not been found.

During the War of 1812, with hostile British again on the bay, slaves belonging to Henry Margaret Ogle sought refuge, and freedom, with the enemy. Henry Margaret went aboard a British ship requesting the return of the runaways, but she was unsuccessful. Years later her estate received $3,402 from the British government as recompense for her loss under the terms of the Treaty of Ghent.

Landon Brooks, an early surveyor and resident of the community of Bay Ridge, used to explain the presence of Scotch broom on the bayside cliffs by saying that seeds of the plant had been brought ashore by British horses in 1814. While there is no evidence of military action on Tolly Point during the war, it is certainly possible that British men, or even horses, landed there.

Henry Margaret Ogle died on August 14, 1815, leaving her Annapolis Neck land to support a daughter and her children. The next month her son advertised the sale of her estate including slaves, cattle, farm animals, and equipment "at the farm called 'Tally's Point' " along with the 470½ acre farm itself, a dwelling, and barns. In October of that year, Henry Maynadier of Anne Arundel County purchased Ogleton and some of the Horn Point land for $32.75 an acre. He also bought Lewis Duvall's 301-acre tract, Cedar Grove, which adjoined Ogleton on the west.

Henry Maynadier, the third generation of an Eastern Shore family, had served as a surgeon in the First Maryland Regiment of the Continental Army during the Revolution. He is said to have removed a ball from the leg of Henry Margaret Ogle's "clever" General Lafayette at the battle of Brandywine. In 1781 Dr. Maynadier married Elizabeth Key, a St. Mary's County girl who had spent much of her childhood with her aunt Elizabeth Ross Scott in Annapolis and at Belvoir on Generals Highway. The Maynadiers had two daughters, both of whom died in infancy and were buried at Belvoir. Elizabeth Maynadier inherited an interest in Belvoir through her aunt, but in 1815 she agreed to transfer that interest to her husband in exchange for the sole rights to the Ogle and Duvall land on Annapolis Neck.

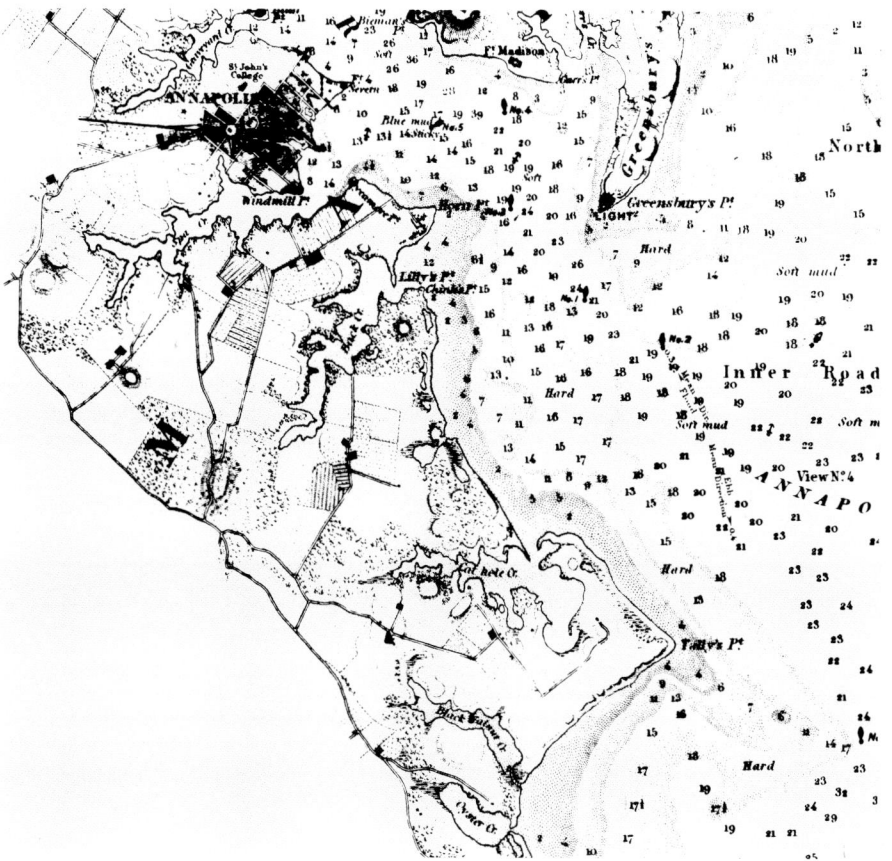

Fig. 5. Detail from a chart of the Annapolis Harbor dated 1884. The typography is the same as that of an 1846 chart.

The Maynadiers obtained the patent to Ogleton in 1828, but their permanent residence remained in Annapolis. Edward Baldwin was living on Tolly Point in 1819 when he took up a drifting "batteau" and advertised for its owner in the *Maryland Gazette*.

Just as she had been informally adopted by her childless aunt, Elizabeth Scott, so Elizabeth Maynadier became "Aunt Maynadier" to her grandniece, Maria Lloyd Key, daughter of Francis Scott Key. Maria Key made extended visits to the Maynadier home in Annapolis and to their land on Annapolis Neck. It was probably during one of these visits that she fell in love with Henry Maynadier's dashing nephew and namesake, Henry Maynadier Steele. They were married in 1823 and lived for a time near Elk Ridge. Sometime after 1840 the Steeles moved to Tolly Point Farm, which Maria had inherited from her great-aunt in 1832. The 1850 census shows Henry M. Steele farming 650 of their 850 acres on the peninsula. His principal crops were corn and wheat, and the farm's livestock included horses, cattle, oxen, sheep, and swine. Tradition says that crops were shipped to market from a dock at the head of the lake.

Fig. 6. Henry Maynadier Steele c. 1840

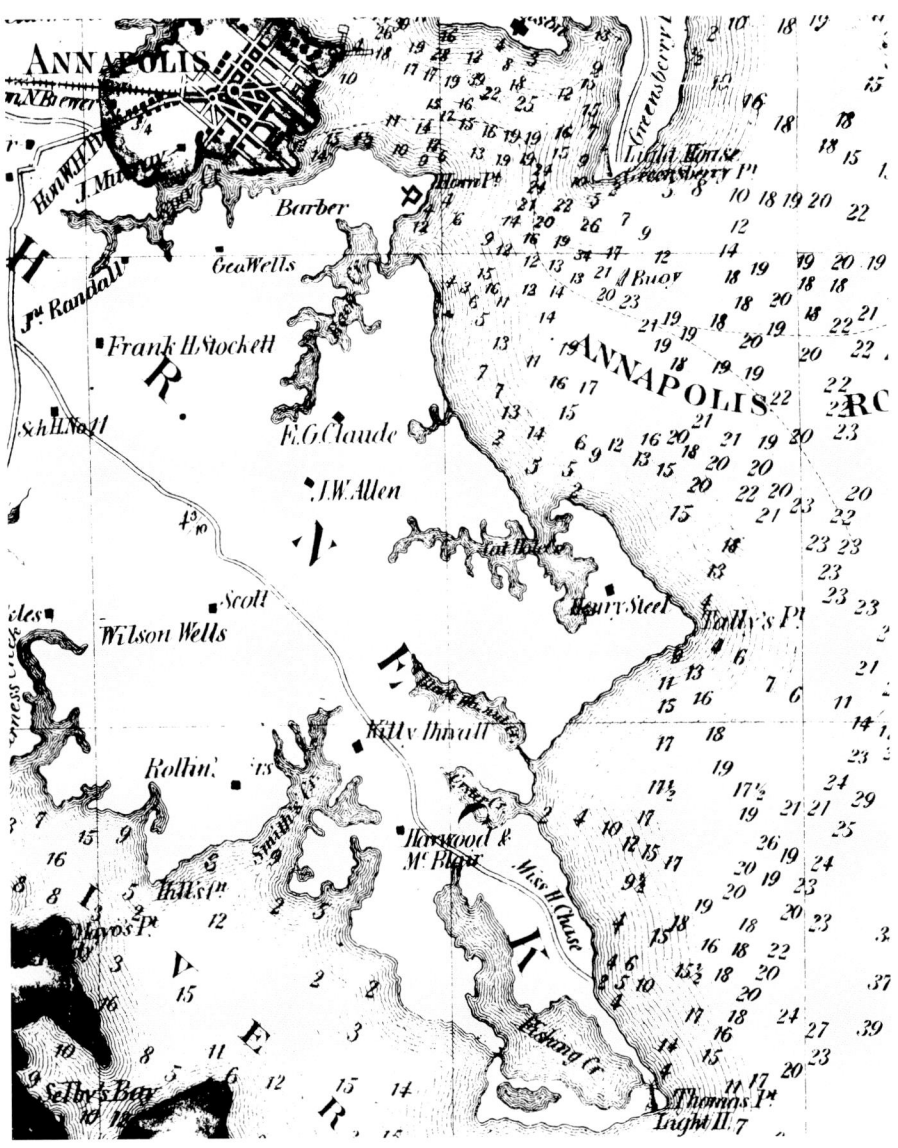

Fig. 7. Detail from Simon J. Martenet's Map of Anne Arundel County, *1860*

The reminiscences of Maria and Henry Steele's fifth daughter, Anna Key Steele, recorded lovingly by her granddaughter Anna Key Bartow Cumyn in *The Bartow Family: A Genealogy*, give a clear and poignant picture of her father and their life on Tolly Point Farm over a hundred years ago.

> My earliest recollection of him [Henry Maynadier Steele] was when in his prime and vigor he rode off each morning to make the round of his estate—a tract of eight hundred acres on Chesapeake Bay. Through the woods gate, through embowered shady roads, on to the fallow fields, the wide acres of wheat and corn, past the serried ranks of tobacco above the bay shore, often stopping beside a plowed field to give an approving word to a novice young negro for the plumb straight line of his furrow across a sixty acre field.
>
> We children loved to walk with him and our mother. In the quiet lanes and forest roads we learned the names of simples, even the names of weeds and how to distinguish the forest trees by their bark and leaves. . . . The beach was a delight with its hard sand and smooth washed driftwood. There were stratas in the high bluffs of the shore of fine black sand that we carried home to fill the sand box on Father's desk. No blotters in those days, only black sand shaken out of a perforated box to dry the heavy ink lines of a quill pen. Also a strata of Fuller's earth, like fine grained white putty out of which we molded bricks and marbles to dry in the sun. And as Father sat on the beach with Mother he carved out tiny boats of drift bark for each with a leaf through the mast for us to sail on the inlets here and there.
>
> Henry Maynadier Steele died at the height of the Civil War, his end hastened by his anxiety for Mother and me, surrounded by encampments of Yankee troops. On one of the last days that we drove in to Annapolis, as we passed through the lines of tents and soldiers on either side of the road they called after us "there goes old secesh and his daughter." I saw his nostrils flare and his color blaze and he said to me "we will not drive in again—we will go in by bateau."
>
> Towards the end of the winter in 1863 his heart trouble increased and caused him much distress. I helped Mother to nurse him. He would eat a few oysters or mushrooms that I cooked for him over the open fire or take an egg nog or frozen cream if I made them while he looked on. . . . He died at one o'clock in the day on the 29th of March, 1863 and was buried from St. Anne's Church, Annapolis. Through a light fall of snow the winter wheat showed green and springlike as he was taken away from his home. His own slaves were his pallbearers and sat either side of his coffin in the church. I was twenty three years old and to lose my father seemed like the end of the world.

Fig. 8. Anna Key Steele (1840–1927) at the time of her marriage to Jacob Field Bartow, January 1864

The family suffered greatly during and after the war, and the year after Henry Steele's death, Maria sold part of Tolly Point Farm to Jacob Brandt, Jr., of Baltimore City for $6,500. Brandt's purchase of 146 acres was the land of the 1728 Tolly's Point patent, including the West Lake Drive peninsula. His bounds crossed the peninsula from Cat Hole Creek to the bay side near the south end of a row of cedar trees, apparently planted years before to mark the division between Tolly's Point and Withers Durand. Buildings

Fig. 9. Detail from G. M. Hopkins's Atlas of Anne Arundel County, 1878

Fig. 10. 1886 plat showing the first two parcels of Bay Ridge land purchased by James H. Vansant

and improvements were included in the sale—presumably the house shown on the 1860 Martenet Map. Brandt was to have a right of way through the rest of Tolly Point Farm to the main county road.

A suit against Jacob Brandt in the 1870s forced the auction of his 146 acres, and in March 1879 the land was sold to James H. Vansant of Annapolis for $2,190. It was here that Vansant's Bay Ridge Company would build a grand Victorian resort.

In 1885 James Vansant purchased an additional 137¾ acres of Ogleton from Maria Steele. This piece cut across present-day Bay Ridge from Black Walnut Creek roughly along Dewey Drive to Lake Ogleton opposite Kass Park and extended north to the tract already owned by the Bay Ridge Company. There were a barn and dwelling on this second parcel, probably in the neighborhood of Wainwright Avenue.

The next year Vansant bought the final 103¼ acres of what is now Bay Ridge from Maria's son Frank Key Steele for $5,500. These last two parcels from the Steeles comprised, roughly, the original Withers Durand patent of 1663. Maria Steele kept the rest of her land, and her grandchildren spent holidays at the farm, gathering memories of their own, until her death in 1897.

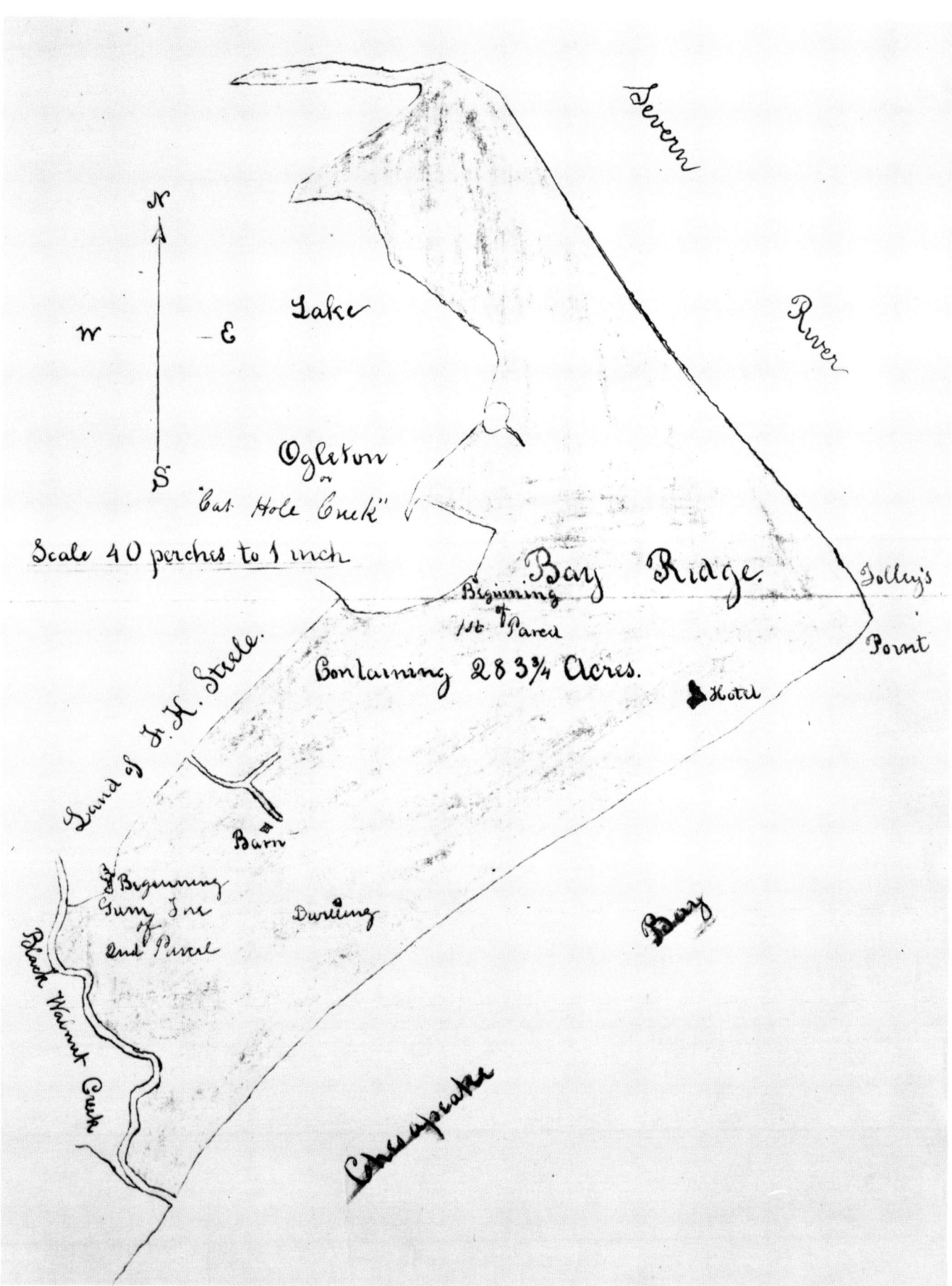

Bay Ridge resort, seen from steamship pier c. 1888

2. The Victorian Resort

Along the bay the steamboat's whistle pierced the silence of even the most remote river to meet and harmonize with train whistles on shore. Spawned by new technology, steam had conquered water and land, taking crops to market and returning the goods of industry to farms and small towns throughout the tidewater. Passenger and freight steamers, with flags flying and smokestacks streaming, bustled off to appointed destinations on schedules set by the great competitive steam packet lines—Weems, Tolchester, and the Maryland Steamship Company. To provide deep-water landings for these large boats, long piers were constructed at ports-of-call along the Chesapeake's shallow shores. At the same time, railroads virtually criss-crossed the state to link up with the major ship lines. Together, the steamboat and train enabled people to travel with an efficiency and speed not previously imagined. Bay resorts became more accessible and enormously popular. Sharing the waters with the steamboat, a large navy of sailing workboats unique to the Chesapeake—skipjacks, bugeyes, small schooners, and sloops—continued to harvest what seemed then to be an unending plentitude of fish, oysters, and crabs. Here and there a sailboat or motor launch heralded a new era of pleasure yachting yet to come.

CHAPTER 2

The Victorian Resort

CAROL CUSHARD PATTERSON

Fig. 1. Dapper excursionists posed for a tintype at Bay Ridge c. 1895.

The years after the Civil War brought rapid prosperity to America, a prosperity imbued with both Victorian morality and a national pride that found full expression in the Gay Nineties. These were the lavish years of the big railroads, of new marvels in electricity, of the grand hotel, and of entertainment on a large scale. These were the years of ladies in high-necked blouses, sedately elegant in long skirts and bustles; of men in high starched collars and knobby straw hats, men with money in their pockets, ready to travel, to vacation, to enjoy the most peaceful, romantic years America had known. The traditional Sunday "outing" evolved into the "excursion" as railroad magnates, turning the times to profit, created attractive recreation parks and elaborately appointed hotels in conjunction with the rail lines, thereby catering to the national enthusiasm for vacationing on a scale never before possible.

In Bay Ridge these were the resort years, the years when people came by the thousands to a grand hotel and amusement park on Tolly Point overlooking the Chesapeake Bay. They came to relax, to swim, to dine, to be amused and entertained. Following the dictates of Victorian propriety, they came to picnic in their Sunday suits and long waist-cinched dresses and to swim in their modest bathing costumes. They came to enjoy the concerts at the bandstand, the moonlight dances on the pavilion deck, and the fireworks displays over the water and under the stars. They came by horse and carriage, by rail or steamboat; and the memories they carried home with them are to be envied. For two shining decades they came, until the century turned and all of the excitement of the Victorian era churned slowly to an end as the nation faced the sobering concerns of World War I.

It is not surprising, considering the location, that in the late nineteenth century when the Steele family began selling off portions of their land, Bay Ridge was developed into a lavish amusement park with the financial support of the Baltimore and Ohio Railroad. This transformation was expedited, in large measure, by an energetic young entrepreneur, James H. Vansant, the Annapolis Adams Express agent and owner of the Annapolis–Bay Ridge Hiring and Livery Stables located opposite the train depot on West Street in Annapolis. It was Vansant who, as the moving force behind the Bay Ridge Company that developed the resort, bought Tolly Point in 1879. That summer a grand hotel was built on the bluff overlooking the Chesapeake Bay. In 1880 the resort was opened to the public on a modest scale, serviced by one steamer from Baltimore, the *Theodore Weems* of the Weems Line. Vansant's subsequent purchases of Steele land in 1885 and 1886 provided room for expansion as the resort flourished. With a contract signed on March 27, 1886, Vansant secured the rights-of-way for a connecting rail line from Annapolis to Bay Ridge. Completed and operating by early July 1886, the line was named the Bay Ridge and Annapolis Railroad, with Vansant as a member of its first board of directors.

By the summer of 1886, Bay Ridge—approximately 387 acres on the Annapolis Neck peninsula—had been transformed into what local newspapers called "The Queen Resort of the Chesapeake." Thousands of people came daily by train and steamship from Baltimore, Washington, D.C., and Annapolis. It was not long before Bay Ridge also became popular with excursionists from the Eastern Shore and Frederick, from Pennsylvania, Delaware, and even New York. During these years before the age of the automobile, vacationers traveled to Annapolis by train on either the Washington,

Fig. 2. James H. Vansant c. 1887—a studio portrait by George R. Buffham, Bay Ridge resort photographer

Fig. 3. Ancestors of modern day resident Polli Barker Rodriguez relaxed at Tolly Point beach—"Aunt Sadie, Mr. Campbell, Mrs. Campbell, Aunt Mamie, Mr. Godfried. Bay Ridge, Summer, 1887."

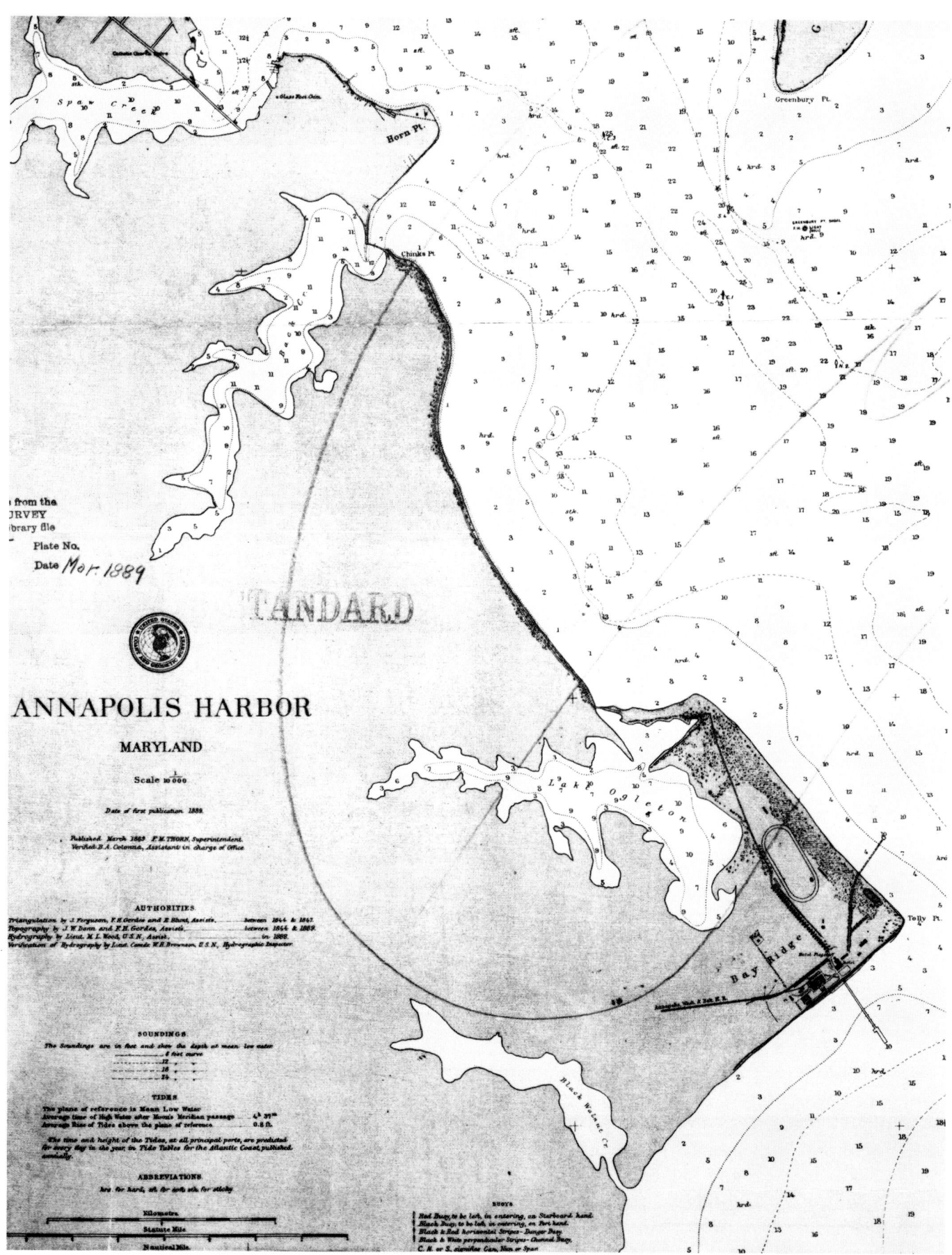

Fig. 4. U.S. Coast and Geodetic Survey Chart #385, March 1889, shows a well-developed resort at Bay Ridge complete with buildings, piers, trackage, and racetrack. The Bay Shore Drive along the water from Annapolis to the resort included bridges over Back Creek and the mouth of Lake Ogleton.

Baltimore and Annapolis line or the rival Baltimore and Annapolis Short Line Railroad. Most Baltimoreans preferred the Short Line, which extended down the Severn River's scenic northern shore to bring vacationers from Camden Station in Baltimore to the Bladen Street depot in Annapolis. The Short Line offered a "Business Men's Special" leaving Baltimore in the late afternoon as well as an optional rail-steamboat ticket by which a passenger might travel to Bay Ridge by steamer and return by train or the reverse. From Annapolis, passengers then boarded the Bay Ridge and Annapolis connecting line to Bay Ridge. This single track railroad passed along what is today Amos Garrett Boulevard, crossed a trestle bridge over Spa Creek and then continued through fields and farmland for approximately four miles to the Bay Ridge inland station, located in the vicinity of what is now the Mayo Avenue and Farragut Road juncture. By the summer of 1887 the terminus in Bay Ridge had been extended one-quarter of a mile to a spot behind the hotel, a convenience welcomed by guests arriving with heavy baggage.

Simultaneously, with the construction of these rail lines, Annapolitans wishing to travel to Bay Ridge by "private conveyance" campaigned for a county horse-and-carriage road along the water from Annapolis to Bay Ridge. They were successful, and Bay Shore Drive, begun on August 5, 1886, was completed on July 2, 1887. This road involved the repair of the Spa Creek Bridge from Annapolis to Fourth Street in Eastport and the construction of two new bridges, one crossing Back Creek at Horn Point and the other crossing Lake Ogleton near the entrance to the channel.

Fig. 5. The Bay Ridge Hotel c. 1893. Wind stirred young trees on a bright summer day as a gardener tended flower beds near an awning-shaded portico.

Fig. 6. Composite lithograph advertising resort attractions for the 1888 season. Compare the artist's stylized version of the hotel with its actual appearance in figures 5 and 28.

Fig. 7. An 1894 promotional lithograph touted Bay Ridge as the "Queen Resort of the Chesapeake" and was chosen by Ben Wills to use as the menu cover design at the present-day Bay Ridge Inn.

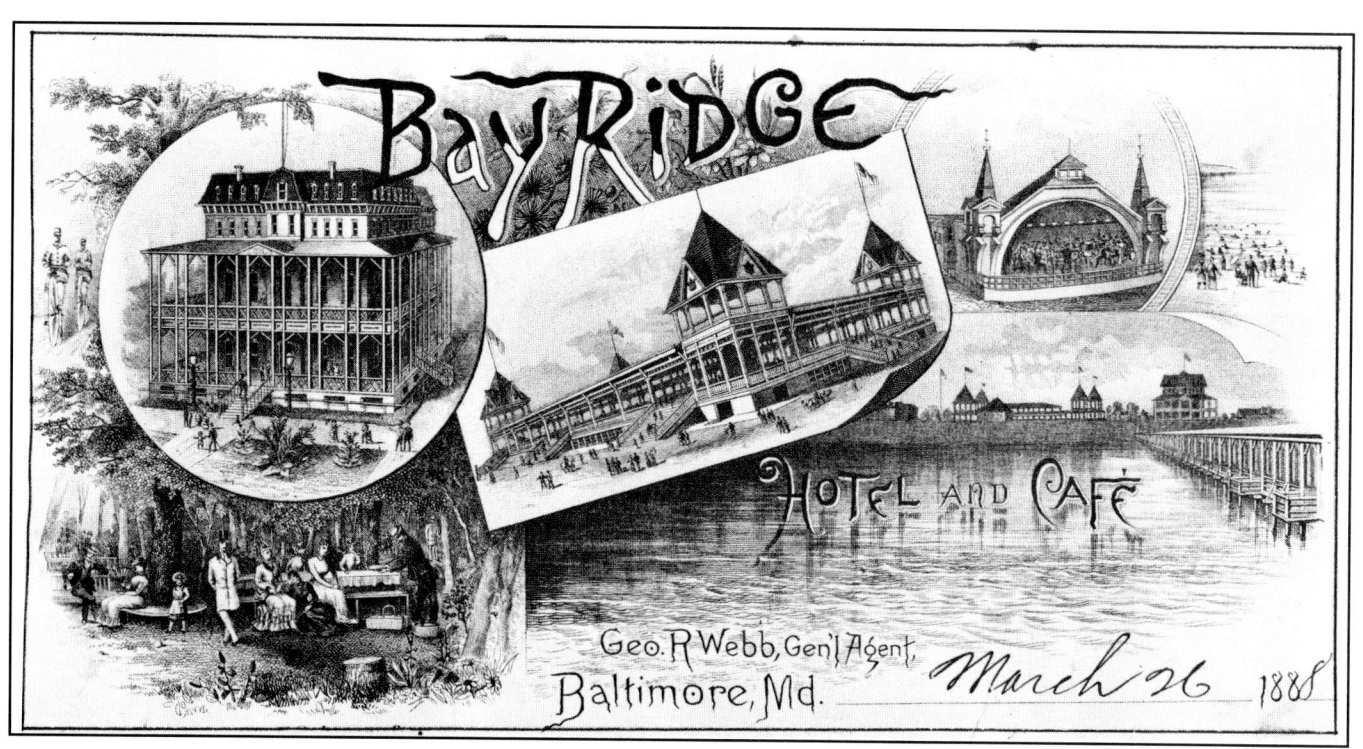

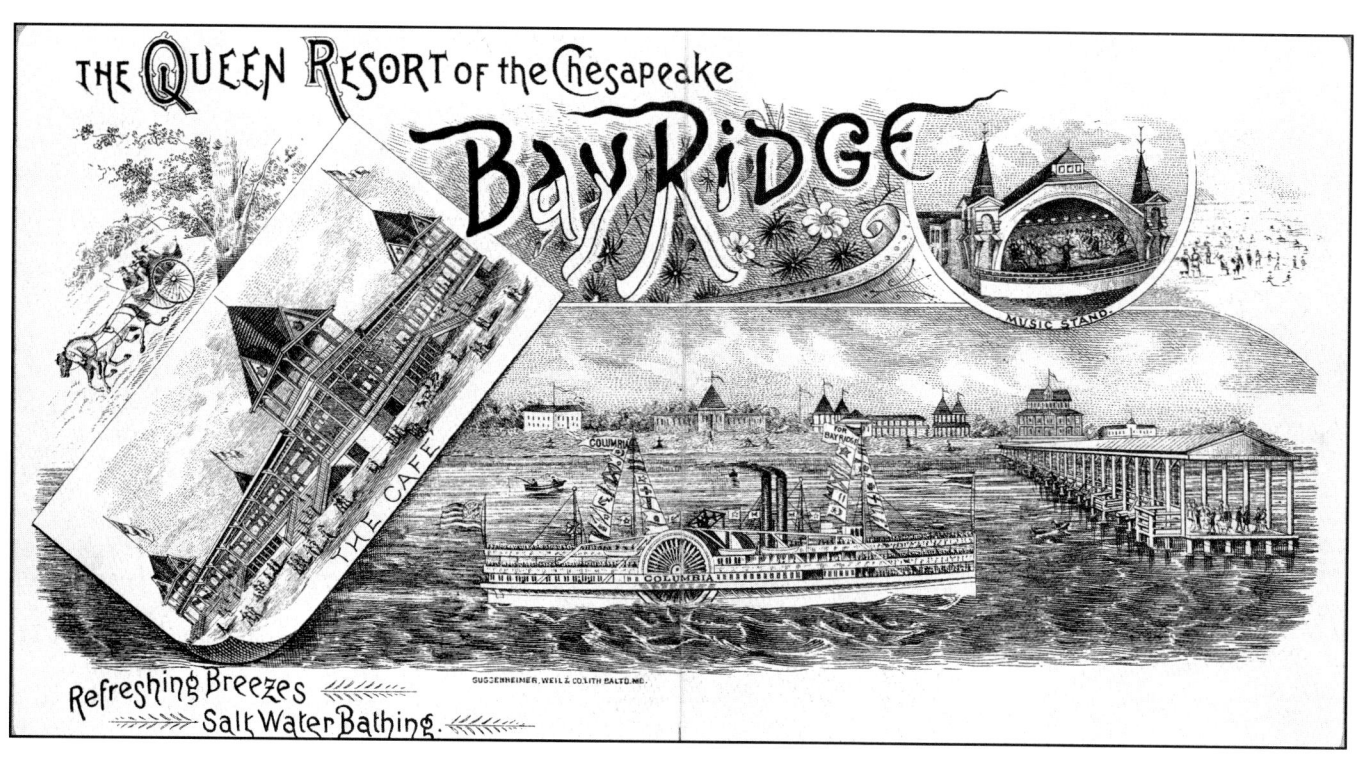

Fig. 8. The Bay Ridge and Annapolis Railroad. "An Annapolis Short Line train waits at the terminal behind the Bay Ridge Hotel, seen at right."— J. E. Merriken, 1981. Dr. Clarence Weaver, grandfather of resident Clarence Kettler, remembers traveling on this train and that in 1898, when Admiral Dewey was in the Philippines, the train's cake vendor would chant up and down the aisles: "Up the river, down the lake,/Dewey at Manila, 5¢ a cake!"

BAY RIDGE.

On and after THURSDAY, July 26th, 1889, the A., W. & B. R. R., will take charge of the Passenger business between Annapolis and Bay Ridge. Trains will leave depot of the A., W. & B. R. R., as follows :

DAILY, (Except Sundays.)

Leave Annapolis 6.10 a. m., 10.15 a. m., 2.35 p m., 4 p. m., 5.40 p. m. and 7 p. m.

Leave Bay Ridge 6.25 a. m., 10.40 a. m., 3 p. m., 4.50 p. m., 7 45 p. m. and 8.50 p. m.

SUNDAYS ONLY.

Leave Annapolis 7.30 a. m., 10.55 a. m., 2.30 p. m. and 7 p. m.

Leave Bay Ridge 7.50 a. m., 11.30 a. m., 3.40 p m., 7.45 p. m and 9 10 p. m.

Fig. 9.

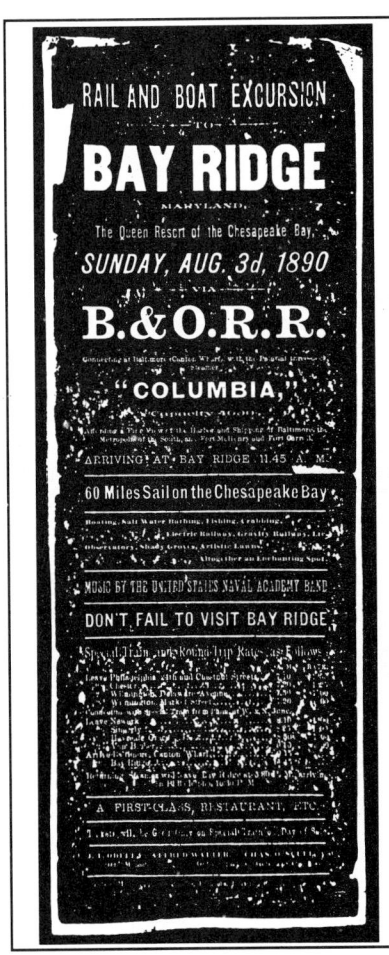

Fig. 10.

TIME TABLES.

ANNAPOLIS AND BAY RIDGE.

On and after Sunday, June 15, 1890, trains will leave A. W. & B. R. R. Depot for Bay Ridge, as follows :

LEAVE ANNAPOLIS—Week Days, 6.00 a. m., 10.00 a. m, 2.00 p. m. and 4.00 p. m.— Sundays at 6.00 a m, 10.20 a. m. and 2 20 p. m.

RETURNING, LEAVE BAY RIDGE—Week Days, 6.20 a. m., 10.20 a. m., 7.45 p. m. and 9.10 p. m. Sundays at 6.20 a, m., 3.30 p. m, 7.45 p. m. and 9.10 p. m.

JAS. H. BROWN, G. T. & F. A.

Fig. 11.

PASSENGERS FOR BAY RIDGE!

Private Families or Persons taken to Bay Ridge or any place desired during the Summer and brought back at any time. Good driver and safe team. Charges moderate.— Orders left at the Postoffice will be called for every morning and evening and attended to promptly.

GEO. H. BRITTON,
6 9   Eastport, A. A. County.

Fig. 12.

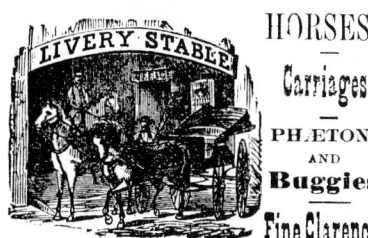

Fig. 13.

Fig. 14. James S. Vansant, Sr., son of James H. Vansant (see figures 2 and 13) set out in a horse and buggy of 1911 vintage.

Fig. 15.

Fig. 16.

Providing a delightful drive, but constantly in need of repairs and "shelling" because of its close proximity to the water, the road proved to be a mixed blessing in the end. Nevertheless, the opening of Bay Shore Drive initiated a business boom of sorts for the Annapolis and Eastport hiring and livery stables, as reflected in their many newspaper advertisements heralding the event.

Similarly, the boat-hiring and sailing-party business in Annapolis took on new life, advertising a more leisurely form of transportation to Bay Ridge. Captain W. H. Burtis's business was so popular that outings on his boats frequently made the society pages of the Annapolis *Evening Capital*.

Even before direct train service to Bay Ridge was available, vacationers could come to Bay Ridge by excursion steamer from Baltimore or Annapolis. As early as 1880, the *Theodore Weems* made two trips daily, at 9:00 A.M. and 4:00 P.M., at 50¢ and 25¢ rates, leaving from Pier 8 at Light Street in Baltimore, and, on Mondays and Fridays, from the Maryland Steamboat Wharf in Annapolis.

In 1881 Bay Ridge was advertised as a "park of 150 acres with a first class hotel" and could boast two steamers, the *Weems* and the *Louise*, with three trips each per day on a two and one-half hour run. Aboard the *Weems* a band provided music during the long bay crossing. From the very first, Bay Ridge drew crowds, as in late July 1881, when the *Weems* transported four thousand visitors to "the Ridge" for an afternoon jousting tournament and

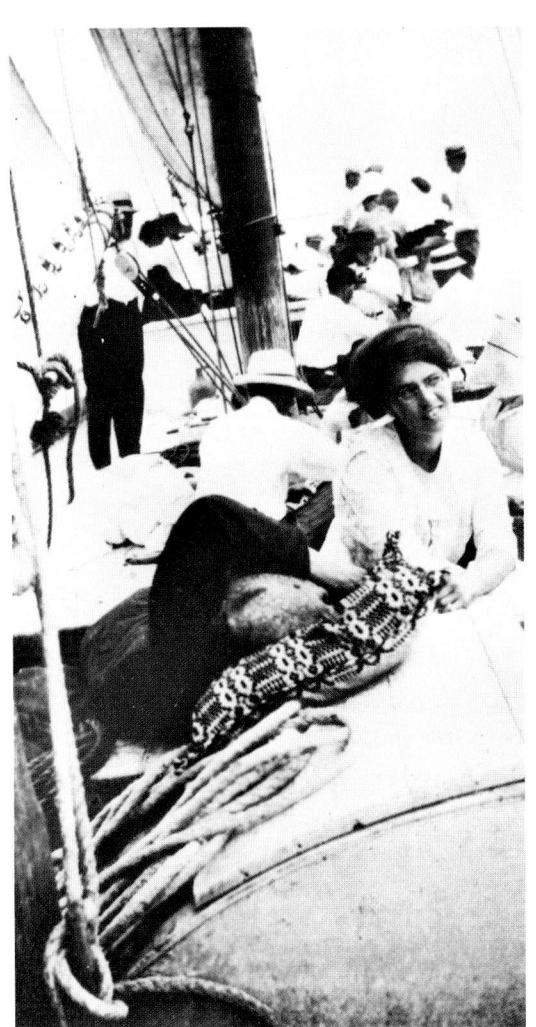

PLEASURE BOATS TO HIRE.

W. H. BURTIS, Foot of Prince George Street, is prepared to furnish Pleasure Boats, Row-Boats, Sail-Boats, Fishing Tackle, Bait, &c., on the most reasonable terms. Will furnish a man to row or sail boats when required.

W. H. BURTIS,
5 9   Foot of Prince George Street.

Fig. 17. Sailing excursion to Bay Ridge. A group of friends played cards on deck as the schooner heeled on the port tack c. 1903.

Fig. 18. Bay Ridge was a popular destination for Capt. Burtis's sailing parties.

Fig. 19. The view from the bow facing aft reveals Capt. Burtis himself, standing left. This photograph and figure 17 above are both taken from Sandy Brooks Newark's family album, proof of a family's long-term association with Bay Ridge, c. 1903.

Fig. 20. Above, opp., At the birth of pleasure boating, but before the invention of leisure sportswear, Capt. Burtis, third from left, and a sailing party of eleven set sail for Bay Ridge. Aboard were friends and relatives of Margaret Taylor Randall, who photographed the group c. 1891.

Fig. 21. Below, opp., Margaret Taylor Randall, mother of Margaret and Virginia Worthington of Annapolis, again captured Capt. Burtis on film, here leaning on the boom to the right. Among the group are: seated, the Reverend George Savage of St. Anne's Church, Annapolis, with Ellen Jenkins, and standing, third from left, Betsy Webster c. 1891.

evening fireworks display and dance. In 1882 the large strange-looking steamer, *Excelsior*, owned by the Potomac Steamboat Company, was engaged to handle the crowds, while the *Samuel J. Pentz* made daily stops at Bay Ridge on her trips up and down the bay. Two steamers, the new *H. L. Baya* and the *Theodore Weems*, were employed to carry passengers to Bay Ridge in 1883. A host of steamboats joined these early pioneers in the peak resort years, either owned or engaged by the Bay Ridge Company or chartered to make regularly scheduled Bay Ridge runs from the Eastern Shore or elsewhere. These included the *Ida, Bergen Point, Jane Moseley, Tred Avon, Empire State, Bay Ridge, Columbia, John A. Bemis, Port Deposit, Thames River, Emma Giles*, and *Tockwogh*. Without a doubt the most popular of these steamers at Bay Ridge was the beautiful side-wheeler *Columbia*, secured in New York by the Bay Ridge Company in May 1888 and sold on Monday, July 17, 1899. When built, the *Columbia* was the largest steamboat in the United States, 262 feet in length and 69 feet abeam. She boasted a carrying capacity of four thousand people and could travel from Baltimore to Bay Ridge in one hour and forty-five minutes at fifteen knots. Attractively appointed with the luxuries of the day, she featured band concerts and vaudeville acts on an upper deck stage in a roof garden. While serving Bay Ridge, her captain, John Thomas, was honored for his record of twenty accident-free years at the helm.

In order to provide an adequate and more convenient landing for these large boats, the Bay Ridge and Annapolis Railroad

Fig. 22. SS Empire State, *built in 1848, stern view, c. 1886. An additional 200 feet were added to the 1,000-foot steamship pier at Bay Ridge to accommodate this boat whose history of running aground just short of the pier (laden with vacationers) had become an embarrassment to the company.*

48

Fig. 23. The ferry-transfer steamer, Thames River, *awaited a train. For one year (1890–91) she ferried passengers and trains from a western shore terminal at Bay Ridge to Bay City (later named Claiborne) as a link in a consolidated line of railroads running from Baltimore to Ocean City.*

Fig. 24. Excursionists disembarked at the Bay Ridge steamship pier c. 1885.

Fig. 25. Between May 1888 and July 1899 the SS Columbia *carried vacationers between Baltimore and Bay Ridge. First licensed to carry 3,500 passengers, she was refurbished in 1893 to carry 4,000 passengers. See also figures 29, 30, 64, and 65.*

Fig. 26. Above, opp., SS Emma Giles *c. 1893. Annapolitans became irate when on Friday, June 14, 1901 they learned that she would not be stopping in Annapolis for passengers on her way to Bay Ridge as planned.*

Fig. 27. Below, opp., SS Tockwogh *brought passengers from the Eastern Shore. Her name is an Indian word for sassafras.*

Company built, in time for the June opening of 1885, a new pier directly in front of the hotel. An additional two hundred feet were added in July 1886 to accommodate the *Empire State*, whose history of running aground just short of the pier had become an embarrassment to the company. The pier was equipped with electric lights for after-dark departures and was partially covered to provide shade for people fishing and crabbing from the little side balconies and benches constructed for that purpose. An incline elevator, hoisted by a stationary steam engine, transported luggage and cargo some sixty feet up from the pier to the hotel. This little boiler engine was also used to steam the guests' hard crabs, caught from the pier.

For one brief year Bay Ridge was actually designated as a bonafide commercial port, operating as the western shore ferry-transfer terminal for a line of consolidated railroads running from Baltimore to Ocean City. The Baltimore and Eastern Shore Railroad's large passenger steamer *Tockwogh* made the first run on this line on Monday, August 25, 1890. By October 1891 the western shore terminal had been relocated to Baltimore. In a 1981 issue of the *National Railway Bulletin* railroad historian Lt. Col. John E. Merriken described this terminal (located near the Farragut–Mayo–

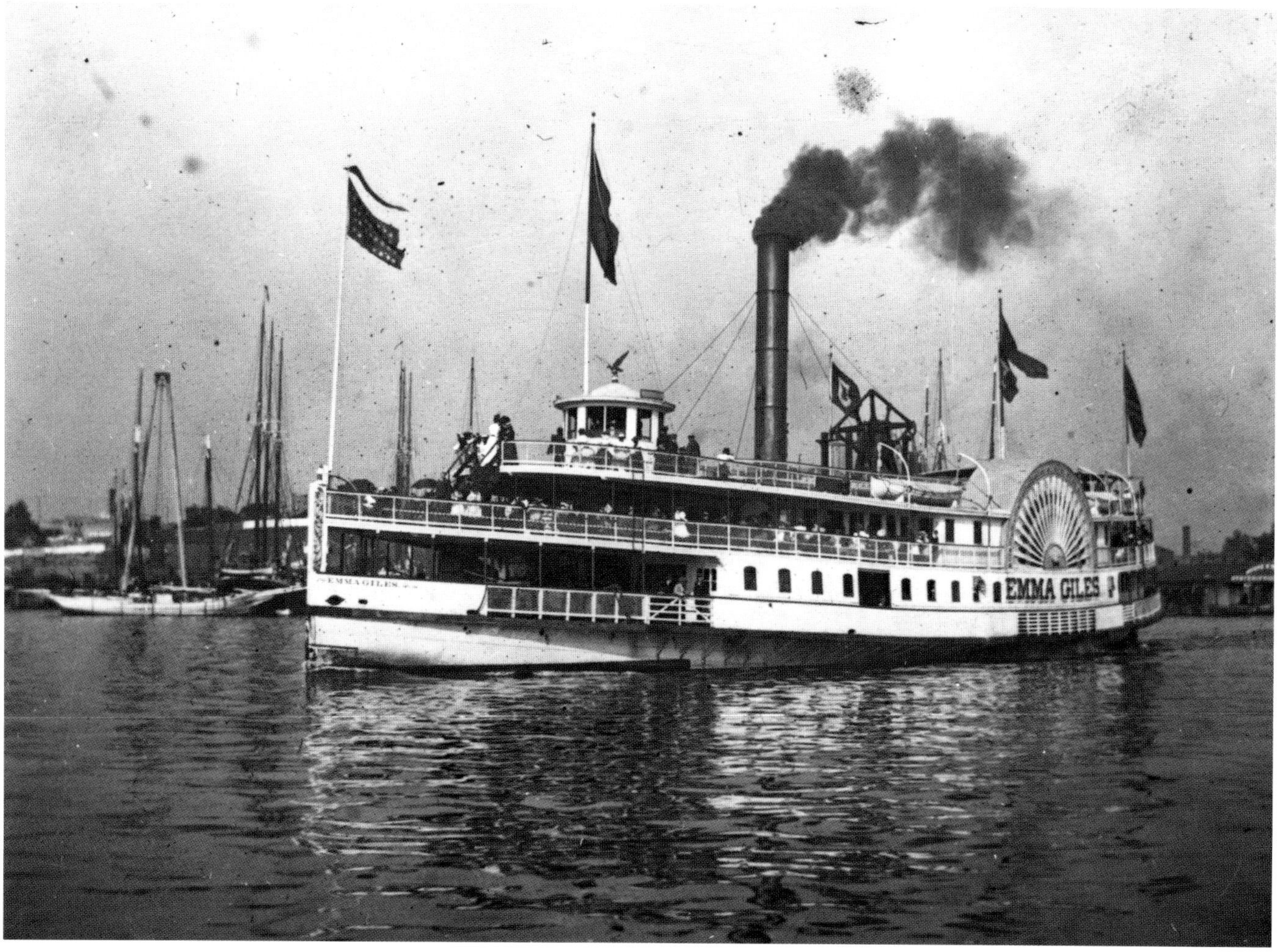
EMMA GILES
EMMA GILES

TOCKWOGH
WICKFORD LINE

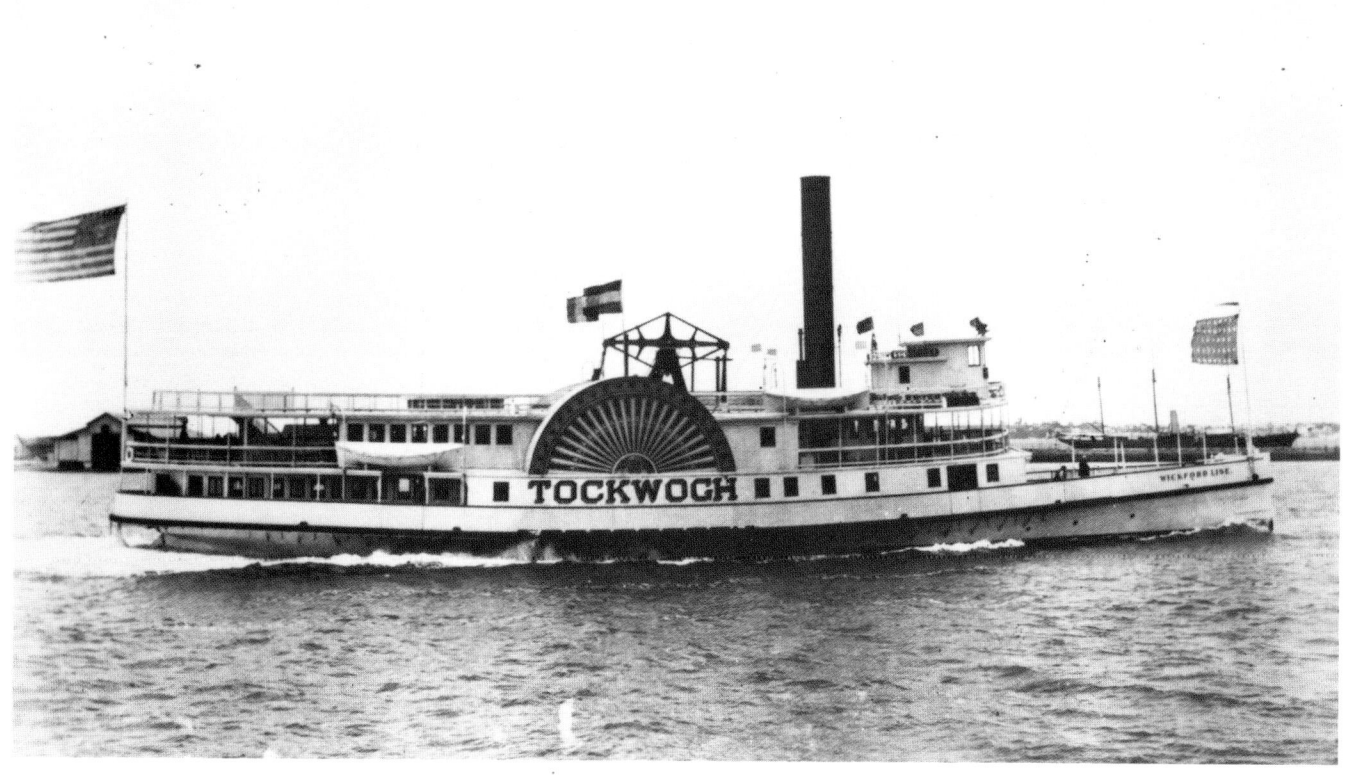

Fig. 28. Visitors enjoyed the scenery in front of the Bay Ridge hotel c. 1900. The hotel was part of a large resort complex attracting many people at the turn of the century. On the Fourth of July, 1891, 10,000 excursionists came to Bay Ridge by steamboat and train—sixty-five passenger coaches came from Washington, D.C., bringing passengers to a terminal in back of the hotel.

Fig. 29. Above, opp., SS Columbia *waited at the Bay Ridge steamship pier below the hotel.*

Fig. 30. Below, opp., The resort viewed from Arundel-on-the-Bay, showing the Columbia *at the long pier in front of the hotel. Margaret Taylor Randall prepared to take a photograph. Tracks of the little private train that carried summer residents of Arundel-on-the-Bay to and from Bay Ridge can be seen in the foreground; and in the middleground is the railroad ferry wharf with the dispatcher's office near the end c. 1891.*

Bay Drive juncture) and the ferry pier (located at the Mayo Avenue beach to the right).

From the Bay Ridge terminal, a spur track was built out onto a railroad pier and, at the eastern end of the 12-mile crossing, another railhead was established in Talbot County at Bay City, later renamed Claiborne. To coordinate the two halves of the railroad with its maritime link, a temporary telegrapher's desk was set up in the cafe at Bay Ridge until a proper dispatcher's office could be built on the wharf. The western shore terminal included a large wye layout and three yard tracks leading into the trainshed and ferry slip located offshore.

This juncture or "crossing" was also the Bay Ridge terminus for yet another operation, the Arundel-on-the-Bay Railroad (or Chesapeake and Columbia Street Railway), consisting of one locomotive and four little red cars traveling on a small single track extending three miles south through the fields and blackberry brambles along the water's edge to a point just opposite Thomas Point Light in Arundel-on-the-Bay. Completed on July 11, 1892, as the brainchild of Thomas W. Smith, the new summer colony's mayor, this "blackberry train" or "the summer cars" carried residents of Arundel-on-the-Bay to card parties, dances, and evening entertainments at the Bay Ridge hotel. In spite of a schedule frequently disrupted by shifting sands and summer squalls, the railroad was good-naturedly well patronized.

The Bay Ridge grand hotel was situated on top of the bayfront cliff near what is now 95 Bay Drive. A large four-story building, it was adorned with the charming architectural gingerbread much admired in the Victorian period. It furnished overnight accommodations for several hundred people, expensive meals, alcoholic beverages, and gambling not offered elsewhere in the park. Because

Fig. 31. McDowell's pier opposite 63 Bay Drive at low tide (April 1974). Extending beyond the pier are the piling stubs of the Baltimore & Eastern Shore railroad ferry wharf built in 1890.

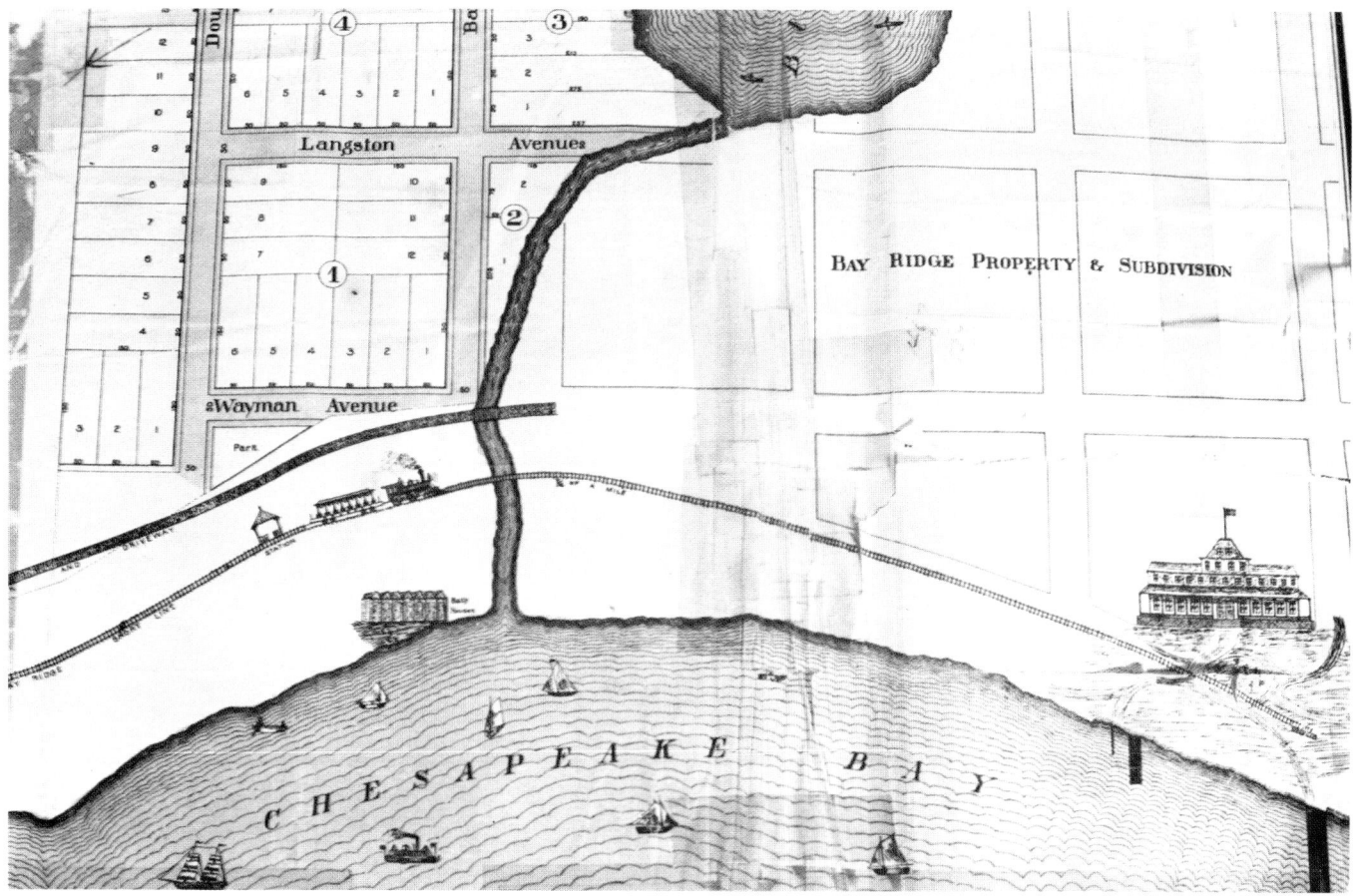

Fig. 32. An 1894 plat of Highland Beach depicted "the summer cars" chugging to Bay Ridge from Arundel-on-the-Bay and ready to cross the narrow entrance channel of Black Walnut Creek. The drawing of the hotel was doubtless rendered "sight unseen."

the resort as a whole catered to family picnics and large group outings, liquor was available only within the hotel for hotel patrons. Infractions of this strictly upheld policy were rare and always "made the papers." A special permit was required for the annual German beer and song fest; and even at that rollicking event participants on the grounds remained respectfully sober. Small-scale dances, euchre card parties, musicales, and various small entertainments were given in the large hotel parlor for boarders who enjoyed socializing privately with specially invited residents of Annapolis and Arundel-on-the-Bay. The hotel management also arranged sailing parties and hay rides for its patrons.

The grounds in front of the hotel were laid out with gravel walks and flower beds, including a special bed of variegated annuals arranged in the shape of the steamship *Columbia*. "Emerald green" parade grounds and lawns were carefully maintained. The banks along the bathing shore were terraced and sodded, and in 1895 a breakwater was erected in front of the buildings. An extensive boardwalk fronted the bluff, connecting the various buildings, and the entire area was planted with literally thousands of shrubs and shade trees. Artistically positioned within these cultivated gardens were little gazebo–like structures of "picturesque architecture" intended for elegant family picnics. At night the boardwalk and garden paths were illuminated by the latest electric street lamps.

To the right of the hotel, facing the bay, was the enormous, two-hundred-foot long restaurant pavilion, or café. The red roofs

Fig. 33. Six hundred young trees were planted at the resort in May 1884, and electric lighting was first installed on Monday, July 12, 1886—facts which help date this scene of the hotel (facing the bay) and the restaurant pavilion (facing the bandstand). Bleacher-like restaurant pavilion steps provided spectator seating during the concerts and variety acts held at the bandstand.

Fig. 34. The mammoth restaurant pavilion (café) and hotel (far right). The restaurant could seat 1600 diners at a time, served by a crew of 80 waiters and waitresses.

Fig. 35. Facing south towards Arundel-on-the-Bay, a walkway with railings fronted the bluff. Here and there charming gazebos of "picturesque architecture" were situated, amidst beautifully landscaped gardens, for the convenience of "pic-nickers." Three thousand gardeners and horticulturists from Washington, D.C. and Baltimore toured the grounds on July 30, 1890.

of the twin turrets on either end always sported festive flags to welcome the crowds arriving by water or land. A covered upper deck, providing shelter from the elements, housed an immense restaurant that could seat 1,600 guests at one time, as well as a spacious and lengthy promenade enwrapping the whole pavilion. This deck could be reached by steps surrounding the building that doubled as bleachers during band concerts and variety shows, which were held at the bandstand directly in front of the pavilion on the bay side. The restaurant was staffed by an army of some eighty waiters and waitresses who served such specialties of the house as crab cakes, soft crabs, fried chicken, clam chowder, vegetables and fruits grown on the property, and homemade pies. Obtaining a refreshing beverage on a hot day was rarely a problem since the resort was equipped with a large cold-storage system, seven mammoth wells, and an ice-making machine producing five tons of ice daily. In the early days, before the resort's electrical plant was installed, the restaurant's gas lights were frequently extinguished by the wind. The management, as an emergency measure, ingeniously solved this problem by using locomotive headlights.

On the ground level under the café was a large lunchroom where "basket parties" or picnickers could find tables (including fourteen marble-topped ice cream tables) and order what they wanted from the café above. Here, too, were refreshment stands that sold licorice

Fig. 36. Prof. Charles A. Zimmerman

Fig. 37. The bandstand with awning extended faced the restaurant pavilion. Here Prof. Zimmerman conducted his 50-piece Naval Academy Band—daily during summers. For the July Fourth 1889 program, the band provided music for a "Grand Jubilee Concert" which included "singing of the national airs, accompanied by the discharge of artillery. . ., the ringing of the mammoth bells, and the discharge of novel fireworks at night."

sticks, ice-cream phosphates, sarsaparilla, lemonade, and flavored snowballs. The souvenir stands, the Museum of Natural Sciences and Curiosities, Jolly's Waxworks, the billiard room, the shooting galleries, the bowling alley, the "wargraph", the camera obscura, and George R. Buffham's photographic gallery also shared this vast space.

The bandstand on the bay side of the restaurant was the site for afternoon background music and the evening band concerts and vaudeville acts that entertained weary vacationers waiting for ships and trains to bear them home. It was said that the band shell was so shaped that music was directed to even the far reaches of the resort's grounds. While many bands performed at Bay Ridge, the most memorable was the Naval Academy Marine Band, engaged every summer from 1880 to 1891 and for a few scattered years thereafter, most notably under the direction of Prof. Charles A. Zimmerman, Naval Academy bandmaster from 1887 to 1916. Professor Zimmerman, whose home is now preserved at 138 Conduit Street in Annapolis, served as bandmaster at the first Inaugural Ball when William McKinley assumed office in 1897. That same year Zimmerman was asked to succeed John Philip Sousa as conductor of the U.S. Marine Band, an honor he declined, preferring to remain at his post in Annapolis with time to compose as well as conduct music. His best-loved composition undoubtedly is *Anchors Aweigh*.

Fig. 38. Swimwear, June 1901

Fig. 39. Swimwear, June 1901

At Bay Ridge, Zimmerman and his superbly talented band—fifty men strong in "cadet" uniforms and caps and sporting identical black handlebar mustaches—provided the ambience for everything that went on. Classical and popular music of the day was performed during the week and sacred music on Sundays. Vocal and instrumental guest soloists, small ensembles, and massive choral groups were frequently engaged, all accompanied by the band. Just imagine for a moment the vacationers relaxing here at the end of the long day and listening to an evening concert, while, as darkness closes in, the pier lights below glitter in a long line out to where the steamer beckons and, on shore, train whistles announce departure times to the cities.

To the right of the café and bandstand were the bathhouses. As saltwater "bathing" gained popularity, the original three hundred dressing rooms were increased to over twice that number. Here, hot and cold saltwater bath facilities were available for invalids, and bathing suits and caps could be rented. The ladies' stairs leading down to the beach from the bathhouses were covered with canvas, affording protection from the sun's heat and "the gaze of the curious." A covered observation pavilion nearby was provided for those who wished to watch the bathing and beach activities below. Proving to be one of the resort's top attractions, five toboggan slides promised thrilling, swift rides from the top of the cliff far out into the water, where lifeguards kept a watchful eye from lifeboats. The shore in front of the bathhouses for half a mile in either direction and the bay bottom in the swimming area were regularly dragged and scraped to remove sharp stones and shells.

To the left of the hotel, facing the bay, stood the building that housed resident employees. In 1900 it was converted into a hotel annex by the Chautauqua Literary and Scientific Circle, which briefly managed Bay Ridge at the time.

The next building toward Tolly Point was the dancing pavilion, ruled by dance master Professor Auer, who conducted the twice-weekly hops, special moonlight dances, and grand balls. He also presented youth ballet performances and offered instruction in "fancy dancing." This dance hall was decorated with "life-like figures in wax and marble representing Terpsichore and other fun-loving deities" and boasted a dance floor "smooth as glass." Here, Chinese lanterns lent a touch of magic to soft and balmy summer nights.

Near the resort entrance was Carvel Cottage, a private home that was the scene of casual socializing and card parties. The resort also had a U.S. Post Office, which opened on February 13, 1899, with a postmaster appointed by President McKinley. Here, too, on the other side of the tracks, directly behind the hotel, was the photography studio and home of George R. Buffham, the British-born resort photographer, the owner of the Naval Academy Photography Studio on Maryland Avenue in Annapolis, and the last manager of Bay Ridge. This two-story frame house [now 11 Barry

Fig. 40. George R. Buffham home and photography studio—the only remaining resort building, built May 1893, now 11 Barry Avenue

Fig. 41. Reverse of figure 2

Avenue], built in May 1893, is the only resort building from those years still standing.

On the inland side of the grounds the resort maintained riding stables and a half-mile racetrack with adjoining grandstand and parade field, a baseball diamond, lawn tennis grounds, the "razzle-dazzle," the patent swings, the summer theater with its nightly offerings by the Bijou Opera Company, a small zoo and zoological gardens, and the bear pit.

The resort's amusement park was also located inland. Its featured rides and moving attractions included a seventy-five-foot, twenty-car Ferris wheel and a merry-go-round or "flying horses," complete with steam organ. The early pride of the park was the oft-repaired, rebuilt, extended, and possibly relocated gravity railroad which paralleled a tree-lined walkway extending straight to Lake Ogleton from the back of the hotel. An early form of roller coaster, it was built along an elevated structure and advertised as the world's second largest.

Bay Ridge was also one of the first American amusement parks to have an electric railway or trolley. Built on the Sprague System by Henry Wellington in 1889, it was first a two and one-half mile loop along the river and the lake and later extended as a five-mile scenic ride. The trolley system originally consisted of two motor cars and three trailers, each with seven benches. Another car was added when the route was lengthened. Three covered stations—Hotel, Point, and Lake—provided convenient stops for vacationers traveling to the Lake Ogleton picnic grounds and back. In time, new stations were added on the river side.

Like the bay, Lake Ogleton was in itself a special attraction. Its banks and wooded areas were regularly cleared of undergrowth and then raked to create rustic picnic groves and overnight campsites. Patrons arriving at the Lake Station could rent rowboats

Fig. 42. Bay Ridge Electric Railway—a resort attraction. A 10¢ ticket (figure 43) bought a 16 m.p.h. ride on this trolley, which circled the grounds along the water with stations at the hotel, point, and lake. Built on the Sprague system of motors by Henry Wellington, the trolley is seen c. 1889 above and, in figure 44, at the station c. 1897.

Fig. 43.

Fig. 44.

Fig. 45. Groups of excursionists congregated in shady groves to relax and picnic. A tree limb served as a handy coat rack on a warm day c. 1903.

Fig. 46.

or one of the fifteen sculls at the boathouse from Mr. Quade and row to various landings and "picturesque locations" around the lake "where it is most shady and inviting."

Special entertainments at Bay Ridge ranged in scope from simple vaudeville and variety acts to extravagant pyrotechnical dramas and even the first two Anne Arundel County Fairs—resembling a combination agricultural fair and Chesapeake Bay Appreciation Day—held the last week of August in 1888 and 1889. Other crowd-pleasers included a Wild West Show, special dances and concerts, "championship" sporting events, regattas, jousting tournaments, and programs of marching drills, target shooting, and field maneuvers presented during Military Day and the military encampments. Visiting baseball teams also competed at Bay Ridge, attracting fans to a new national pastime in its infancy. Those in search of knowledge and moral uplifting enjoyed the programs of the National Chautauqua Assembly in 1900 and 1901.

Many thousands of people came daily to see these events and to participate in or observe the annual celebrations of the countless large conventions, societies, associations, and fraternal lodges that gathered at Bay Ridge. A continuous stream of Sunday schools chose the resort for their outings. These groups typically included several hundred children, parents, and teachers with picnic baskets in hand, and were fondly called "the basket brigade" by the management. Military groups such as state militias, national guards, and the Civil War veterans of the Grand Army of the

Fig. 47. Cycling act at Bay Ridge. Vacationers watched a cyclist ride upside down in the loop-the-loop while another cyclist waited poised to descend the incline into the loop c. 1895.

Republic added to the crowds and generated a general excitement with their marching and field music.

During this era genteel leisure sports activities that could be enjoyed by both sexes increased in popularity. Horseback riding, lawn tennis, and croquet were among the favorites, and resorts such as Bay Ridge catered to these interests. In the 1890s bicycling became a national craze. Ladies enjoyed this sport to the extent that new outfits with bloomers were designed for safety and comfort at the urging of physicians. The racetrack at Bay Ridge was used at times for cycling races sponsored by the League of American Wheelmen, while Bay Shore Drive proved to be the less-hurried cyclists' Sunday afternoon route of choice.

Fig. 48.

Fig. 49. Cycle races in 1892 and 1893, sanctioned by the League of American Wheelmen, were held on the racetrack at Bay Ridge. The Annapolis Evening Capital *(July 14, 1892) reported that "the Baltimore Wheelmen [seen here, left], about 300 strong, will give a tournament in Bay Ridge. . . ."*

Fig. 50. Groups of Sunday school children came in droves to picnic under the trees and enjoy a day of rides and games.

Fig. 51. Rowing regattas were a popular resort attraction. Here, scullers practice at the mouth of Spa Creek, perhaps to compete in races at Bay Ridge sanctioned by the Association of Amateur Oarsmen (July 15–18, 1886) at which the winner's purse was $400. Visiting teams were quartered in the old Steele mansion at the head of the course on Lake Ogleton.

Over the years various companies managed Bay Ridge, usually under a lease arrangement with the railroad syndicate that owned the property. These companies—the Bay Ridge Company, the Bay Ridge Improvement and Transportation Company, the Bay Ridge Electric Park and Steamboat Company, and Chesapeake Chautauqua at Brighton Beach—operated on a shoestring and often faced end-of-the-season financial woes. As early as 1894 there were thoughts of developing the land around the resort as a summer community in order to offset company losses. By 1903 it became clear that the railroad syndicate no longer intended to invest money in Bay Ridge. Steamboat service had ceased and, except for the merry-go-round, the rides had been shut down because they were in disrepair and therefore not safe. At the close of 1903 train service on the Bay Ridge connecting line was cancelled. From 1904 to 1915 the resort was left in the hands of George Buffham, who lived on the premises and who, from time to time, made arrangements for picnic and camping groups to use the grounds. Big plans

Fig. 52. Lake Ogleton was also a popular spot for rowing at a more leisurely pace.

in 1914 to revitalize Bay Ridge as a hotel-marina complex were never realized. On March 3, 1915, a disastrous fire raged through the park, and the hotel burned to the ground. Only Mr. Buffham's wife, Ethel, and several farmers were on hand to witness the resort's final and most spectacular performance. Sadly, Mr. Buffham's prints and negatives—an entire photographic history of the resort years—were stored in the hotel and, consequently, were consumed in the flames.

And so this resort and all that happened there have, like Camelot and Brigadoon, vanished, seemingly overnight, with little left to remind us of their existence at all. Still, somehow, it is wonderful to know that for a brief time, just a dream ago, there was at Bay Ridge a grand resort on a high bluff overlooking a vast bay where people congregated for pure pleasure, a place where religious organizations of every faith sang the praises of their Creator, where military associations gathered for mass expressions of patriotism, and where individuals and families came by the thousands to celebrate the goodness of life in a country of their own making, secure in the knowledge that "God's in his heaven—All's right with the world." These words of Robert Browning, in the greater sense, speak for the ebullient spirit of an era, an era innocent of war to come.

Fig. 53. Annie Riley (Mrs. Earl A.) Smith of Annapolis, seated second from the left at age 4, remembers this day well. She was camping with her family and close friends at Bay Ridge and had walked through the woods along the Bay Ridge side of the lake entrance channel to the point where the lake widens. Here, under a tree, Annie's father, George W. Riley, posed the group for a photograph because he thought the ladies were so beautiful with freshly picked wildflowers in their hair. Left to right (seated): Jennie F. Riley, Annie Riley, Blanch Finkle, Roy Martin, Mamie Martin with baby, and (top to bottom) George, John, and Alva Riley. Left to right (standing): Phoebe Hardesty, Bessie Riley, Annie Mitchell, her husband William Mitchell, July 1899.

Bay Ridge

The Diary of a Victorian Resort

Fig. 54.

This diary of the Bay Ridge resort has been compiled especially for those who may wish to take their own express excursion back in time to learn exactly what happened, week-by-week, year-by-year, during the two decades the resort flourished. It is based on information carefully recorded in the pages of the Annapolis Maryland Republican *(1880–83) and the Annapolis* Evening Capital *(1884–1915). These newspapers, now on microfilm at the Maryland State Archives, not only provide details long forgotten but create a wonderful sense of "being there" for the reader who wishes to learn about Bay Ridge directly from eyewitness sources. Another type of immediacy is created by the journalistic style of that era, which, with subjective insights and attitudes not found in modern news coverage, has a charm of its own. Where possible this style has been preserved in direct quotations, but for the sake of reasonable brevity much of the material has been condensed or paraphrased. Because many of the events included here either occurred annually or often, only the most representative accounts were selected.*

1880

SATURDAY, MAY 8: "On Monday last a number of gentlemen [from Philadelphia] interested in the new hotel and bathing grounds at Bay Ridge visited the site. They arrived here in the cars [rail] at 10:30 a.m. and were taken to the hotel by boat . . . [and] returned to Baltimore on the 4:20 train."

1881

SATURDAY, JUNE 18: "Bay Ridge opens June 20. . . . Free from malaria, the air is fresh and invigorating. . . ."

SATURDAY, JUNE 25: The Fifth Regiment Band provides music aboard the *Weems* which made her first trip of the season. A Naval Academy Band "of ten pieces" provides music on shore. " . . . first class bathing, fishing, boating . . . a billiard saloon, bowling alleys, flying horses for children, patent-swings and a shooting gallery . . . hotel and restaurant elegant, employing a skilled caterer . . . Mr. M. A. Osbourne, general manager."

SATURDAY, JULY 9: For the 4th of July, Annapolitans came "by vehicles and by boat . . . 4 excursions from Baltimore . . . 6000 people . . . enjoyed . . . the performance by Avery and Larus on the horizontal bars, and Mike Alma on the trapeze . . . lunch stands were erected on the grounds . . . crowded dining rooms."

SATURDAY, AUGUST 3: A Jousting Tournament was held at Bay Ridge last Monday and Tuesday. "The track where the knights competed for the honor of crowning some fair lady queen was decorated with bunting and flags, and would have been in good condition save for the drouth [sic], which made the grounds dusty and heavy. . . . The chivalric men who contended for the honors were Thomas Quill, Knight of Columbia; James C. Hewett, Knight of Carroll; R. G. Chaney, Knight of Bay Ridge; Charles Pearce, Knight of Silver Star; William Brown, Knight of Hunter's Chance; W. B. Pearce, Knight of Deerfield; William Quill, Knight of Howard; F. R. Smith, Knight of Annandale; William Anderson, Knight of Rippling Wave; R. Wiley, Knight of Harford and D. M. Hite, Knight of Baltimore. . . . Miss Mollie LeBron was crowned Queen of Love and Beauty, with the usual complement of maids of honor. . . . The coronation address . . . and the charge to the knights [preceded the competition]. . . . At night there was a ball which was largely attended." On Tuesday 4,000 came for the second day of the Tournament, which culminated with a coronation ceremony at which the queen and maids of honor were crowned and prizes of a silver tea set, silver pitcher, silver goblet and silver mug were awarded. "At night a grand display of fireworks by Bond took place, which was witnessed by a large crowd." The steamer *Port Deposit* brought Annapolitans in the evening to see the fireworks but was unable to land at the wharf "because of the heavy sea."

1882

SATURDAY, MAY 27: Mr. J. C. Toner, manager of the Mansion House at Druid Hill Park, will also manage Bay Ridge this season.

1883

SATURDAY, JUNE 23: "Through the courtesy of Messrs. Hamilton Disston, of Phila. and Jas. H. Vansant, of this city [a reporter from the *Maryland Republican*] had the pleasure of visiting the Ridge, going down on Mr. Disston's steam yacht, *Mischief*. Dr. G. O. Glavis, late of Red Sulphur Springs, is manager this year . . . a large dancing pavilion has been erected . . . a race track and baseball ground laid off."

SATURDAY, AUGUST 11: "A grand family excursion was given to the Ridge, gotten up by some of our citizens . . . quite a crowd. . . ."

SATURDAY, SEPTEMBER 1–SATURDAY, SEPTEMBER 8: "The world renowned Levy," cornet soloist, backed by Professor Emerich's twenty-five piece orchestra, performed on Sunday at no extra charge. "The programme embraced selections from Mendelssohn, Offenbach, [Von] Weber, Donizetti, and Gounod." Levy played many encores including "Nearer My God to Thee," "Swanee River," "My Maryland," and "Yankee Doodle." The Ridge will be closed for the season on September 3 "which will be Grand Army Day, the numerous posts of this organization in Baltimore having full control of the grounds on that day." "Companies of the Washington Light Infantry, National Rifles and Union Veterans Corps of D. C. attended . . . shooting matches were held . . . and a fine punch bowl was won by the Washington Light Infantry team."

1884

FRIDAY, MAY 23: "The Bay Ridge House has been handsomely repaired. Six hundred trees have been planted . . . and the vegetables needed at the hotel have been raised on the farm." Mr. Jerome Durham is manager. "A party composed of young people will give a hop to-night at Bay Ridge, and will leave here by way of [hansom] cabs."

SATURDAY, MAY 24: "The hop given last night at Bay Ridge, by Mrs. Vansant and daughter to their numerous friends, was an excellent affair. The hotel was thrown open to the guests and everything tended to make the evening pleasant and agreeable to the young people—Dancing began at 10 o'clock, music was furnished by several pieces of the Academy Band under the direction of Mr. Schryer. A handsome collation was served at 1 o'clock in the spacious dining hall of the hotel. There were between forty and fifty present from Annapolis and several from Baltimore. Dancing continued throughout the evening, and it was not until the 'Monarch of the East' heralded the approach of day that the weary ones returned home."

THURSDAY, MAY 29: At the resorts this season, "Fashionable and dressy parasols are very gay, very large, and very much trimmed with lace and flowers."

TUESDAY, JUNE 10: "The proposition to construct a narrow-gauge railroad from this city to a point on the Chesapeake is being discussed with considerable energy by several capitalists of this city. . . . This proposition is a good one . . . if the route should pass through our city and terminate at Bay Ridge. . . ."

Fig. 55. Mrs. James H. Vansant c. 1887

MONDAY, JUNE 16: "Mr. James H. Vansant has just caused to be completed a line of telephone communication between his livery stable in this city and Bay Ridge. The next enterprise we hope to hear of in conjunction with this is the commencement and completion of the new line of railroad from here to Bay Ridge, a charter for which was granted by the last legislature. Van is an energetic and enterprising fellow and generally succeeds in anything he undertakes."

MONDAY, JULY 7: "Through the efforts . . . of Mr. James H. Vansant, who is ever on the 'qui vive' to do everything looking to the enjoyment of the pleasure seeker of our city, the proprietors of the steam ferry boat, *Bergen Point*, were induced to run excursions daily to Bay Ridge . . . leaving from the foot of Prince George's St."

TUESDAY, JULY 8: "It was intimated some time ago that the Annapolis Improvement Association had in contemplation the opening of a new road along the beach leading from Chinck Point, opposite the gut leading into Back Creek, to Bay Ridge. If this idea is carried out . . . a beautiful drive would be afforded to our people . . . an excellent opportunity to sniff the balmy and invigorating salt air from the bay and return home via the county road. . . . Where is our enterprising fellow citizen, Jas. H. Vansant? Van is just the fellow to enlist his energies in such an enterprise. Come to the front, Van!"

MONDAY, SEPTEMBER 22: A special committee has recommended the building of a "sea-shore road to Bay Ridge resort" from Annapolis, to be a "tramway along the sea shore with a width of 30 feet, together with a ten foot road on either side of the main thoroughfare for pedestrians. On either side of the road there are to be planted beautiful shade trees. . . . With a road of character . . . Bay Ridge . . . would . . . be courted by many in quest of health."

TUESDAY, SEPTEMBER 30: Mr. Dennis C. Thompson, "fishing off Tolly's Point in a flood tide . . . in a very short time had hauled up 105 fine large rock . . . each over a foot in length. . . ."

1885

TUESDAY, FEBRUARY 24: "The creeks and rivers were crowded yesterday all day with skaters, including many ladies. Several ice-boats on runners with sails, were also on the river, and made lightning speed. Every one that could raise a pair of skates, took advantage of the day—many skating as far as Bay Ridge."

SATURDAY, APRIL 18: "This beautiful summer resort has fallen into new hands, who, it is hoped, will make radical improvements in its management. . . . The first season of its opening gave hopes of abundant success, but . . . was so parsimoniously conducted, that visitors became disgusted, and at the close of the season the managers were sadly disappointed in their returns for the outlay, and threw up their lease in disgust. . . . The lessees for this season are Baltimoreans, and are said to be gentlemen of ample capital, with large experience . . . to cater to the public taste.—We hope this may be so. . . . The *Capital* wishes them great success."

FRIDAY, MAY 15: Miss Jennie Calef with her guests day-cruising on the schooner, *Mary A. D. Night*, Capt. R. T. Kelly, "after sailing around some time on the bay . . . stopped at Bay Ridge, where they met a cordial welcome from those in charge. . . ."

Fig. 56. Sailing excursion to Bay Ridge c. 1903

MONDAY, MAY 25: "Five of the incorporators of the proposed Annapolis and Bay Ridge Railroad Company met . . . among the incorporators are James H. Brown, John Ireland and J. H. Vansant of Annapolis."

WEDNESDAY, JUNE 3: "Mr. Thomas J. Hurley, president of the Bay Ridge Improvement and Transportation Co. [now managing Bay Ridge], closed with the owners of the *Jane Mosely* for the use of that steamer for the season. . . ."

Fig. 57. SS Jane Moseley

TUESDAY, JUNE 9: "A splendid pier has been built in front of the hotel and will be covered for 1,000 feet to allow ladies and children to fish in the shade...." The hotel dining room will now "accommodate 400 persons."

FRIDAY, JUNE 19: "Bay Ridge is being thoroughly and elegantly equipped.... Several of the popular 'Heinkampt' pianos have just been procured...."

THURSDAY, JUNE 25: "Bay Ridge opened today! The steamer *Jane Mosely* came into Annapolis this morning with flying colors, with a large party of Baltimoreans on board and took about a hundred from Annapolis."

FRIDAY, JULY 3–MONDAY, JULY 6: "About 5,000 visitors" were at Bay Ridge for the Fourth of July. "Brass and string music [was played] on the boat and also on the ground during the entire day.... The steamer *Ida* ... carried a large excursion from Easton, Cambridge, and Oxford.... The *Pentz* ... and the *Jane Mosely* ... also carried a number from this city and continued to run between the Ridge and Baltimore during the day with crowds more." The managers of Bay Ridge are to be praised for a successful Fourth and for maintaining sobriety on the grounds. The "bathing grounds" are "the finest on the bay shore and the surf almost equal to that of Cape May ... the grounds are artistically laid off with gravel walks and beautiful flower plots."

SATURDAY, JULY 11: "The company now managing Bay Ridge is entitled to a great deal of credit.... But there is one real nuisance which should be positively quickly abated, if the company proposes to continue to invite respectable organizations and people as its guests. I refer to the prohibition of inappropriate bathing suits. None but woolen material of good texture, and full suit should be allowed. The incomplete and very thin suits used to some extent there now are positively indecent. They should not be permitted at a shore where ladies and gentlemen bathe together. There was a great deal of earnest criticism of this 'nasty feature,' while the excursionists of last Thursday were there. The company will probably see that it is abated. For in its deserved success it will doubtless recognize that this is due to a decent public opinion."

TUESDAY, JULY 14: "The steamer *Bergen Point* excursion to Bay Ridge on July 15, 16, 17, will leave Ferry Wharf at 12:00 sharp so Annapolitans can spend 7 hours at the Ridge and enjoy the fine concerts to be given by the famous Mexican Band, considered one of the finest musical organizations in the world. The Band, composed of twenty-one noble

Fig. 58. July 2, 1885

Mexicans, is adorned with the national Charros costume, gorgeously trimmed with silver layers and large sombreros, with silver cord and tassel, will make a picture never seen before at any summer resort in this country."

MONDAY, JULY 20–FRIDAY, JULY 24: "The guard of James A. Garfield Camp, No. 1 Sons of Veterans, will go into a Camp of Instruction at Bay Ridge for 5 days starting July 20–24 inclusive, under Gen. W. E. W. Ross. A grand field dress parade will take place... attended by military from Baltimore, Washington, Towson and Alexandria. Col. W. G. Moore of D.C. is in charge of the visiting military. Strict military discipline will be enforced." July 21: "Special excursions will be made to see the encampment of the Grand Army of the Republic...." July 22: "The Union Veterans Corps, 'Old Guard,'... will travel from D.C. to Annapolis and Bay Ridge via the A & E Railroad tomorrow. They will take the steamer *Pentz*... down the Bay [and will] land at Bay Ridge." July 23: "It is estimated that 4000 persons were at the Ridge today" for the military display dubbed "Camp Arnold." July 24: A dress parade was held in the morning. "Resolutions were read on the death of Gen. Grant.... Minute Guns were fired today in memory of Grant."

WEDNESDAY, JULY 29: "The steamer *Pentz* inspector was forced to turn away 200–300 excursionists in Annapolis for the season's largest Sunday school excursion to Bay Ridge. Excursionists were seen wending their way homeward with their picnic baskets on their arms. It was sad to see the little ones who had anticipated a day of enjoyment at Bay Ridge." Mercifully, at noon, the *Bergen Point* arrived to take the "children-left-behind" to Bay Ridge on a special run.

Fig. 59. View of resort from steamboat landing with visitors ascending steps to hotel. The pier, constructed in time for the 1885 season, was covered for 1,000 feet to provide shade during the long trek ashore, and side balconies were added for fishing and crabbing.

THURSDAY, JULY 30: An "observer" at Bay Ridge writes to the *Capital* commending the managers of Bay Ridge for the recent change to appropriate rental bathing suits, the former having been "too ridiculous for anything.... Instead of the flimsy material heretofore used, a dark woolen material of good texture, loosely fitting, had taken place of the former 'nasty feature.' The company managing Bay Ridge this year is to be commended."

THURSDAY, AUGUST 20: "The success of Bay Ridge and the necessity of having quick communication between it and Baltimore have given impetus to the short line railroad movement."

FRIDAY, AUGUST 21: Mr. John F. Anderson, state railroad commissioner; Mr. C. W. Richardson, Boston; Mr. John Goodwin and Col. Underhill, Baltimore; plus New York gentlemen met at Bay Ridge yesterday concerning the contemplated Short Line Railroad.

SATURDAY, AUGUST 22: "The large water tank that supplies the Bay Ridge hotel, gave way yesterday, letting all the water escape, and rendering it necessary to carry the water in the hotel by hand. The grounds near the hotel were temporarily flooded.... A party ... caught over 3 bushels of hard crabs off one of the piers at the Ridge, and remarked that it paid to go to Bay Ridge."

THURSDAY, AUGUST 27: "A grand display of fireworks" will be held tomorrow evening under the direction of Prof. Wm. Bond, and will last one hour. "A grand military band of 20 pieces will play music during this pyrotechnical display."

THURSDAY, SEPTEMBER 10: "Bay Ridge closed yesterday for the season. The number of visitors for the season was in excess of 80,000."

1886

FRIDAY, MARCH 19: James H. Vansant is listed as a member of the board of directors for the Bay Ridge Railroad. "It will be a 10 minute ride from Annapolis to Bay Ridge on a 5-mile track. Mr. Vansant secured the right of way and has expedited the details. Construction will begin soon and the road will be finished in 30–40 days."

MONDAY, MAY 3: Baltimore musicians have complained in writing to the Secretary of the Navy in protest of the Naval Academy Band's accepting professional employment outside the Navy, that is, for accepting a summer engagement to play at the Bay Ridge resort. "The Secretary of the Navy has declined to prevent the Naval Academy Band at Annapolis from playing for the Bay Ridge Company ... [explaining that] the band does not play outside as a body, but the members make engagements, as they are allowed to do...."

SATURDAY, MAY 15: A sum of $250,000 was recently invested for resort improvements and for construction of the Bay Ridge Railroad by the Bay Ridge Company, and two fine steamers have been chartered, the *Empire State* and the *Bay Ridge*.

THURSDAY, MAY 20: "The first consignment of 600,000 feet of lumber for the Bay Ridge improvements arrived at Jackson's Wharf, Baltimore, yesterday from Pennsylvania. It will be shipped to Bay Ridge in bay vessels.... A large raft of piles for the Annapolis and Bay Ridge R.R. were taken up the Spa this morning for the bridge over that creek.... The Baltimore and Annapolis Short Line R.R. has begun laying rails."

TUESDAY, MAY 25: "Hundreds of city people daily visit the construction of this [Bay Ridge] railroad."

Fig. 60. SS Bay Ridge *moored in front of a warehouse in Baltimore harbor c. 1886*

FRIDAY, MAY 28: "Thousands of feet of building materials have landed at the Bay Ridge wharf for the addition to the hotel . . . ." The company has received letters confirming arrangements for the rowing regatta which will include a race between Gauder and Hamm and Teemer and Courtney, "the fastest double scullers that this country has ever produced."

WEDNESDAY, JUNE 2: "The cross-ties for the Bay Ridge Road are being distributed along the route preparatory to being put into position. . . . A large vessel load of steel has arrived at the Bay Ridge wharf."

MONDAY, JUNE 14: The steamer *Pentz* brought to Bay Ridge "three large bears, 2 alligators, a wildcat, eagles, owls and some fine aquatic birds to be placed in a large building as a part of the collection for the zoological exhibition."

WEDNESDAY, JUNE 16–TUESDAY, JUNE 22: The 30-piece Austrian Military Band has been employed by Bay Ridge for the summer in addition to the ever popular Naval Academy Band. They will begin their new duties next Monday, providing music for the passengers traveling by steamboat to and from the resort.

THURSDAY, JUNE 17: The Governor has commissioned Edward K. Tryan, of Baltimore, as Chief of Police at Bay Ridge with five policemen under him.

TUESDAY, JUNE 22: Mr. J. M. Hill, lessee and manager of the Opera House in Annapolis, "has secured the privilege of the Bay Ridge Opera House," and will open the season on July 1st with the "Bijou Opera Company."

MONDAY, JUNE 28: "The first engine with 4 freight cars ran over the Bay Ridge road on Saturday evening as far as Primrose. . . . Hundreds of people witnessed, for the first time, an engine and cars passing over Spa Creek, and through the fertile fields of adjacent farms. As it passed along, the crowd that stood upon the banks on either side of the road waved their hats and handkerchiefs and gave three cheers to those on the engine [Mr. Gable, engineer, A. Musterman, fireman]. It was the opening of a new era in the history of our city, and county. . . ."

TUESDAY, JUNE 29: Today the grading was finished on the Bay Ridge Railroad. The official opening will be held on July 3 with the mayor, city council, and invited guests from Baltimore, Washington, and Annapolis attending.

Fig. 61. SS Bay Ridge *redesigned and rebuilt for safety and comfort*

THURSDAY, JULY 1: The new steamer *Empire State* plying between Baltimore and Bay Ridge, "ran aground within thirty feet of the wharf [at Bay Ridge] and was unable to unload her passengers." She was still aground at 9:00 p.m. "The *lusus naturae*—white snake, captured in the lower part of this county, arrived," having been purchased for "the Zoological Collection."

FRIDAY, JULY 2: "The *Empire State* was aground until 1:00 a.m. . . ." The Bay Ridge wharf "is to be run out 200 more feet making it altogether 1,200 feet in length in order to accommodate the steamer *Empire State*." The steam pile-driver, now in the Severn working on the construction of the Short Line Railroad bridge, will be used to construct this addition to the steamship wharf. "Plumbers and laborers are laying pipes connecting the hotel with buildings for the purpose of sewage."

TUESDAY, JULY 6: For the Fourth of July there were 9,000 people on the grounds. The *Bay Ridge* and the *Empire State* made two runs each to Baltimore. Many came in small private boats. "The Naval Academy Band was loudly applauded . . . at night a brilliant display of fireworks took place and was seen for miles around. In the display a number of fire balloons were sent up bearing tags of Bay Ridge. . . . Cars will run on the Bay Ridge Railroad next Thursday."

WEDNESDAY, JULY 7: "The first steam engine with construction cars came to Bay Ridge yesterday as far as the gravity railroad, the terminus of the new road."

SATURDAY, JULY 10: "Raceboats have arrived... for the 17th and 18th races... teams will practice daily until the day of the races.... Their quarters will be in the Ogleton Club House, formerly the old Steele mansion, which is situated at the upper end of the course." Because "many carpenters failed to return after the Fourth to finish the Opera House [there are] only 50 workers left... it will now take 2 weeks to finish the Opera House and Bandshell."

MONDAY, JULY 12: "Fire, discovered by nightwatchman, Thos. Holliday, in the old shanty [on Tolly Point] known as the 'Home of the Friendless,' occupied by laborers, severely burned two sleeping men, one of whom died later. Most of the building was burned and was destroyed." Holliday alerted the managers who arrived too late with fire extinguishers. The injured were taken to the hotel doctor and were sent to Baltimore City Hospital aboard the steamer *Bay Ridge*. It was determined that "the fire was caused by the explosion of a coal oil lamp which was left burning...."

MONDAY, JULY 12: "About 4,000 people were on the grounds" for the big band competition. "The Marine Band opened with a great concert on the pavilion.... Their rendition of 'The Mikado' was loudly applauded by the spectators. The Austrian Band followed with a sacred concert, equally applauded and quite a contrast!" At Bay Ridge "the white snake shed its skin and is even whiter."

TUESDAY, JULY 13: "Machines for electric lights have been adjusted and the grounds were illuminated with electric lights for the first time last night."

WEDNESDAY, JULY 14: The oarsmen, "men of fine physique," have been practicing for the scull regatta. "The view from the porticoes of the hotel and other elevated positions on the grounds" are recommended to those who will watch the regatta. Annapolitans are unhappy about the new Bay Ridge edict prohibiting private sailboats from landing on the beach. The *Capital* is in favor of the edict. "The Bay Ridge Company doesn't propose to give the rights of their ground free to every sailboat on the bay and rivers [having] gone to great expense to provide a train." A little Baltimore girl, delighted and charmed with her visit to Bay Ridge, asked her mother, "Mama, do all good people go to Bay Ridge when they die?"

THURSDAY, JULY 15–SATURDAY, JULY 17: Large crowds of over 5,000 have arrived for the Rowing Regatta. The race purse is "... for $400 in the final heat. $150 for the consolation purse." July 17: The "great double scull race for the championship of America" was held at 5:30 p.m. "Lake Ogleton was perfect, not a ripple [and] Ross beat Teemer by a length in 18:10."

MONDAY, JULY 19–FRIDAY, JULY 23: On Sunday, "music of a sacred character" was played to a "beach and hotel crowded with [4,000] promenaders." July 22: Bay Ridge now lighted by electricity "presents a magnificent appearance at night. The view from the bay is simply grand.... Now 3 trains travel to Bay Ridge a day—25c round trip from Annapolis." July 23: "The Howard Zouaves, a military organization of N.E. Baltimore, will camp at Bay Ridge Aug. 2–7th" with about 52 members. "Mrs. Phillips, going down the steep steps to the bath-house shore, slipped and fell headlong to the beach, was picked up by Officer Frazier and helped to the ladies' dressing room of the bathhouse. A physician and apothecary came to her aid on the spot.... A turntable for trains is soon to be built at this end of the road."

WEDNESDAY, JULY 28: "Permission was given the Bay Ridge Company today to land their steamers... at the Naval Academy Wharf so Bay

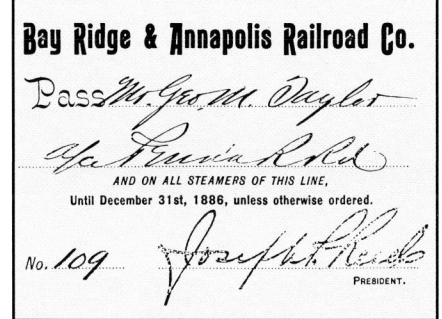

Fig. 62. Rail-steamer pass, 1886

Ridge guests could attend the unveiling of the DeKalb statue.... The Bay Ridge Railroad will also run special trains for the occasion."

THURSDAY, JULY 29: "The Grand Pavilion was crowded due to refreshing breezes there. A baseball game ensued. The Red-stocking Nine of Baltimore defeated the Brown-stocking Nine of Bay Ridge, 1–0. The Bijou Opera Company will ... introduce 'Banker's Luck.' "

FRIDAY, JULY 30: The rights-of-way have been secured for the Bay Shore Drive to Bay Ridge which "will be a treat to our women and children who need fresh, pure air in the hot season, and will give the beaus a delightful drive, with their sweethearts, in the cool of the evening."

FRIDAY, AUGUST 13: Between 7–8,000 persons were on the grounds and there was "considerable confusion at the depot tonight [with] the passengers getting on wrong trains [as] no less than four trains were leaving at about the same time."

FRIDAY, AUGUST 20: "A large portion of the farm [will be laid off] for the purpose of an agricultural fair, upon which will be erected suitable buildings, for stock" and farm produce exhibitions. A "first class race course" has been proposed for the fair.

TUESDAY, SEPTEMBER 6–THURSDAY, SEPTEMBER 8: There is no band at Bay Ridge due to non-payment for services rendered. The Naval Academy Band is owed $1,800. September 8: It is the end of the season and "Bay Ridge without the music of the Naval Academy Band is tame indeed."

WEDNESDAY, SEPTEMBER 15: At a Bay Ridge Company creditors' meeting in Baltimore yesterday it was learned that the total liabilities of the company are $168,000 totally unsecured and $58,000 partially secured through rights of the mechanics lien law. "All the bonds represented by the mortgage [300], of the par value of $1,000 each, were claimed to be issued.... The creditors agreed to desist from enforcing claims for a time because the working of the company was yielding a handsome profit on the actual cost of the investment."

TUESDAY, NOVEMBER 8: "Mr. Robert Garrett, president of the B & O R.R. Company, yesterday purchased the controlling interest in the Bay Ridge summer resort and the Annapolis and Bay Ridge Railroad. The consideration is said to be $150,000—The improvements at Bay Ridge are to be completed, and the resort will be operated under the B & O management with transportation by railroad and steamboats. The officers of the Bay Ridge Company were in Baltimore to complete the formal transfer. The company's liabilities have been put at about $168,000 and the $150,000 sale is expected to turn out well for the creditors."

1887

SATURDAY, MARCH 5: The Annapolis Local Improvement Association committee has "permission from Bay Ridge to bridge Lake Ogleton and land on Bay Ridge territory."

WEDNESDAY, APRIL 27: The survey for extending the Bay Ridge Railroad to the hotel was completed and work has begun. Soon passengers will be spared the 1/4 mile walk to the center of the resort. J. L. Colvin is manager this season.

WEDNESDAY, JUNE 22: "Bay Ridge started off with a boom ... and is already booked for the season.... The steamers are *Theo. Weems* and *Jane Mosely*...." Good fare at Bay Ridge: "... soft crabs and fried chicken, all fresh meats are brought to Bay Ridge daily by boat and placed in the large ice house ... coffee, tea, bread and butter ... always fresh."

SATURDAY, JUNE 25: Between 5,000 and 8,000 people witnessed "the World Championship Jousting or Mounted Sword Contest between Ross and Walsh whereby the mounted men dash towards one another. . . . Professor A. J. Corbessier, fencing master at the U.S.N.A. was referee."

Fig. 63. Back Creek Bridge, a link in Bay Shore Drive—the horse and buggy route from Annapolis to Bay Ridge (see figure 4).

SATURDAY, JULY 2: "The Bay Shore Road leading from Back Creek to Bay Ridge around the bay shore is now complete . . . "

THURSDAY, JULY 21: Professor Bond will present his fireworks again this year. "The view from the hotel will be beautiful and as the boat steams from the wharf a grand illumination of red, green and blue lights will be made. . . . A shower of rockets, followed by a bombardment of shells, will open the ball."

THURSDAY, JULY 29: Frederick N. Innes, the great trombone soloist, has been engaged at Bay Ridge for a week. His repertoire includes "The Sea Shell Waltz," "Goodbye Sweetheart," "The Palms," and "Dixie."

THURSDAY, AUGUST 18: The Championship Tub Race was held between 6 and 7 p.m. on Lake Ogleton, witnessed by at least 2,000 persons. All the contestants were Annapolitans: Messrs. C. Jickling, Robert Redmond, Thos. Tydings, Jas. Strange, Ed Stevens, Martin Brady, Edward Abbott, and Frank Geraci. "Three of the contestants became entangled in the grass and their tubs sank. A gold-lined silver cup inscribed 'Tub Race, Bay Ridge, Aug. 17, 1887' was given to the winner, Mr. Robert Redmond. Many ladies and gentlemen from Annapolis were present including Dr. Thos. Welch, Mr. and Mrs. Benj. Watkins and family and Mr. H. M. Murry."

TUESDAY, AUGUST 23–MONDAY, AUGUST 29: Large crowds, including the Sodality of St. Andrew's Church and the Lord Baltimore Society, enjoyed the main attraction this week, "The Mandoline Quintet, composed of the Tipaldi Bros. who rendered selections such as 'Zanobia,' a march; 'Pique Dame,' an overture; and 'Valse Estudiantina,' . . . soft and delicate mandoline music wafting in a strong wind from the spacious porches of the restaurant." August 29: ". . . the music in tone is delicate and sweet, and the exquisite strains will long be remembered by those who wandered down the sandy beach."

Fig. 64. SS Columbia

1888

THURSDAY, MAY 10: The steamer, *Columbia*, a new boat from Baltimore is now engaged for Bay Ridge service. She is very large and is licensed to carry 3,500 people, which is 1,300 more than the other steamers at Baltimore. Mr. Charles Webb is general manager.

THURSDAY, MAY 17: According to the minutes of the Annapolis Local Improvement Association, Mr. Randall has submitted a resolution to locate an Anne Arundel County Fair at Bay Ridge in the fall on a permanent basis. Bay Ridge authorities have offered the use of grounds and buildings. Leading members of the County Grange are enthusiastic, stating that the fair will be a great success "if Bay Ridge be the chosen land."

TUESDAY, JUNE 19: A Baltimore man broke his left leg in two places "from a fall from a horse at Bay Ridge yesterday.... Dr. [Joseph Muse] Worthington [future husband of Margaret Taylor Randall who often photographed the resort] sent the man to the steamer *Columbia*, where the leg was set," by Dr. A. S. Warner of Baltimore assisted by Dr. Worthington.

Fig. 65. SS Columbia *at Bay Ridge pier*

MONDAY, JULY 2: "Between 10 and 15,000 persons were on the grounds at one time during the day attracted by the visit of the Great United German Saengerfest Association of Baltimore, whose chorus of 3,000 voices would echo through the air with instrumental music." By special permit, the large Opera House was converted for the day into a German lager beer saloon, where persons were admitted "on presentation of a ticket which could be had for the asking... between 800 and 1000 kegs of beer were drank [sic] during the day, to say nothing of soft drinks. The saloon was crowded from start of day till the last car and boat left the grounds.... [Surprisingly] there was little drunkenness to be seen...."

TUESDAY, JULY 31: The first Anne Arundel County Fair will be held at Bay Ridge. In preparation there will be constructed a covered grandstand, racehorse stable, open stables for 30 horses and 50 cattle and a half-mile racetrack for horses.

TUESDAY, JULY 31: A corps of carpenters and mechanics are now building a large music stand and a special platform for the Great Music Festival to be held August 5 through 19. Professor Innes will direct the Thirteenth New York Regiment forty-piece band and a featured chorus of 350 voices. The main feature will be "the Military Congress of All Nations, comprising 350 people dressed in the garb of the nations represented. Eight guns will be fired simultaneously when the congress assembles in front of the music stand."

THURSDAY, AUGUST 2: The Governor's Guards marched to Bay Ridge in full dress because they missed the steamer to their encampment with the Frederick Rifles and Howard Zouaves named "Camp LeCompte."

FRIDAY, AUGUST 10: Innes' production, "The Military Congress of All Nations" has attracted the most visitors for any week since the history of the resort. It "opens with a fanfaronade by trumpets in the distance followed by a vivid rendition of the 'Star Spangled Banner' with cannon accompaniment. After a pretty dance refrain by the band, the 'figures' march up to the music stand headed by a Russian contingent in full costume with national flag flying, followed by the representatives of other nations in costume, headed by separate bands of flags, the Scottish contingent having bagpipes. When the colored calcium lights are lowered, all present arms and the cannons again boom to 'My County 'Tis of Thee' followed by storms of applause."

MONDAY, AUGUST 13: "The Grand Pyrotechnical Battle at Bay Ridge: The attraction for this week will be the fireworks drama on Tuesday and Thursday evenings and again on Sunday evening of the great Naval battle between the Merrimac and Monitor. This exhibition shows the boats in position and steaming about, discharging their cannons, throwing bombs in the air and finishing up with the sinking of the Merrimac."

TUESDAY, AUGUST 14: Many people inspected "the machinery and other paraphernalia for the great fireworks drama."

WEDNESDAY, AUGUST 15: Six thousand persons "viewed Prof. Thayer's pyrotechnic panorama... a spirited and exciting show."

THURSDAY, AUGUST 16: "Manager Webb advertised No Extra Charge! No Extra Charge! in the *Baltimore Sun*. But then he erected toll gates and collected tolls on the public roads to Bay Ridge at 25c for adults and 15c for a child.... [There is] a tollgate on every road into Bay Ridge with a tollgatherer demanding payment for everyone entering Bay Ridge by *other* than rail or steamboat."

FRIDAY, AUGUST 17: "Over 9,000 persons, including 1,200 from this city, witnessed [the fireworks drama]... 80 waiters were kept busy all day

---

PROGRAM OF ATTRACTIONS

At the Anne Arundel Fair, Bay Ridge.

The following is the program of attractions during the Fair at Bay Ridge:

TUESDAY—11 A. M., Batteau Races.
   2 P. M., Trotting Races.
   5 P. M., Tub Race.

WEDNESDAY—11 A. M., Bugeyes and Canoes.
   12 M., Crabbing Skiffs.
   2 P. M., Racing.

THURSDAY—11 A. M., Sloops.
   12 M., Field Trials, Dogs.
   2 P. M., Trotting Races.
   4.30 P. M., Rowing Races.

FRIDAY—11 A. M., Pungies and Schrs.
   12 M., Plowing Match.
   1 P. M., Clay Pigeon Shoot.
   2 P. M., Trotting Races.
For catalogues, &c., address George T. Earle, Jr., Annapolis, Md.

Fig. 66. The first Anne Arundel County Fair was held at Bay Ridge.

EXCURSION TO

Bay Ridge.

The Annual Pic-Nic of Wesley Chapel M. E. Sunday School will be held at Bay Ridge on

THURSDAY, July 12th,

Train will leave depot at 10.10 A. M. returning, leave Bay Ridge at 8.15 P. M.
Tickets, Adults 25 cents, Children 15 cents, for sale by J. S. M. Basil, Goodman & Marcy, George W. Jones, and scholars. Tickets good on all trains. 76

Fig. 67. July 11, 1888

feeding the multitude.... At 7:30 the large open field was filled by thousands who cheered lustily at the brilliant display.... When the Merrimac steamed out amid the strains of 'Dixie,' there proved to be a great deal of Southern sentiment in the crowd, for 'The Bonnie Blue Flag That Bears a Single Star' was loudly applauded. New varieties of pyrotechnics were introduced. The crowd was lost in admiration and could say nothing but, 'Ah!' The appearance of the Monitor amid 'Hold the Fort' was greeted with loud hurrahs; and when after a terrific conflict of colored fire balls the Merrimac was enveloped in red fire and the Monitor steamed around to the tune of 'Yankee Doodle,' the crowd shouted."

TUESDAY, AUGUST 21: "The exorbitant and unreasonable charge by the Bay Ridge Co. for all Annapolitans and others coming on their grounds in private vehicles, boats, or on foot, has caused a great falling off in the teams that play ball in the afternoon ... a blow to Annapolis livery men who did such a thriving business. Bay Ridge has now withdrawn the toll on passengers but has doubled it on all teams."

WEDNESDAY, AUGUST 22: "Every day during the Fair, sailing races will be held on the bay in front of the bluff at 11:00 a.m. ... every day, trotting and running horse races at 2:00 p.m. ... On Tuesday, a tub race on the lake ... on Wednesday, a crabbing skiff rowing race in front of hotel... on Thursday, a series of rowing races will be held on Lake Ogleton for the rowing clubs ... plus there will be the usual agricultural attractions ... and trials for dogs."

TUESDAY, AUGUST 28: Batteau Race today ... "Early this morning, the City dock and the harbor were alive with the white-winged sailors preparatory to their departure for the Bay Ridge races.... Every master of his little bark was confident of success.... [The first day of the Fair] stock of all kinds [are] passing through Annapolis en route to the fair ... teams have been passing through the city since daylight this morning, loaded with sheep, hogs and poultry. Elegant race horses arrive in line with stolid curried cattle."

WEDNESDAY, AUGUST 29: "Bugeye and canoe races ... horse racing ... dairy, fruit and vegetable exhibits ... display of farm implements and machinery."

THURSDAY, AUGUST 30: Trotting races on the new half-mile track are held along with boat races on the bay.

1889

FRIDAY, MAY 24: Mr. Chas. Webb of J., manager, invited guests from Baltimore on the *Columbia* for a pre-season trip to see the new electric railway or trolley. "... the line ... extends all around the grounds, giving a fine view of the Bay, Annapolis, Naval Academy, Severn River ... the whole trip is 10c.... While the gentlemen inspected the buildings and improvements ... the ladies took possession of the fields and groves, and gathered wild flowers in profusion ... wild daisies and clover blossoms."

MONDAY, JUNE 24: Jules Levy, "greatest living cornetist ... played a number of ... popular airs and was loudly applauded. [His finale was] 'Home Sweet Home' and the last few bars were played amid the greatest enthusiasm."

TUESDAY, JULY 2: Large crowds observed the Swimming Match held at Bay Ridge. "The distance was over a mile and occupied about 45 minutes from start to finish."

WEDNESDAY, JULY 3: "The Grand Jubilee Concert" July 4th program by the fifty musicians of the Naval Academy Band, Professor Charles A. Zimmerman conducting, will include, "singing of the national airs, accompanied by the discharge of artillery, and the ringing of the mammoth bells, and the discharge of novel fireworks at night."

FRIDAY, JULY 5: Seven thousand visitors witnessed this event for which the Naval Academy superintendent had lent the Bay Ridge Company "four 12-pound guns and had also detailed a detachment of marines to fire off the pieces while 'The Star Spangled Banner' and 'Hail Columbia' were played." A fireworks display followed in the evening. Today a repeat of yesterday's concert was held, at which "300 voices and the Anval [sic] Chorus" performed.

TUESDAY, AUGUST 6: The midsummer musical festival was again presented. "Prof. Auer's Juvenile Corps de Ballet of Baltimore, did the national representation and dances in costume equal to stage veterans. . . ."

WEDNESDAY, AUGUST 7: The Anvil Chorus in costume added greatly to the program. Mr. Innes, trombone virtuoso, other soloists, and the Naval Academy Band were loudly applauded.

MONDAY, AUGUST 12: The next attraction will be a grand pyrotechnic display representing "the attack and fall of Fort Sumter. . . . The exhibition will be given on the boat lake at the end of the gravity road. Fort Sumter will occupy the centre of the lake, with batteries of fireworks. The fort will be attacked from earth works on the shore and by ships of war and steam ram."

WEDNESDAY, AUGUST 14: Approximately 6,000 people attended "The Bombardment of Fort Sumter. . . . A regular fortress was erected in Lake Ogleton from which the American flag was flying, and the spectacle of the ships in battle array was a realistic one. The maneuvering of the vessels was not as perfect as desired owing to the stiff breeze . . . the display . . . was grand and greatly enjoyed by all. . . ."

THURSDAY, AUGUST 15: A successful picnic of the Presbyterian Sunday School was held at Bay Ridge. "Upon entering the grounds, the school children, accompanied by their teachers, parents, and friends . . . proceeded to the beautiful shady grove on the banks of the river, where stationary tables and seats are provided in abundance for such occasions. . . . Soon swings and hammocks were swung in the trees, and the merry hearts of the children were delighted with the scenes around them. Near to the grove is the steam merry-go-round or flying horses, while the electric railroad is every now and then passing around the grounds with its merry passengers. Beautiful walks lead in every direction of the grounds and everything is brought into easy distance. Manager Webb is obliging and accommodating . . . a more delightful place . . . could not be found in the State." The children returned in the evening to see the "Bombardment of Fort Sumter" on the Lake. "The school realized between $7 and $8 after expenses."

MONDAY, AUGUST 20: The Anne Arundel County Fair plans include "a Wild West Show every day at 11:00 a.m.; a regatta on the 30th with entries from D.C., Annapolis and Richmond; trotting and running races for horses . . . a grand ball on the last night of the Fair to patrons of the Fair, with 600 invitations sent out . . . and a rowing regatta open to all amateur oarsmen in many events . . . senior single sculls, junior single sculls, semi 4-oared shells, junior 4-oared shells and 4-oared gigs. A gold medal will be presented to winners and a silk banner to clubs that they represent. Rules adopted by the Naval Association of Amateur Oarsmen will prevail."

THURSDAY, AUGUST 22: Special guests "invited to witness the working of the Sprague Electric Railway, travelled the road at 16 m.p.h. and were then banqueted at the cafe where guest speaker, Mr. O. T. Crosby [later to become the first president of Potomac Electric Power Co., Washington, D.C.] described the workings of the Sprague System of electric motors . . . used by more than 60 street railway companies."

SATURDAY, AUGUST 24: Pawnee Bill's Wild West Show will be featured at the Fair and will include "reckless riding, the attack on the old Overland stage coach, the capture and burning of the trapper's cabin, the descent of the Indians on the emigrants' train and the opportune arrival of the cowboys who rescue those in peril, feats of horsemanship [wherein] handkerchiefs, hats, and coins are picked up from the backs of ponies running at full speed, bucking mustangs and ponies, Pawnee Bill, himself [a former member of Buffalo Bill's Wild West Show], and cowboys and scouts . . . an Indian Village . . . home customs of Indians, chiefs, braves, squaws and papooses."

Fig. 68. Ancestors of Sandy Brooks Newark enjoyed a family outing at Bay Ridge, late 1880s. The Indian headband and feather worn by the child suggests she may have attended Pawnee Bill's Wild West Show, August 1889.

TUESDAY, AUGUST 27: The 2nd Annual Anne Arundel County Fair begins today. Farmers will be addressed from the West Portico in the rear of the cafe. Events include trotting races; Wild West Show; horse races; sailing races between bugeyes, batteaus, sailing canoes, schooners, sloops; and a display of poultry. "The race track has been smoothed and hardened by large iron rollers."

WEDNESDAY, AUGUST 28: The "sailing races presented a beautiful scene from the cafe and the Hotel verandas. . . . The excursionists were very loathed to give up their dancing pavilion" for use as an agricultural exhibit hall.

THURSDAY, AUGUST 29: Live-stock awards, horse races, sailing races were held. There was also a "bag race" for small boys in front of the grand stand on the racetrack in which "little boys run in loose fitting bags tied about the waist." The sailing races took place from Bay Ridge wharf to Sandy Point and back, a distance of 7 miles.

FRIDAY, AUGUST 30: In the shooting matches the Annapolis Gun Club beat the Patuxent Gun Club for a gold medal. Today's events include a "big cattle exhibit . . . work horse exhibit . . . produce exhibit . . . trotting races . . . a special train assigned to bring invited guests to the Ball."

SATURDAY, AUGUST 31: In the afternoon the exhibits were removed from the pavilion, and floors were waxed for dancing at the Ball. The Fair Ball, attended by persons from Washington, Philadelphia, Baltimore and Annapolis was a success. "The large dance pavilion . . . [was] decorated with potted flowers and ferns . . . innumerable Chinese lanterns were hung from the ceiling . . . guests began to arrive at 9:00 p.m. . . . The programme began with a march, headed by Mr. and Mrs. Charles Webb. The costumes worn by the ladies were costly and beautiful. . . . Music was furnished by the Naval Academy Band, directed by Charles A. Zimmerman. . . . Dancing continued until nearly midnight, when it was announced near train time, and all began to leave the ball-room for the train. . . ."

FRIDAY, SEPTEMBER 6: Word has it that Bay Ridge is to change hands to become a health spa, that a New York syndicate has secured a 99-year lease on all Bay Ridge Company property.

SATURDAY, SEPTEMBER 7: Mr. Hugh L. Bond, president of the Bay Ridge Company, denies the rumor that Bay Ridge has been leased to a New York syndicate.

MONDAY, SEPTEMBER 9: Bay Ridge closes after a successful season. In spite of the many rainy days "the gross receipts will exceed those of 1888." Mr. Webb is "the right man in the right place." Today, "the *Theo. Weems* was destroyed by fire at her wharf in Baltimore."

1890

MONDAY, MAY 19: "A number of our citizens took advantage of the delightful weather yesterday to walk to Bay Ridge." Their attention was attracted to "the long pier to the right of the Bath House, which extends out quite a distance from the beach . . . rails are laid up to the pier, upon which ties are partly laid for a double track."

TUESDAY, JUNE 3: The Eastern Shore Railroad will be in operation during the season and more guests will be coming to Bay Ridge from the Eastern Shore. The first ball of the season at Bay Ridge was "given by leading citizens of Annapolis." A special train at 8:00 P.M. carried "the elite of city and Naval circles" and returned the party to Annapolis "at an early hour this morning."

MONDAY, JUNE 16: "It is stated that over 50 teams, single and double, passed through Annapolis to Bay Ridge yesterday."

TUESDAY, JUNE 17: The county commissioners were given a petition signed by citizens and taxpayers to repair and shell the Bay Shore Drive between Annapolis and Bay Ridge.

SATURDAY, JULY 5: "Train after train passed over the Bay Ridge road yesterday with 6, 8, 10, 12 coaches with excursionists from Philadelphia, Baltimore and Washington plus 600 from Annapolis. . . . At least 10,000 people were at Bay Ridge yesterday. . . ."

SATURDAY, JULY 12: The Juvenile Corps de Ballet exhibition of fancy dancing, in costume, directed by Prof. Auer, featured "Swedish, plantation, skirt, tambourine, cachuca, chime, and rope and sword dances" on the Opera House stage. The Naval Academy Band provided the music.

MONDAY, JULY 28: Large crowds attended the Operatic Concert at which Maffail in costume sang "Heart Bowed Down" from Balfe, "Bohemian Girl" and "In Happy Moments" by Wallace. Miss Peddleford sang Molloy's "Only Tonight." H. Judson and Mrs. Webb sang Lesson's "The Daily Question," and Brri and Faye's "The Old Brigade" and "Tell Her I Love Her So."

BALTIMORE AND EASTERN SHORE RAILROAD.

WILLARD THOMSON, Receiver. | A. J. BENJAMIN,
J. M. JACKSON, Gen. Supt. | Gen. Fht. & Pas. Agt. and Auditor.
General Offices—Salisbury, Md.

Mix.	Exs.	Exs.	Mls	*July* 12, 1891.	Mls	Exs	Exs.	Mix.
	P. M.	A. M.		LEAVE] [ARRIVE		P. M.	NO'N	
	†4 55	*7 00		Baltimore ♂	131	10 30	12 25	
	5 50	7 55		Annapolis[1] ♂	104	9 30	11 30	
	6 15	8 15		Bay Ridge ♂	99	9 15	11 15	
P. M.	P. M.	A. M.		LEAVE] [ARRIVE		P. M.	A. M.	A. M.
†2 30	†7 45	*9 50	0	Claiborne[2] ♂	87	7 45	9 50	11 42
2 36	..	..	1	McDaniel	86	..	..	11 36
2 43	7 50	9 56	2	Harper	84	7 30	9 35	11 29
2 53	7 55	10 02	5	St. Michael's ♂	82	7 25	9 30	11 18
3 02	..	..	6	Riverside	81	..	..	[illegible]
3 12	8 02	10 11	9	Royal Oak ♂	78	7 18	9 23	10 59
3 22	8 05	10 15	10	Kirkham	77	7 15	9 20	10 50
3 32	8 10	10 21	12	Bloomfield	75	7 10	9 15	10 45
4 00	8 15	10 27	15	Easton[3] ♂	72	7 05	9 10	10 27
4 10	..	..	19	Turner	68	..	..	9 50
4 20	8 29	10 42	22	Bethlehem	65	6 51	8 56	9 40
4 30	8 35	10 49	25	Preston ♂	62	6 45	8 50	9 30
4 37	8 40	10 55	27	Douglass	60	6 40	8 45	9 25
4 55	8 48	11 04	31	Hurlock[3½] ♂	56	6 32	8 37	9 08
5 06	..	..	34	Ennalls	53	..	..	8 57
5 13	8 56	11 13	35	Rhodesdale ♂	52	6 21	8 29	8 50
5 42	9 09	11 26	42	Vienna ♂	45	6 11	8 16	8 25
6 00	9 18	11 36	46	Barren Creek ♂	41	6 00	8 07	8 07
6 20	9 23	11 46	51	Hebron ♂	36	5 51	7 57	7 50
6 30	..	..	52	Rock-a-Walkin	35	..	..	7 43
6 50	9 40	11 58	57	arr. Salisbury[4, 5] lve.	30	5 39	7 45	7 25
7 20	9 40	11 58	57	lve. Salisbury arr.	30	5 39	7 45	6 40
7 43	a	..	[illegible]	Walst[illegible]	25	..	..	6 17
7 53	a	12 14	[illegible]	Parso[illegible]	23	5 25	..	6 08
8 07	a	[illegible]	[illegible]	Pitt[illegible]	[illegible]	5 18	..	5 54
8 27	a	..	72	New [illegible]	15	..	..	5 33
8 34	a	12 33	74	Whaleyville	13	5 06	..	5 25
8 50	a	..	77	St. Martin's	10	..	..	5 10
9 05	10 27	12 47	80	Berlin[5] ♂	7	4 53	6 58	4 55
9 30	10 40	1 00	87	Ocean City	0	*4 40	†6 45	†4 30
P. M.	P. M.	P. M.		ARRIVE] [LEAVE		P. M.	A. M.	A. M.

* Daily; † daily, except Sunday; a stops to let off passengers from Baltimore. ♂ Telegraph stations.

CONNECTIONS.—[1] With Annapolis & Baltimore Shore Line R.R.; Annapolis, Washington & Baltimore R.R. [2] With ferry to Bay Ridge. [3½] With Philadelphia, Wilmington & Baltimore R.R. [3] With Philadelphia, Wilmington & Baltimore R.R.—Delaware & Chesapeake Division. [4] With New York, Philadelphia & Norfolk R.R. [5] With Philadelphia, Wilmington & Baltimore R.R.—Delaware, Maryland & Virginia Branch.

Fig. 69. Bay Ridge—a bonafide commercial port for one year. Vacationers could travel from Baltimore to Ocean City via Bay Ridge in less than six hours.

WEDNESDAY, JULY 30: The 3,000 gardeners and horticulturists of the combined garden clubs of Washington, D.C. and Baltimore will tour the Bay Ridge gardens. Half came on the *Columbia* from Baltimore and half by train from D.C.

MONDAY, AUGUST 4: An "added attraction" of "Optical Illusions" will take place including "The Witches and Goblins of the Magician's Cauldron, rising moon, rippling waters, blooming flowers, storms, falling snow, volcanoes in action, ship-wrecks, rainbows. . . ."

WEDNESDAY, AUGUST 20: Mr. Mezzick, manager, was presented with a large gold watch and chain from his employees "as a token of respect, love and esteem" today in the hotel lobby. "He was overcome by the surprise. . . . The *Columbia* will remain at Bay Ridge until 10:00, giving the lovers of dancing three hours of amusement at the Ridge, and two hours on the steamer, returning in time to take the last cars for home."

THURSDAY, AUGUST 21: Those waiting at the steamship pier in Baltimore to meet their loved ones were unaware of the special late departure of the *Columbia* and became very concerned that the steamer had not arrived. A rumor spread among the crowd that the boat had sunk. The hotel was telegraphed in alarm, and the situation was explained to the relief of all.

WEDNESDAY, AUGUST 27: The 4th Annual Dinner of the Bay Ridge Company to the officers of the *Columbia* was held aboard the steamer at Bay Ridge today. The officers of the ship gave Mr. C. R. Webb a gold watch and the ship physician, an umbrella. Mr. Webb, in a speech, stated that he will sever his connection with Bay Ridge at the close of the present season after four years with the company.

1891

WEDNESDAY, JUNE 17: Mr. Samuel Fort, "well-known theatrical manager" is in charge of Bay Ridge amusements. This week free entertainment will be held daily on the bandstand stage: "Ramza and Arnold—horizontal bar performers, a juggling act, a bell-ringer, Prof. Burke and his trained dogs, Bijou Quartet, Mr. Eastwood with his imitations of the late J. K. Emmett with songs and dances and 3 concerts by the Naval Academy Band. . . ."

FRIDAY, JULY 3: The Naval Academy Band assisted by the ninety-piece Fourth Battalion Infantry Field Band will present "a potpourri of national airs," Prof. Auer and twenty young ladies in a national dance, Brothers Weston in a cornet duo and "the entire entertainment will be accompanied by Japanese bombs thrown in the air by 4 batteries of artillery brought from the Naval Academy, discharged by electricity by J. Frank Eline."

MONDAY, JULY 6: On the Fourth of July 10,000 people came to the Ridge, by steamboat and train—65 passenger coaches came from D.C.

SATURDAY, AUGUST 1: Forty-two men of the District of Columbia National Guard have arrived for their military encampment, having marched from D.C. to Annapolis and thence to Bay Ridge. They have erected 20 tents in the open field at the rear of the cafe and will practice military maneuvers and drills.

The state's attorney served notice on Manager Mezzick stating "no more concerts on Sunday under penalty of the Sunday Law." Mezzick stated "that he was not aware that the sacred concerts given by the Band on Sundays were in violation of the Sunday Law."

MONDAY, AUGUST 3: The Sixth Battalion went into camp today and will remain until August 10th.

TUESDAY, AUGUST 4: "The commanding officer, Maj. George Bartlett put the men to work erecting tents and digging trenches around them . . . on the lawn in the rear of the cafe . . . 16 officers' tents, 3 guards' tents, 8 servants' tents, close to 50 tents to include the rest . . . . Reveille is at 5:50 and taps is at 10:30." The men "are delighted with the amusements [but the main purpose] is to familiarize the men with the extended order drill adopted by the regular army."

FRIDAY, AUGUST 7: A military ball will take place tonight, given by the Fourth Battalion.

THURSDAY, AUGUST 27: The Oyster Navy is being reviewed at Bay Ridge today. Many excursionists came to witness the regatta between schooners, sloops and other boats of the Oyster Navy. The steamer *Thomas* was used as the referee boat with "one whistle given as notice to hoist sails and two blasts for to start. . . . Thousands flocked to the bluffs of Bay Ridge to witness the start and interest never flagged until the white sails swelling under a sharp breeze could be seen dashing back toward the starting point" at Tolly Point. The sloop, *Daisy Anchor*, Captain [Emil] Hartge, won the race. It was a 14 mile course.

Fig. 70. "Racing at Bay Ridge"

FRIDAY, AUGUST 28: Shortly before 2:00 p.m. the Review of the Oyster Fleet transpired. ". . . the vessels pulled up in line opposite the long pier, and as the flagship with its inspectors passed by, each saluted with a report from the cannon on deck. . . . Later in the afternoon, the men were dismissed and the crews of the various batteries 'took in' Bay Ridge."

WEDNESDAY, SEPTEMBER 2: "The large water tank or reservoir on top of Bay Ridge Hotel gave way yesterday flooding the rooms . . . and doing other damage."

THURSDAY, SEPTEMBER 8: Bay Ridge closed yesterday for the season after a very successful run. A post-season hop will be held on the steamer *Columbia* Thursday night, September 10.

1892

FRIDAY, MAY 20: Professor Paris Chambers' Great Southern Band is engaged to furnish music at Bay Ridge this summer as Professor Zimmerman and the Naval Academy Band are now engaged at Atlantic City. "Mr. W. H. Vansant's genial face will be seen again at the Ridge in charge of the race course." [W. H. is the son of James H. Vansant.]

THURSDAY, JUNE 9: "1000 new bathing suits ordered ... the merry-go-round is equipped with a new organ ... the gravity railroad has been rebuilt and lengthened 80 feet, making it nearly ½ mile long. New cars have been put on the track. ... The boat house at Lake Ogleton has been rebuilt and 15 new shells have been placed in it. ... The several islands in the lake have been raked and benches and tables placed in position. ... The race course has been ploughed and rolled and is now perfectly level. Even the cyclists will enjoy a run over its smooth expanse. ... The flower beds have been changed ... the notable one being the steamboat *Columbia* in variegated flowers. ... The shade trees ... now shade the walks in the cool breezes. ... The first Moonlight Hop will be held on the 29th. ... The railroad track from Bay Ridge to Arundel-on-the-Bay is completed—20c for the round trip."

THURSDAY, JULY 14: "A party of 100 gentlemen and ladies came by special train for a fish and crab supper and dancing till midnight. ... The Baltimore Wheelmen, about 300 strong, will give a tournament in Bay Ridge. ... The summer car with its donkey engine, distance 3 miles to Arundel-on-the-Bay is well patronized. ... The run is delightful around the Bay Shore to opposite Thomas Point Light."

WEDNESDAY, AUGUST 3: The Elks of Baltimore Lodge No. 7 swelled the crowds to see six finalists compete in the cakewalk under direction of William Neal, D.C. "It was a treat to watch the stately step of the dusky couples as they trod the boards." The winner received a medal inscribed "Bay Ridge, Aug. 2, 1892, Cake Walk."

THURSDAY, AUGUST 11: The District of Columbia National Guard has encamped. "A veterinarian will join the company to care for the horses. ... The routine includes revolver practice in the a.m. and mounted drill in the p.m. The 25 men have pitched tent. They came with two Gatling guns, two caissons, an ambulance, one baggage wagon, each drawn by 4 horses and 9 saddle horses." The Fourth Regiment Band and Field Music of sixty pieces will be on hand.

FRIDAY, AUGUST 12: The Fourth Regiment Maryland National Guards arrived for Military Day with eight full companies in white trousers, blue blouses and fatigue caps, aboard the *Columbia*. They marched up the pier at the route step and formed on the parade ground in back of the hotel, where they received a 21 gun salute from the District of Columbia National Guard already encamped there. A complimentary hop was given the men in the large pavilion, attended by ladies from Baltimore, Washington, and Annapolis.

WEDNESDAY, AUGUST 24: The Iroquois Cycle Club of Baltimore will race at 5:00 p.m. today on the new racetrack. "According to former agreements Bay Ridge goes into the hands of the B & O Railroad after this season. ..."

1893

THURSDAY, MAY 18: Many improvements have been made at Bay Ridge. "... a new pier. ... The Fifth Regiment Band will give concerts ... and will furnish music on the steamer *Columbia*. The steamer has been repainted and renovated and will carry 4,000 people. ... Wright's Band [has been] engaged for the pleasure of persons wishing to dance. ... Bay

Ridge Improvement Co. has been incorporated.... H. S. Bond, Jr., Thos. C. Musgrove, C. K. Lord, Walter Ancker, C. A. Lagen, W. H. Earstan and W. Burton...."

TUESDAY, MAY 23: "Many improvements ... extension of the gravity road 120 feet.... Mr. T. C. Musgrove, of Philadelphia, B. F. Bond and W. S. Woolford of Baltimore will lease the resort this season as the Chesapeake Resort Company. Messrs. Buffham Bros. are erecting a two story frame building near the electric road where they will have their photographic gallery.... The syndicate of Baltimore and Philadelphia capitalists [Henry S. Paul, Thomas C. Musgrove, Charles A. Lagen] that recently purchased Bay Ridge are known as the Bay Ridge Re-Organization Committee. They have appointed M. E. S. Hooper ... general superintendent of the grounds."

SATURDAY, JUNE 10: "Royal Arcanum Day will be celebrated ... an excursion.... The 4,700 members in the State will wear badges.... It is thought that all summer resorts may suffer a little this year on account of ... the World's Fair at Chicago.... Nearly all the employees at the cafe are girls from Philadelphia and New York who act as cashiers, clerks and waiters...."

TUESDAY, JUNE 13: "The cycle races under the auspices of the B & O Pattern-makers and the sanction of the L. A. W. [League of American Wheelmen] took place yesterday at Bay Ridge. There were 3 events, each of which was hotly contested."

WEDNESDAY, JULY 5: "It is estimated that from 10,000–12,000 persons were at Bay Ridge during the day [July 4].... The grove to the right of the dancing pavilion was filled with pic-nickers before noon.... The great attraction in the afternoon were the TWO EXPERT SWIMMERS, Miss Bertha Goodwin and Miss Katie Anderson, now engaged by the manager, to give exhibitions in swimming and to teach ladies how to swim. They made their appearance on the bath-house steps at exactly 3 o'clock, in pink and flesh-colored tights with dark trimmings, and attracted the attention of the crowds that lined the banks from the bath-house to the pier.... They gave exhibitions of double floating—feet to feet, then head to head, walking on their hands with feet above the water;

Ho! For Bay Ridge.
Private families or persons taken to Bay Ridge and back with safe teams, for 25 cents, by   J. G. CRANE,
*   Eastport, A. A. Co., Md

Fig. 71. July 21, 1893

Fig. 72. "Camp Out at Cat Hole Beach" c. 1893. George W. Riley, a tombstone carver and amateur photographer from Eastport, pitched tents with family and friends near the mouth of Lake Ogleton.

the double somersault; the leap-frog dive, the bicycle float, the rescuing act . . . every evening during the season from 3–5 p.m. . . . The Philadelphia Yacht Club sailed yesterday to Bay Ridge . . . [with] seven sailing vessels and two steam yachts."

MONDAY, JULY 17: "The extremely hot weather yesterday brought crowds of people . . . from the heated cities. The trains rolled into the resort from Philadelphia with every coach filled. Many . . . came down [from Baltimore] on the morning and evening boat and by rail. . . . They found however that it was quite warm at the Ridge, and men, women and children could be seen under the shade of trees, or sitting on the large pavilion enjoying the music. Fans were readily purchased for 10c each. . . . All amusements were in full blast and the electric road seemed to be doing the bulk of the business. The waitresses . . . hustling to and fro for the patrons of the cafe . . . all dress uniformly in black and deep white collars and cuffs, white aprons and lace caps, and are designated by numbers pinned on their shoulders. . . . An old man sits on the pavilion grinding a hand organ and singing . . . while Wright's Band gives . . . better music from the band stand. . . ."

THURSDAY, JULY 20: "The Celtic Club of Baltimore gave their excursion at the Ridge yesterday . . . for the home rule cause in Ireland."

WEDNESDAY, JULY 26: "Yesterday was the day set for the Laurel Guards' picnic at Bay Ridge. The guards were composed entirely of ladies, and presented a novel sight. They were repeatedly applauded while drilling."

MONDAY, JULY 31: "A regatta will be held at Bay Ridge on Aug. 5, between the Ariel and Neptune Boat Clubs of Baltimore and the Severn Club of Annapolis."

TUESDAY, AUGUST 1: A Washington train brought a Chinese Methodist picnic excursion yesterday. Baltimore associations booked at Bay Ridge include the Oddfellows, Ancient Order of Hibernians, Catholic Literary Society, and the Improved Order of B'nai B'rith, as well as the Frederick Rifles and numerous other societies and associations.

MONDAY, AUGUST 7: "Many of the officers, cadets and sailors from the Italian cruisers which are at anchor off Bay Ridge, spent the day taking in the amusements."

WEDNESDAY, AUGUST 16: "A private hop was given at Bay Ridge last night to the young ladies of Arundel-on-the-Bay and Brighton Villa by the young gentlemen of Annapolis. The orchestra from Annapolis furnished the music and dancing continued till morning. A delightful evening was spent and it was remarked by an onlooker that the collection of youth and beauty on this occasion excelled that of any previous event. . . ."

TUESDAY, SEPTEMBER 5: Excursionists "crowded into the dancing pavilion, to witness a sparring exhibition by two Baltimore pugilists. Considerable slugging was done and the 'bout' did not end until the principals were tired out."

1894

SATURDAY, MAY 19: A heavy rain and hail storm struck the county. "At Bay Ridge the storm was severe. A portion of the long pier was carried away and also the hotel and cafe and other buildings were greatly damaged by the breaking of glass and unroofing of portions of the building."

MONDAY, MAY 28: The big bicycle craze is here: "Yesterday on every road bicyclists could be seen spinning along on the silent steed. A number rode to Bay Ridge, where they spent the day with excursionists from Baltimore."

MONDAY, JUNE 25: "Bay Ridge [is] under the management of Mr. C. G. Musgrove, a Philadelphia capitalist . . . [and] is in the charge of Superintendent H. F. Meyer. . . . Yesterday was Catholic Day and the exclusive use of the . . . steamers was obtained for the celebration . . . nine societies participating. . . . 5,000 happy picknickers."

TUESDAY, JULY 2: "Tomorrow a grand excursion will be given to Bay Ridge for the benefit of St. Vincent's Male Orphan Asylum, of Baltimore. . . . A grand welcome chorus will be rendered by the little orphans. A splendid concert will be given on the boat and grounds, under . . . Prof. Thomas F. McNulty."

WEDNESDAY, JULY 25: This resort season, the fashionable young man wears "white duck trousers . . . a double breasted blue serge coat and a cartwheel straw hat . . . a white collar tied about with a plain string bow."

TUESDAY, AUGUST 7: "Certification of incorporation of the Annapolis, Brighton and Bay Ridge Electric Railway [trolley] is now being prepared." The incorporators are Messrs. T. C. Musgrove, James H. Vansant, Gadd, Melvin, Saunders, Rehn.

TUESDAY, AUGUST 29: "The Baltimore excursionists on the steamer *Columbia* had an experience which they will remember for some time, says the *Baltimore Herald*. The steamer was caught in a storm which created a panic among the passengers.

"No one was able to control the frightened crowd, and above the din of battle waged by the elements could be heard the prayers, and even curses of the frightened. . . . Women and children fainted, and the stoutest hearts on the great boat quaked with fear. . . . The boat was completely at the mercy of the waves. The engines were stopped, and in the darkness of the hour the billows rose high around her. The rain came down in torrents. Those on deck were drenched to their skin. After the storm had somewhat spent itself the passengers were carried into the state rooms by the crew of the boat and everything done for their comfort.

"Never . . . has such a crowd of sick, frightened and thoroughly drenched people been landed at Bay Ridge. Many . . . refused to return by boat. . . . Among the number was the Chorus of Innes' Band numbering about 80 people. They absolutely refused to return by boat. . . . Three [extra] trains were sent down and about 1,000 of the frightened excursionists returned that way. . . ."

Fig. 73. Annapolitans (left to right) Ellen Jenkins, Betsy Webster, and Alexander Burton Randall often visited Bay Ridge, coming by horse and buggy along Bay Shore Drive in the company of family and friends. Here they posed for the camera of Margaret Taylor Randall c. 1893.

1895

MONDAY, MAY 27: New attractions . . . "The Mammoth Ferris Wheel [purchased for] $10,000 is the exact prototype of the Famous Wheel . . . [at the] World's Fair. . . . It will revolve at a height of 75 feet enabling passengers to obtain a view of Annapolis. . . ."

MONDAY, JUNE 10: The Water-toboggan Slide "is constructed next to the bathing pavilion and extends from the bluff to the water, a distance of about seven hundred feet. Five toboggan courses are in operation, which furnish a delightful and safe amusement."

FRIDAY, JULY 5: On the Fourth of July "Everyone seemed bent on having a good time, and teams were brought into requisition from every quarter, decked off with flags and bunting. Some went one place and some to another—but all Annapolis and Anne Arundel County appeared to have emptied itself into the beautiful grounds of Bay Ridge for the day. What the railroads could not carry were conveyed in double and single-horse teams with every conceivable vehicle. It is estimated that fully ten thousand people were at the Ridge. The groves and summer houses on the ground, the cafe and every available place was crowded with picnickers, and all the amusements were well patronized.... The Ferris Wheel appeared to have the advantage of some of the older amusements, and its swinging cars were ... filled with passengers.... The toboggan slide is a new feature to the bathhouse this season.... An attractive programme of music was presented. It included the presentation ... by the Congress of Nations.... The music was furnished by Prof. Charles E. Wright's full military orchestra.... In addition ... a musical number entitled 'Columbus' Discovery of America' [was performed] ... at about 6 o'clock a number of figurative fire-works were sent off from the bandstand on the beach ... a loud explosion would take place in the air, from which would come formations of fish, birds, images, the American flag, liberty bell, and various figures, which would float in the air for some distance and then drop in the water off the long pier.

"As train and boat time approached, the crowd was immense, and car after car was filled. The large steamer, *Columbia*, was crowded to her full capacity.... The only accident ... during the day ... was the accidental discharge of a pistol in the hands of a young man...."

THURSDAY, JULY 18: "A musical and literary entertainment was held at Bay Ridge Hotel last night which was highly enjoyed by the guests ... and others from Arundel-on-the-Bay. Solos were sung by Miss Katie Carr of Baltimore and Miss Baker, and recitations given by Miss Mabel Robinson and Mr. Dorsey. A dance followed ... in the large parlor of the hotel."

SATURDAY, JULY 20: A free minstrel entertainment was held in the dance pavilion complete with banjo, guitar, and comedians. The programme concluded with a farce entitled "The Coming Man." A dance followed.

FRIDAY, AUGUST 2: "A delightful sail was given on Tuesday night by guests at the hotel.... When near Greenbury Point light-house about eleven o'clock, a small row boat was picked up containing 2 ladies and 2 gentlemen [who] had lost their oars while skylarking and were fast drifting out in the bay.... The young ladies were very much frightened.... Wednesday night a straw ride was given by the guests at the resort. The party came through Annapolis blowing horns and singing, making merry the night along their route. After spending some time at Camp Parole camp-meeting they returned to Bay Ridge at a late hour."

MONDAY, AUGUST 5: "A young lady from Baltimore made a narrow escape from drowning while boating on Lake Ogleton Saturday afternoon. She was seized with a spasm and rolled over and fell into the water. Her escort was unable to render any assistance as he could not swim. Messrs. Robert Welch and C. W. Martin, of Annapolis, rescued the lady and took her to the Bay Ridge Hotel."

TUESDAY, AUGUST 6: "Managers Baker and Woolford plan a grand balloon ascension Saturday next by a world renowned aeronaut."

WEDNESDAY, AUGUST 7: Mr. Arthur Grollman of Bay Ridge was presented a gold-watch for rescuing the two couples adrift in the rowboat. It was given by the families of the young ladies. Further excitement this week took the form of "a sail from the Ridge, Monday night. About 20 ladies and gentlemen left the pier at 8:30 o'clock and sailed down the bay on a sloop yacht. The party stopped at Arundel-on-the-Bay, where an enjoyable hour was spent attending a lawn fete, given by a number of the Arundel ladies. The sail then continued down the bay. When off Thomas Point a vessel was sighted aground. While near Poplar Island the party was overtaken by a severe storm. The night became suddenly dark and the bay was brilliant from the vivid flashes of lightning. It was thought to be unsafe to return until after the storm had subsided, and the boat was run ashore at the Island. By this time it was raining in

Fig. 74. Sailing party to Bay Ridge c. 1903

torrents and all of the party were drenched. The ladies took shelter in an old fishing shanty near shore and remained there until four o'clock in the morning when the party ventured out on the bay in their craft and safely landed at Bay Ridge at half-past six o'clock. The absence of the party during the storm had caused much excitement at the hotel, and many persons remained awake all night waiting for their return."

FRIDAY, AUGUST 9: "The Frederick Rifles, Company A of the First Regiment, M[aryland] N[ational] G[uard] held their 12th Annual Excursion to Bay Ridge yesterday . . . friends and members . . . seven hundred . . . left Frederick . . . [to go] to Baltimore . . . where they took the steamer to the Ridge. Music was furnished on the train and the boat by the Yellow String Band . . . and the Hopeland Band . . . from Frederick. . . ."

FRIDAY, AUGUST 16: Nearly 7,000 excursionists came as the "Ancient Order of Foresters celebrated the anniversary of its independence from the present order in Great Britain by going on an excursion to Bay Ridge."

FRIDAY, SEPTEMBER 6: "Mr. Baker [co-manager] met with a serious accident last night at the Bay Ridge Hotel. He fell against a hat pin, which penetrated his back. Dr. H. R. Walton of Annapolis was summoned and rendered medical aid."

1896

MONDAY, MAY 25: "The toboggan slides at the bathhouses have been lengthened and a novel kind of sled will be run upon it. A number of fancy bathing suits have been procured. Organizations booked for the season include the United Baptist, United Presbyterian and Episcopal Churches, the Heptosophs, Maryland Christian Endeavor Union, Young Catholic Friends Society, Grand Army of the Republic Reunion, and many other associations. . . ."

TUESDAY, AUGUST 18: "Bay Ridge closes on Monday, August 31 with a grand ball. . . . The managers say it was not a successful season."

1897

TUESDAY, MAY 26: ". . . carpenters and painters are busy repairing storm damage to the buildings . . . last fall's storm badly damaged the electric line of cars. . . . [Plans for the season include] sports events, hops, variety shows, musicales, parades. . . ."

MONDAY, JUNE 28: ". . . 5,000 were at Bay Ridge for St. Leo's Gymnasium Field Day. . . . There will be track and field events for the State Records."

TUESDAY, AUGUST 3: "Mr. Henry Wellington, of New York, has come to stay at the hotel and is interested in the electric road which was built by him about 9 years ago."

THURSDAY, AUGUST 5: Big crowds came for Grand Army Day. "In the afternoon religious services were held in the grove. . . . Addresses in which old war stories were recalled, were made. . . . Old songs were sung by all the veterans." Later a baseball game was held "between the fat men and the thin men."

WEDNESDAY, AUGUST 18: "Manager Woolford has employed 3 musicians to furnish dance music every evening in the dining hall of the hotel, which has been converted this year to a ball room." Annapolitans by special invitation come to socialize with the boarders and for the evening dancing.

SATURDAY, AUGUST 21: The Severn Cycle Club is spearheading a drive to collect subscriptions to shell the Annapolis to Bay Ridge Bay Shore Drive.

Cyclists have collected $60 and solicit help from all Annapolitans. "The horseman should help the wheelman: So, horsemen, pitch in too and help along... for the purpose of having a cool pleasant ride all during the summer."

FRIDAY, AUGUST 27: "Bay Ridge Musical Day... has proved a great success.... The second musical excursion took place yesterday when the gems of 'Cavaleria Rusticana' were given away to ticket buyers at the steamer *Columbia* office."

SATURDAY, AUGUST 28: The B & O Railroad announces that it will check bicycles aboard for free.

[The *Evening Capital* for 1898 is missing.]

1899

MONDAY, MAY 29: "Large sums of money have been spent to make the place more attractive than ever."

MONDAY, JUNE 5: "A roof garden is a new feature on the *Columbia* this season.... On a stage erected on the upper deck a continuous vaudeville performance, under the direction of Oliver C. Ziegfield will be given both going and returning from Bay Ridge.... [In addition there will be] a miniature railroad, complete with engines and passenger coaches... a gipsy camp; a sea-shell bazaar, an oriental theatrical troupe... C. L. Peter's Illusions, 'Galatea' and 'The Maiden of the Mist;' the wargraph... a resident physician, Dr. R. L. McNeer.... A post office... has been opened and Major J. J. Pennington, of Baltimore has been appointed postmaster by President McKinley."

SATURDAY, JUNE 10: Bay Ridge has opened under the management of "The Bay Ridge Electric Park and Steamboat Company."

MONDAY, JUNE 12: *"BAY RIDGE WIDE OPEN"*: [Front page headline] "Over 6,000 [are on the grounds].... The recreation pier in the German Village is not completed, but refreshments in the way of beer were sold yesterday and Saturday.... Deputy U. S. Marshall C. R. Martin closed the German Village on account of no government licence... for the sale of liquor."

TUESDAY, JUNE 13: "Yesterday Sheriff Revell made his appearance on the grounds... to investigate reported violation of the liquor law, but found everything quiet and orderly...."

MONDAY, JUNE 19: The "Clan-na-Gael excursion is at Bay Ridge... the combined patriotic Irish societies of Baltimore, Washington, D.C., and Wilmington, Delaware."

SATURDAY, JULY 1: *"FINANCIAL STRAITS OF BAY RIDGE"*: [Front page headline] "... an order signed... Bay Ridge must show cause for why a receiver should not be appointed for the Bay Ridge Electric Park and Steamboat Company.... The company was incorporated with a capital stock of $60,000. It is alleged in the bill of complaint that its business is being conducted at a great loss... alleged to be hopelessly insolvent, its assets being of little value and consisting principally of furniture, the lease of Bay Ridge and rights under certain contracts...."

MONDAY, JULY 3: The management denies Bay Ridge is insolvent. "... 8,000 came on the 3rd.... The company will charter the *Thomas S. Morgan* for the rest of the season to help with the crowds on the 4th of July and on holidays and weekends."

WEDNESDAY, JULY 5: "From early dawn, indeed the day before, until midnight of the Fourth, the booming of cannon and firing of crackers was heard on every side.... With the sunrise large parties of picnickers

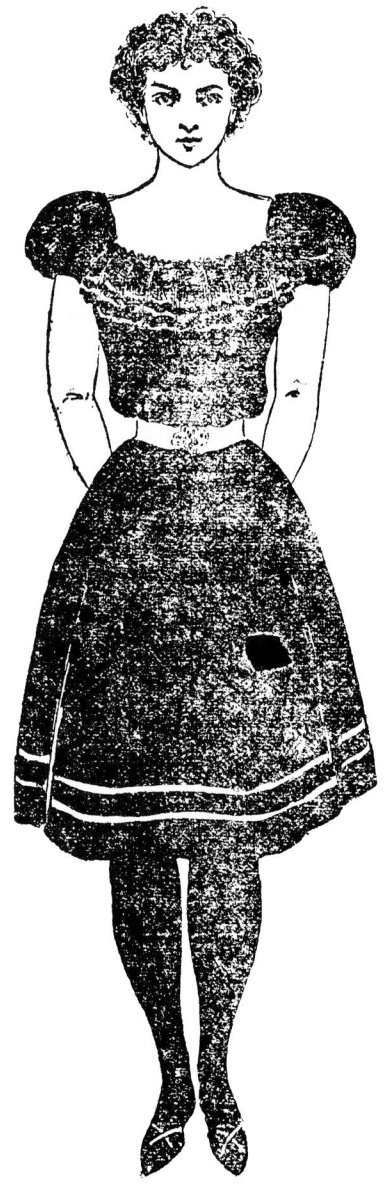

Fig. 75. June 6, 1899

Fig. 76. "July 4, 1899." Annie Riley Smith remembers that her family and their friends camped out at Bay Ridge for a week each summer, arriving by "locomotive" and bringing their own hammock. They stayed at a small cabin on stilts near the mouth of Lake Ogleton (also called "Cat Hole"). The group dined on "just caught, just cooked fish" at their July Fourth picnic supper. Left to right: Annie Mitchell, her husband William Mitchell, Blanch Finkle, John W. Riley, Alva Riley, Phoebe Hardesty, Willie Martin, Mary Martin, her husband William Martin, Bessie Riley, and "Angy" (Annie A. Riley Smith at age 4, daughter of Jennie and George W. Riley).

```
        WILL TAKE YOU
   To Bay Ridge
            —OR—
    Pic-Nic Grounds,
            —IN—
      Buss or Wagons
         AT REASONABLE COST.
           ZACH. MERRIKEN,
   6 12tf            32 Charles Street.
```

Fig. 77. June 19, 1899

and excursionists wended their way to the country and the surrounding shores in wagons and by sailing craft. Every size and fashion of vehicle was called into use yesterday and the favorite place of destination was Bay Ridge.... In the afternoon large parties went to Bay Ridge by trains. At this popular resort... [there were] 10,000 people."

MONDAY, JULY 17: "BAY RIDGE SALE OF COLUMBIA": [Front page headline] The daily trips of the *Columbia* between Baltimore and Bay Ridge are discontinued on Monday, July 17, 1899. The B & O Railroad sold her to the Cape May and Delaware Navigation Company. The Bay Ridge management had an option to buy the *Columbia* but "finding her too massive and expensive... decided not to purchase her.... [The management] has arranged for the use of the steamer *John S. Morgan* [sic], Philadelphia, Capt. Isaac Kirby...." Bay Ridge is owned by the Bay Ridge Improvement Co. of which the B & O is the main stockholder. It is leased by the Bay Ridge Electric Park and Steamboat Company.

MONDAY, JULY 17: "The Electric Road, which was damaged beyond repair by the storm of last winter, has been removed and the rails and cars are being shipped to Savannah."

THURSDAY, JULY 20: The Bay Ridge management was unsuccessful in its attempt to engage the steamer *Thomas S. Morgan*.

FRIDAY, JULY 21: "Nearly all the workmen at Bay Ridge are on strike.... Yesterday there was no music... the crowd of excursionists was disappointed."

WEDNESDAY, AUGUST 9: "A detachment of the Naval Academy Band will begin to furnish music under the new management at the Ridge today.... For several weeks past [with] no music at Bay Ridge, visitors began to materially fall off... the company, in order to save the reputation of the place [stepped in and took over].... Hereafter... music will be at the Ridge daily, and ice water in abundance for the visitors."

MONDAY, AUGUST 14: "BAY RIDGE TROUBLES": [Front page headline] The Bay Ridge Electric Park and Steamboat Company is defunct and will go into receivership.

1900

FRIDAY, APRIL 27: "Rev. Dr. C. C. McLean, president and chancellor of the Chautaqua [sic] ... will conduct it [Bay Ridge] as part of the National Chautaqua.... On May 10th Chesapeake Chautaqua will be opened and on Decoration Day ... will begin to inaugurate the Chautaqua Program ... covering the course of the Chautaqua Literary and Scientific Circle. Also there will be assemblies and exercises appropriate to church, Sunday school, temperance, national army and navy literature and art.... Dr. McLean will live at Brighton Beach, which is the title under which the property will be known in the future."

FRIDAY, MAY 25: "A number of rooms have been built in the rear of the dancing pavilion.... The building for the help has been renovated as an annex to the hotel...." Many excursions are booked for the season including the Maryland State Teachers Convention to be held July 3–5. The management is still looking for a steamer.

MONDAY, MAY 28: "The resort offers a varied program of exercises, entertainments, schools of study including art, music, elocution, literature and the Bible.... The surrounding influences will be elevating and refining."

THURSDAY, MAY 31: "The buildings will accommodate about 500 persons overnight.... Boats will be placed on Lake Ogleton ... parties can enjoy a sail around to the steamboat wharf ... a fresh start, no debt.... The old German Village has been made into a recreation pier, where twilight and moonlight services will be held ... music is provided by the Naval Academy Band."

SATURDAY, JULY 21: "Music, lectures, entertainment will be free on 'Annapolis Day'—one evening a week is set apart for the entertainment of Annapolis visitors to the Beach, local talent assisting in the programme."

WEDNESDAY, JULY 25: "All entertainments are free. Go and enjoy a literary and musical treat together with breezes from the Chesapeake."

WEDNESDAY, AUGUST 8: The gas boat, "*The Mystery*, Capt. Roe, taking parties of about 50, is now running excursion parties to Arundel-on-the-Bay, Indian Landing, Round Bay and Chautaqua Beach."

MONDAY, AUGUST 13: "Few people were at Chautaqua Beach yesterday.... Most of the help at the Beach has been dispensed with.... The season has not been a prosperous one, numerically or financially."

1901

TUESDAY, JUNE 11: "Chautaqua Beach will formally open Saturday, June 15 with an excursion on the *Emma Giles*, touching at Annapolis on her way to the Beach."

FRIDAY, JUNE 14: "The *Emma Giles* will stop at the new pier, east of the ground.... *Emma Giles* will not stop at Annapolis for passengers as planned.... Those of our citizens who would visit the Beach during the season must either swim, row, walk, drive, or go by rail in the evening.... Annapolitans are given no consideration.... It is time our people were drawing the line...."

FRIDAY, JUNE 21: Col. Musgrove is now in charge of a fleet of pleasure boats at Chautaqua Beach. He bought a "new gasoline launch" for use as a pleasure boat by visitors. It will be run on lake, river and out in the bay. The boat was christened *Severn*.

MONDAY, JULY 8: Evening concerts have been popular. Miss Ruth Violet Coulter [appropriately] sang "Were I a Violet" by Abt and "The Serenade"

Fig. 78. June 27, 1901

by Schubert accompanied by Mr. Schultz of the Naval Academy orchestra. Afternoon lectures were held. Professor Marshall Lowe, Ph.D. of Heidelberg University spoke on "The Decade's World Battles." Dr. McLean conducted the evening vesper services.

SATURDAY, JULY 13: The "Stereoptican Lecture, 'In the Footsteps of Washington,' by Clarence W. Broomall will be a featured part of the Lutheran Day Program.... Large groups are expected on Methodist Episcopal Day and for the excursion of the Woman's Home and Foreign Missionary Societies of Washington and Baltimore."

FRIDAY, JULY 19: The Presbyterian Sunday school picnic went down at 11:30 on the train, "a party of about 200 Sunday school children, parents and friends. On their arrival ... the woods and groves were open to the choice, for the Presbyterian contingent were the first on the grounds. A pretty little Maypole dance with graceful maneuvers was executed by the scholars of Miss Lottie Gardiner's class. At 4 o'clock ... delicious ice cream and cake [were served] in abundance.... The merry-go-round ... Ferris wheel, shooting gallery, bathing and other sports were liberally patronized.... A large number remained at the Beach until the 9 o'clock train and witnessed the sublime storm with its electrical effects."

Fig. 79. This 19th-century Maypole dance scene illustrates some marked differences between the activities, interests, and dress of children then and now.

FRIDAY, JULY 19: "Last night's storm washed away the long pier at Chautaqua Beach, the old one where the steam boat used to land. The pier parted in the middle and floated out toward the Bay. The excursionists caught in the storm watched the sight from the cafe veranda as the vivid flashes of lightning lit up the water, and showed the wreck wrought by the storm. The pier had been used of late as a crabbing and fishing post, and was crowded yesterday nearly all day with crabbers."

MONDAY, JULY 22: "Chautaqua Beach was yesterday a place of ideal Sunday rest, peace and quiet. The gravity railroad, the merry-go-round and the launch on the lake were still and the salt breezes rustled musically through the trees."

TUESDAY, JULY 23: "The hotel is giving excellent accommodations and lots have been sold on which cottages are to be erected. A number of tents have been pitched near the lake, a few having been there since May. No liquor is sold on the grounds...."

THURSDAY, JULY 25: People from Raleigh, North Carolina; Lafayette, Indiana; New York City, Chicago, as well as Baltimore and Washington are on the hotel guest list.

FRIDAY, AUGUST 21: The Crystal Social Club, Washington, D.C. is camping this week at Chautaqua Beach. The thirty-five ladies in the club are staying at the hotel at night and the men are camping out in tents. "Last night the male members of the club regaled the guests at the Beach with a callithumpian band serenade. Attired in sheets, pajamas and night robes, under the leadership of the giant, J. Cummings, and the dwarf, F. K. Smouse, the gentlemen awakened the guests at the hotel with weird music performed on grotesque instruments. Everybody took the fun in good part...."

MONDAY, SEPTEMBER 2: The Anti-saloon League, Christian Endeavor Society, and the Mapel Fishing Club held Day Outings at the Beach.

[The *Evening Capital* for 1902 is missing.]

1903

TUESDAY, JUNE 30: "Crowds are expected from Washington to spend the Fourth at Bay Ridge. The bathing is in full blast, but besides the merry-go-round, there are no other amusements. Mr. George R. Buffham, the manager, says he is not willing to risk life and limb of his patrons by attempting to use the old gravity road, the Ferris wheel or any of the other amusements at Bay Ridge which are in need of repair, but which the company refuse to have repaired...."

"*A Mean Trick*: Three valuable horses belonging to Mr. George R. Buffham, manager of Bay Ridge, were last night driven away from Bay Ridge or stolen. Mr. Buffham suspects the guilty party to whom strong suspicion points. Detectives are on the track and the guilty party will be punished to the full extent of the law."

WEDNESDAY, JULY 22: "The police schooner, *May Brown*, towed by a Naval Academy steam launch, will take the M. E. Church Sunday School to Bay Ridge for their annual picnic.... Ice cream, lemonade [will be] for sale on the grounds. Round trip—25c."

THURSDAY, JULY 30: At Arundel-on-the-Bay "delightful dances are held every Saturday night. The music is furnished by the Bay Ridge orchestra."

SATURDAY, AUGUST 8: "The season has not been successful so far as that of last year, owing to the unusually cool weather.... A stiff breeze is blowing most of the time and the visitors think Bay Ridge... most delightful... [and are] highly pleased with... Mr. Buffham's management."

TUESDAY, AUGUST 11: "Mr. Buffham, always keenly alive to the enjoyment of Cliff House [current name of the hotel] guests gave last night a straw ride to the children of the families staying there. About 20 little girls and boys were driven by Mr. Buffham in a gaily decorated farm wagon from the Ridge to Annapolis. The large farm wagon they occupied was festooned with red, white and blue, and overhead was a canopy of Chinese lanterns. The children carried large horns, cow bells and whistles and made things lively." The party drove through the principal streets in town to the Tolchester Steamboat Wharf and greeted the businessmen's excursion. "The children serenaded the *Capital* man and his family,

Fig. 80. June 22, 1903

which they appreciated. Mr. Buffham values the press and is, therefore, an up-to-date business man, as well as the successful manager of Bay Ridge...."

SATURDAY, AUGUST 22: "There are only 2 more weeks of beautiful Bay Ridge.... Bay Ridge will close on Monday, Sept. 7. Large crowds are expected for Labor Day."

MONDAY, SEPTEMBER 7: "Bay Ridge closes today. After this afternoon all Bay Ridge trains will be taken off and the popular resort will be closed until next season."

1904

WEDNESDAY, MAY 25: "Bay Ridge will not open this season and there will be no Bay Ridge trains," a fact which has proven a great inconvenience to Arundel-on-the-Bay summer residents. Mayor Smith doesn't think many will return as a result, but that some will "tough it out."

THURSDAY, JUNE 23: "There has been a great deal of trespass of late on the farm of Mr. George R. Buffham, 'Brighton Villa,' near Bay Ridge [not the Barry Avenue residence]. His property has become "a convenient cut through for people going back and forth to Arundel-on-the-Bay." Mr. Buffham only objects because the trespassers leave his gate open causing his live-stock to wander off. He has shut the gate because "he is now farming the land." The gate was then knocked down and stolen.

TUESDAY, JUNE 28: "Special permission was obtained of the Bay Ridge Company, through Mr. Buffham, for the privilege of the Bay Ridge ground [for the M. E. Church Sunday school picnic], the resort not being open to the public this summer."

FRIDAY, AUGUST 26: "A party of young people gave a straw ride last night to Bay Ridge. By special permission they were granted the privilege of the grounds and after reaching Bay Ridge they enjoyed a picnic by moonlight. The party numbered 11 couples, and drove down in one of Chaney's large wagons with 4 horses. The night was ideal...."

1906

WEDNESDAY, JULY 18: "Mr. John T. Barber, D.C., president of the Crystal Social Club will come to camp at Bay Ridge ... the club members have camped there for a number of years."

1914

SATURDAY, MAY 2: "A deal has been closed by which Robert Rennert, son of the late Robert Rennert who built the Hotel Rennert, Baltimore, has obtained control of Bay Ridge, the famous old excursion resort near the city.... It is the intention to make it ... [an] elaborate resort.... A harbor for yachts will be built and the hotel enlarged.... The new Bay Ridge will not be opened for one year ... it ... will be connected by an electric road between Baltimore, Washington and Annapolis, and also by boat from Baltimore and Washington."

TUESDAY, JULY 14: "The Bay Ridge Road leading from Annapolis to Arundel-on-the-Bay has been closed to automobiles by the authority of the superintendent of grounds, George R. Buffham." It is still open to horse and buggy but cars must use the shelled farm road.

WEDNESDAY, JULY 22: Bay Ridge is being cleaned up, shrubbery cut and the camping grounds put in perfect condition for fifty campers from Pittsburgh, members of the "Orient Camping Club," coming August 1st until September "to enjoy the delight of roughing it at Bay Ridge." Mr. Buffham is making the arrangements.

MONDAY, AUGUST 3: The Orient Club, including a band of musicians passed through Annapolis on the way to Bay Ridge.

THURSDAY, AUGUST 6: Farmers take down daily food supplies to the Orient campers. "An ice plant sends a ton of ice daily." They have erected 15 tents and have the use of "a large pavilion for their entertainment and dancing . . . camp, tents, and pavilion are brightly lighted at night . . . ."

1915

THURSDAY, MARCH 4:

FIRE AT BAY RIDGE DESTROYS OLD HOTEL

Mr. Buffham's Great Loss
Started at about 2 o'clock in Western Part of Bay Ridge
Popular Old Resort in Ashes

"No moving picture screen could picture a fire more spectacular or more horrible in its beauty and grandeur than the fire which burned up Bay Ridge Hotel yesterday afternoon and ate itself out in hundreds of cubic feet of dry brush and undergrowth.

"Yesterday afternoon, about 2 o'clock, Mrs. George R. Buffham, who was alone at Bay Ridge, her husband being in Annapolis, moving his effects from the former residence on Maryland Avenue to his home at Bay Ridge where he had taken in the past few days several wagon loads of furniture, discovered the fire. Mrs. Buffham went out to see that the horse was sheltered, as there was a strong keen wind blowing, and to put up her chickens.

"She saw flames creeping up the old gravity railroad to the northwest of Bay Ridge. The undergrowth is heavy, Bay Ridge having been abandoned for some years. This brush fed fuel to the flames, but how did the flames start? [Conjecture follows considering arson as a possibility. This was the last of five mysterious fires in the area, all of which were devastating. The Hambrock house at Bay Ridge crossing was totally destroyed, as was the Hillsmere Farm house, the Hart home in Eastport, and the O'Neille home at Arundel-on-the-Bay.]

"Realizing the danger to her home, a frame cottage near the flames, Mrs. Buffham endeavored to beat back the flames, unassisted, but they spread fiercely. With her own hands, she drew bucket after bucket of water from the well next to her cottage and saturated the surrounding brush and deadened some of the flames, and in almost superhuman manner, saved her cottage [11 Barry Avenue].

"In the meantime the wind spread the flames to the old electric road station, where there was a pile of lumber torn from the old bath houses at Bay Ridge. This dry lumber was more fuel for the flames, and burned rapidly, the burning pieces being driven by the wind toward the old Bay Ridge Hotel which was soon in flames.

"Realizing her inability to cope with that mass of flames, Mrs. Buffham ran to the residence of Mr. H. A. Keyes, about a mile distant, and appealed for help. [Mr. Herbert A. Keyes had owned the house which is now 136 East Lake Drive. He later lived at Cedar Crest Farm, 1131 Bay Ridge Road.] Fortunately Mr. Keyes was at home, and with 3 of his men went immediately to Bay Ridge and lent valuable assistance in preventing other buildings being burned. Through Mr. Keyes' efforts the old cafe was saved.

"The fire had such a hold on the Hotel that it was impossible to save anything. Mr. and Mrs. Buffham lived in the hotel and all their belongings were burned up, including a $450 piano of Mrs. Buffham's. Three valuable Goertz's lenses of Mr. Buffham's, several valuable cameras, films and negatives that can never be reproduced, beds, bedding, down comforters, blankets, dishes, silverware, cooking utensils, all the clothing of Mr. and Mrs. Buffham, furs, overcoats, etc.

"There was no insurance on anything, because insurance companies will not insure 'abandoned buildings' and Bay Ridge was so classed. Mr. and Mrs. Buffham's loss is fully $1,500 or $2,000, without a cent of insurance.... The cow narrowly escaped, but was badly singed.

"It took great effort on the part of Mr. Keyes and his three men to save Carvel Cottage, the property of Mrs. George Carey of Washington, at the entrance of Bay Ridge [of the resort area, see 1894 plat, Ch. 3, fig. 12], but this was finally accomplished. Mr. Buffham was on his way to his home when he was apprised of the fire and was almost overcome."

Fig. 81. Carvel Cottage c. 1915

WEDNESDAY, MARCH 17: "Complying with the request of officials of the B & O Railroad Co. which controls the old Bay Ridge property, much of which was destroyed by fire recently, the County Commissioners, in session yesterday, directed that the assessment against the old hotel and other buildings be stricken from the county tax books.

"The hotel was assessed at $4,000. At the same time the commissioners ordered a reduction of the assessment of the old cafe and restaurant, the power plant and ice-houses, the reduced amount being $1,800."

FRIDAY, MARCH 19: "*Vandalism at Bay Ridge*: From time to time, during the keeper's absence, there has been ... wilful destruction of property of Bay Ridge ... especially ... since the fire ... which destroyed the old hotel property and all of its contents. The ruins have attracted people, especially boys and young men, who have walked from Annapolis and vicinity to see the damage done by the fire.... Some one has broken every globe in the old cafe and broken globes are piled up on the floor three feet high.... The vandals have broken every window glass in the place, and have taken chairs and tables away and even ripped up the flooring in places.... It does seem deplorable that what there is left of old Bay Ridge cannot remain as it is without vandalism of the worst sort being perpetrated."

MONDAY, MARCH 22: "Bay Ridge ... will be purchased by a well-known syndicate and ... the property will be converted into a park and building lots. There is no better site for summer homes than Bay Ridge."

90 River Drive, built by Dr. Stoutenburg, Spring 1926

3. The Summer Colony

The era of the steam excursion playground continued for many years elsewhere on the bay—at Tolchester, Chesapeake Beach, and Betterton—and boarding houses in small fishing villages along the steamboat's route offered home-cooked meals and a relaxed country pace to summer visitors. But the winds of change were already rippling the waters as gasoline-powered engines—whether in boat, car, or truck—refined and individualized transporation. Now, farmers in the counties near Baltimore hauled produce to market by truck, loading baskets of strawberries and bushels of cantaloupes and sweet potatoes before daybreak for the long, dusty trip to the city. Low-slung white workboats chugged out of creeks and inlets before dawn to harvest the bay's bounty. And, as the automobile ventured forth from towns and cities into the countryside, families came to explore, on their own, the quiet beauty of the tidewater. Tentatively at first, and then, after World War I, with increasing boldness, city folk moved outward to build remote summer homes along the rivers of the bay's western shore. These homes, occasionally opulent but most often simple cottages, became treasured retreats from the cares of the city. Vacationers took to the water in speed boats and cabin cruisers; solitary fishermen in small wooden rowboats with outboard motors rocked in the wake of sleek, varnished Chris-Crafts.

CHAPTER 3

The Summer Colony

JANE WILSON MCWILLIAMS

Fig. 1. Visitors to the Brooks home c. 1918 arrived in an elegant roadster.

Down the sandy road along the deserted railroad tracks came little boys, occasionally with a sister or two in tow, to pick blackberries or hard cherries in the fields and woods that had once echoed with the excitement of the old resort. The children might bring a picnic lunch and sneak a swim in the river to cool off when their baskets were full. Sometimes a grandfather would come with them in the horse and buggy and tell them stories of the days when thousands had flocked to the amusement park. Joe Hopkins, Jr., remembers those days and the wine his grandfather made from the berries they picked.

In the early years of the automobile, daytrippers came from Annapolis to swim from deserted beaches or explore the old cart tracks and railroad beds that crisscrossed abandoned fields overgrown with tall weeds and scrub cedar. Some visitors found a more novel conveyance, as the *Washington Herald* reported on May 25, 1910.

Middies Steal a "Joy Ride"
Four Members of the Freshman Class Off on a Handcar

Confined to their rooms in Bancroft Hall, four midshipmen, all members of the freshman class at the Naval Academy, are under arrest and in a fair way to be most severely dealt with by naval procedure.

A stolen hand car, switched by them from a siding and used as a means of accomplishing an inland joy ride, made all the trouble for [the boys].

While out on a cross-country walk in the far reaches of the Academy limits, the quartet found the hand car on a siding of the Maryland Electric Railways Company. They commandeered the hand-propelled vehicle; and in minutes the car was speeding across the frogs [switches] and on to the old disused Bay Ridge branch of the road.

107

An Annapolis policeman saw the joy party flash across a street on the outskirts of town and telephoned the railway office which, in turn, notified the Academy authorities. Lt. Comdr. C. E. McVay, Senior Assistant to the Commandant, hastened out in an automobile, while Midshipman W. D. Lamont, Officer of the Day, was sent out on foot along the crossties. He had walked nearly the whole of the four miles to Bay Ridge, before he met the youngsters coming back.

Making them continue to furnish the motive power, he assumed command of their land craft, and brought them back to the Academy where they were at once placed under arrest.

By 1915 a new hotel, called the Bay Ridge Inn, had been built on the low shore near Black Walnut Creek. Albert Z. Wilson of Lansdowne, who then owned Carvel Cottage, the Victorian house near the old grand hotel, had become involved with Bay Ridge and decided to go into the hotel business. His niece, Mattie Gates, remembers that her father, Mr. Wilson's brother-in-law, built the small Tudor-style hotel. It catered to families who came by car in the summer from Washington, Baltimore, and beyond for a peaceful week or more by the bay. Sunday schools and other city-based organizations could again make Bay Ridge their destination for summer excursions, enjoying the sparkling waters they remembered from earlier years and picnicking now in the groves along Black Walnut Creek. Adventurous hikers followed the wide sandy

Previous pages:

Fig. 2. Bay Ridge, before development, c. 1918

Fig. 3. From a Bay Ridge Realty Company business card, a Bay Ridge road c. 1922

Fig. 4. Tolly Point bluff c. 1922, as shown on another Bay Ridge Realty Company business card. These cards had an illustration on one side and advertising copy on the other and were folded in the middle, which explains the crease lines seen here and in figure 3.

Fig. 5. "Bay Front Looking toward Tolley Point. Lots with old shade trees." Bay Ridge Realty Company brochure c. 1923

Fig. 6. From the Bay Drive cliff, near Upshur Avenue, two children look out over the bay c. 1925

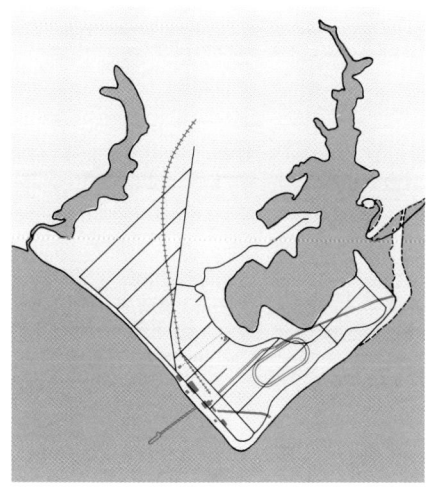

Fig. 7. The buildings and rail-lines of the Victorian resort (see Chapter 2, figure 4) superimposed upon a present street map, showing the relationship of resort features to current streets. Much of the old railroad bed is still discernable today in the woods near Farragut Road.

beach to Tolly Point and scrambled up the bluff to gaze in solitude across the bay. Long past were the crowds, the music, the laughter.

Indeed, by 1920 little evidence remained of that brief halcyon period. George R. Buffham's house stood empty. After his death on August 7, 1915, his widow had remarried and sold the property. An ancient house of mortise and tenon construction beside the lake was now the summer home of Reese and Pearl Abbott of Annapolis, and only a lone section of brick wall stood near the site of Mr. Wilson's Carvel Cottage, which was no more. Workers hired to remove the tracks from the Bay Ridge and Annapolis Railroad had been burning brush on March 4, 1918, when their fire swept out of control and raced along the tracks into the center of Bay Ridge. Carvel Cottage burned to the ground before firemen could arrive from Annapolis.

Later Bay Ridge residents have often found traces of the resort, the railroad, and the two early fires. Sometimes the discoveries are expected—a piece of railroad tie at the corner of a garden on Barry Avenue, spikes in the backyards of Mayo Avenue and Farragut Road, or melted, misshapen fragments of glass buried near Bay Drive and Lawrence Avenue. Sometimes they are intriguing, like the steps to an old cellar in the yard of 11 Barry Avenue, or the remains of wells and cisterns near Bancroft Avenue and in the woods south of West Lake Drive. But occasionally these ghosts from the past loom large and expensive, as when the house at 81 Bay Drive began to tilt into what was probably the cellar of the old bathhouse, with its deep well for the seawater baths filled with burned debris.

111

Fig. 8. 136 East Lake Drive c. 1918. This house, almost certainly the "Brighton Villa" of the resort years, was sold as part of Brighton Beach in 1903 and purchased by the Abbotts in 1914. The original section of the house was set on upended cedar logs.

Fig. 9. The rear of 136 East Lake Drive. Reese Abbott (left) and "Mr. Landon," probably Landon Brooks, looked toward the old barn. The Abbotts continued to keep farm animals for many years—the only Bay Ridge property allowed to do so after 1922.

On February 8, 1922, the Bay Ridge Realty Corporation assumed title to the former resort property of 387 acres. The third in a series of companies that during the previous twenty-eight years had intended to develop Bay Ridge into a summer resort community, Bay Ridge Realty was the only one to succeed. Major stockholders in the company were Thomas R. Bond, Herman G. Odenwald, and Thomas T. Boswell, the first president. The company replaced the 1894 Brighton Beach layout with a slightly less gridlike design and named the streets after naval heroes.

For the romantics, an early plat noted the location of "Skull Hall" near the River Drive end of Sands Avenue. According to local legend, treasure captured by the infamous Captain Kidd had once been buried on the point, and an old recluse living in a nearby house had been killed by treasure hunters. When his skull was found in the basement of the old house, the house and, by extension, the point were referred to as "Skull Hall."

Farfetched though it may seem, the legend may have had some basis in fact. In his recent book, *Pirates on the Chesapeake*, Donald G. Shomette tells of Theophilus Turner, one of Kidd's henchmen, who sailed into the Severn in 1699. Maryland authorities, who had been warned of his arrival on a hijacked ship, arrested Turner and confiscated four hundred pieces of eight from the pirate's chest. After several months' imprisonment in Annapolis, Turner was shipped back to England for trial. The captain of the presumably hijacked vessel was released and apparently disappeared. Who is to say that either Turner or the elusive captain did not sneak

Fig. 10. 81 Bay Drive c. 1932, before Bancroft Avenue was cut through to the lake

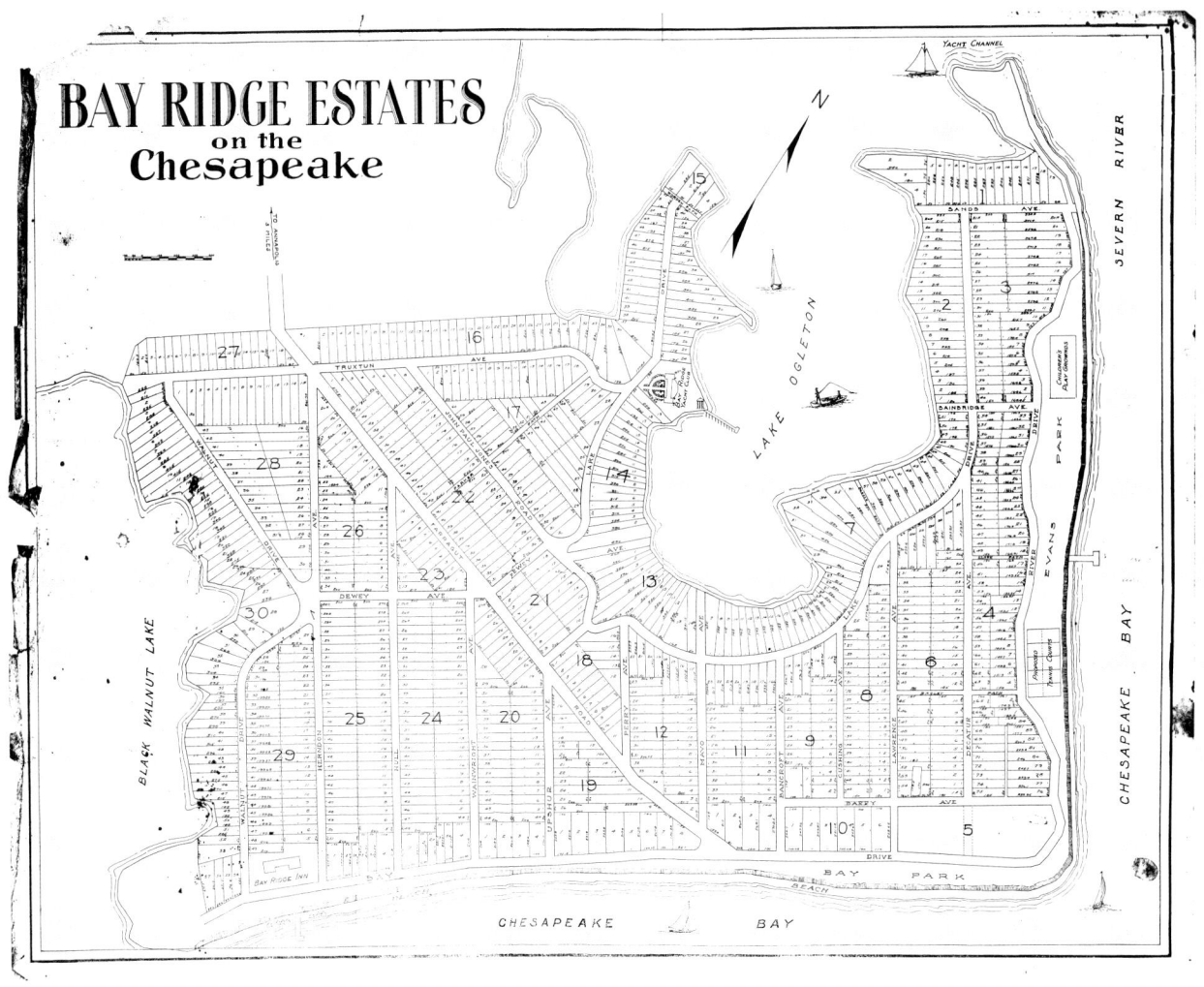

Fig. 11. Bay Ridge Realty Company sales plat of Bay Ridge c. 1922, including proposed development features such as the "Bay Ridge Yacht Club"

Fig. 12. Plat of Brighton Beach proposed by the Bay Ridge Improvement Company of Anne Arundel County in 1894. Only four of these lots were sold between 1896 and 1916 when the company went out of business and the property was sold to the Real Estate and Improvement Company of Baltimore City.

Fig. 13. Landon M. Brooks, surveyor, Bay Ridge, c. 1918

Fig. 14. Artist's conception of an aerial view of Bay Ridge c. 1923, showing the proposed hotel and pier on Bay Drive near the site of the old resort hotel. Many of the streets pictured here have never been cut through.

ashore to bury more of the booty in Bay Ridge? The legend was recounted in a 1927 supplement to the *Evening Capital*, perhaps by a twentieth-century treasure hunter, but the story is not generally known today.

During 1922 thirteen deeds were recorded for lots in the new development. Almost without exception, the land sold was on the riverfront. Those first purchasers included George Kahl, Dr. Hamilton Boyd Wylie, Clifford E. Kettler, Herman G. Odenwald, George W. Daw, and George Engel, all of whom built houses still standing on River Drive. They were followed by fifteen familes in 1923, three in 1924, and twenty-three in 1925. All told, there were 214 sales by 1929, most of them for more than one lot.

The dashing debonair bachelor, Thomas Rollins Bond, followed Mr. Boswell as president of Bay Ridge Realty and by 1927 had assumed complete control of the company. He was also involved in the development of Gibson Island. Both Mr. Bond and Mr. Boswell envisioned Bay Ridge as a "desirable and high class residential section," and early deeds carried the restrictions they felt would ensure this. Although the restrictions varied slightly from deed to deed, in general they excluded minorities and prohibited commercial activities, the sale of wines and liquors, and the keeping of poultry, domestic animals, or "nuisances of any kind." Only hedge fences were allowed, and a garage was the only acceptable outbuilding. While double houses could be built on 75-foot lots, minimum costs for both single and double houses were specified, with those on the waterfront to be more expensive. Houses were required to have indoor plumbing, drilled "artesian" wells, and a four-foot cement sidewalk maintained by the lot owner. Obviously not all of these covenants were adhered to—the only sidewalk in Bay Ridge extends from 15 Mayo Avenue to Farragut Road and was built by Fred Smith, not, as the story goes, to comply with the restrictions but because he didn't enjoy getting

Fig. 15. "A bungalow at Bay Ridge facing Chesapeake Bay;" Thomas R. Bond's house at 43 Bay Drive c. 1923

Fig. 16. 87 Bay Drive, c. 1924. Albert Z. Wilson built this house after his summer home, Carvel Cottage, burned.

Fig. 17. As part of its aggressive advertising, Bay Ridge Realty Company produced several posters and brochures illustrating the qualities of the new community. This one from the mid-1920s features George Kahl's home at 114 River Drive, 108 River Drive, and the house at 1 Barry Avenue built on the site of Carvel Cottage.

his feet dirty walking up from the beach. The only double house still recognizable as such is the house at 6 Wainwright Avenue, built by Judge Robert Moss.

Many of the Bay Ridge pioneers came because they remembered happy childhood days at the old amusement park or had heard their parents reminisce about their visits by steamboat or train to the resort. Some, like George Daw and Henry Porter, had taken picnics from the Bay Ridge Inn up to the point in the days before Prohibition and had seen firsthand the beauty of the area. Now they could build summer homes and make this magic place their own.

The trip from Washington, permanent home for most early Bay Ridgers, was often harrowing. Defense Highway was not opened until 1927, so motorists followed the old winding post road from

Fig. 18. Taking her place with the beauties of 1925 was Miss Bay Ridge. Can you find her? (She's tenth from the right, top row.)

Fig. 19. While on the homefront . . . Bay Ridge ladies posed on the River Drive beach during the Fourth of July festivities c. 1926.

Bladensburg through Chesterfield to Annapolis. The last leg of the journey from Annapolis, across the Eastport bridge at Fourth Street and out onto the peninsula, picked up the route of the old railroad as it came east through what is now Victor Haven and Annapolis Roads. Built over the old cross ties, the one-lane road was truly "like a washboard," says Adelaide Ervin. Her sister, Caroline Josey, remembers their family's stopping for ice at the corner of Bay Ridge and Forest Hills avenues and again for fresh milk and produce at the Keyes' farm. Herbert Keyes lived in the large brown house at 1131 Bay Ridge Road. His horses were a familiar sight in Bay Ridge; they cleared many of the lots for building and, on at least one occasion, dragged sand from the River Drive beach back into the marsh between the beach and the road.

Once ensconced in their summer homes, women and children stayed put and the men traveled back to their jobs in the city, to return on weekends. Few women could drive and had a car at their disposal, but those who did would go into town to pick up their husbands at the railroad station or run errands for their neighbors.

A number of families brought servants or nursemaids to watch the children on the beach. Ladies did not sunbathe in those days. They would don robes or beach kimonos and bathing shoes for the walk across the road to the beach, have a swim, and then retire to their shady porches for coffee, gossip, or cards with their neighbors. Firm friendships were made during those peaceful, lazy summer days.

120

Fig. 20. Watermelon feast near 14 River Drive c. 1925

Fig. 21. Keeping cool on Upshur Avenue beach c. 1925

Fig. 22. Properly attired for serious crabbing c. 1925

Fig. 23. Henry Porter emerged from his beach tent near 14 River Drive ready for a swim c. 1925.

Fig. 24. Back from a fishing trip with the day's catch, fishermen posed in the backyard of 14 River Drive c. 1925.

Fig. 25. The sand-covered boy is missing a great story, Upshur Avenue beach c. 1925.

Fig. 26. Summer sweethearts on the pier in front of River Drive, 1920s

Fig. 27. Clarence Kettler, Sr., and Adelaide D. Ervin, River Drive beach, 1925

Fig. 28. Smiling through it all—River Drive beach scene, 1920s

Fig. 29. Richard and Stanley Hollander (on right) with friends at Bay Ridge Beach, late 1920s

123

Fig. 30. 104 River Drive, summer home of the Edward J. Ervin family, 1927

Fig. 31. The Ervin family first traveled to Bay Ridge in their 1923 Buick.

Fig. 32. Victoria Hollander, Dr. William G. Cushard, Sr., Stan Hollander, and Dan McEllin continued the ritual croquet games into the 1950s.

Weekends were filled with shopping, guests, picnics, swimming, and lawn games. However, no family lawn game had the ritual and continuity of the croquet matches in Dan McEllin's backyard. For more than thirty years the lawn between Hollanders' and Clark Path on Decatur Avenue was off limits to everyone except approved croquet players. After the lawn was carefully mowed with a push mower, Mr. McEllin would trim off any offending tufts with his lawn shears. Summer evenings found Dr. Grant S. Barnhart, George Daw, Mr. McEllin, Henry Porter, at least one Fowler, and invited gentleman guests engaged in genteel but serious battle. Ronnie Hollander notes that her mother-in-law was the only woman allowed in the game, probably because she was a first-class croquet player. Ruth McLaine remembers the dinners that got cold at the Fowler household because Sinclair Fowler could never carve his mother's roast "Until the game is done, Mom."

In 1928 Freeman Paulson and his brother Peter, both tennis champions, cut down twenty trees to build clay courts behind the Paulson home at the end of East Lake Drive. For years spirited matches were held throughout the summer with neighbors and friends.

At the other end of Bay Ridge, Col. Peter M. Anderson rented Judge Moss's cottage on Wainwright Avenue and decided that he

Fig. 33. 33 Bay Drive, built by Col. Peter M. Anderson c. 1924, shown on a 1930s Bay Ridge Realty Company poster with traditional blue hydrangeas in bloom.

had found his "haven." His daughter, Jane O'Meara, writes that her father chose a Spanish style for his summer home, similar to designs he had seen in Arizona while building power plants for the Rural Electrification Administration. While the house was being built, the Anderson family camped out in a twelve-man army tent with six iron bedsteads and a flashlight handy for trips "to the one-holer in the woods." Mrs. O'Meara recalls: "Saturday at 7 A.M. my dad would be at the Annapolis railroad station where the labor pool hung out, to find seven [men] waiting to pack into the Cadillac touring car, ride to Bay Ridge, and work side-by-side with the colonel to build his six-bedroom house." The Andersons built a tennis court on one side of the house, an eighteen-hole miniature golf course on the other, and a sunken garden with fish pond and formal boxwood garden under a cedar tree in the backyard. The house was named Los Cedros, and Mrs. O'Meara remembers there was "a row of red cedars running perpendicular to the bay." Quite probably this is the same row of cedar trees that divided

Fig. 34. Spanish-style house at 17 Bay Drive, built c. 1929 by the Loffler family from a design by Col. Anderson. The first Bay Ridge Jamboree was held in 1945 on the tennis courts to the right.

Fig. 35. "George F. Evans House," 83 Bay Drive, shown on an advertising poster c. 1932

the original Tolly's Point and Withers Durand patents. The four Anderson children were properly dressed in bathing shoes, woolen bathing suits, and kimonos when they walked to the bay on oyster shell roads and took "a fragrant, honeysuckled twenty-five foot winding path down to the clean sandy beach of Chesapeake Bay. Locust trees made an occasional shadow on the beach, and we could hear the locusts and cicadas telling us tomorrow would be hot."

During these early years Bay Ridge was virtually deserted in the winter, its beautiful homes standing empty except for the families' occasional weekend visits. Break-ins and robberies were inevitable. Sometimes owners returning in the spring found to their dismay that their houses had provided winter shelter for unknown and unwelcome guests. Since the development company offered no solution to the problem, the homeowners finally took action themselves. During the winter of 1926–27 they met at the home of Edward J. and Adelaide D. Ervin in Washington, D.C., and

Fig. 36. "Homes on River Drive," shown c. 1932, including the houses of George Daw, Dan McEllin, and Dr. Grant S. Barnhart on the far right

127

formed the Bay Ridge Civic Association. Dr. Grant S. Barnhart was elected the first president; Clarence M. White of Annapolis, vice-president; Adelaide D. Ervin, secretary; and Mary Irene Roeth, treasurer. The following summer Mr. White, Henry W. Wanner of Kensington, and George Kahl of Baltimore County incorporated the association with a board of directors composed of themselves, Dr. Barnhart, and Dr. Hamilton B. Wylie. By-laws were adopted in September 1927. The stated purpose of the organization was "to protect the property of its members in Bay Ridge and to promote and advance the interest of the community as a residential colony." Yearly dues were set at $10 for house owners and $3 for lot owners.

One of the first acts of the new Bay Ridge Civic Association was to engage a community watchman, and one of the first to have this job was Theodore Christenson. By the late 1930s Mr. Christenson and his family were living in the old Buffham house, and he and his horse had become a familiar part of the Bay Ridge

Fig. 37. Looking north from 90 River Drive c. 1930. Long boards were placed across the great marsh so that swimmers could walk to the beach.

Fig. 38. River Drive beach panorama c. 1927

scene. Thomas Bond's niece remembered that, on her visits to Bay Ridge from Baltimore, she would be met at the railroad station in Annapolis by the community postman, surely Mr. Christenson, with his white horse and a wagon to carry her to her uncle's house.

In 1930 there were about seventy houses in Bay Ridge, three-quarters of them located between Lawrence Avenue and the Severn River. Lot sales continued at a steady rate until the mid 1930s, but behind the scenes, the Depression was shaping the community in profound and irreversible ways. The developers' original plan to construct a hotel on Bay Drive between Lawrence and Barry avenues, near the site of the old resort hotel, was given up and the block was platted into lots in 1931. None of these large expensive lots was sold for years, however, because waterfront mansions were giving way to more modest cottages built on interior lots.

This change meant trouble for the Bay Ridge Realty Corporation and eventually for the residents. Thomas Bond had mortgaged the unsold property, plus one thousand shares of the defunct Bay Ridge and Annapolis Railroad Company in 1928, and in 1933 the mortgage was foreclosed. At a public auction that November, Bond managed to buy back his interest in the property for $25,500, but only by immediately remortgaging both land and stock. Unable to satisfy mounting pressure from the residents for decent roads, Bond and his mortgagee, Elsa Loffler, conveyed title to the main loop around Bay Ridge to the Anne Arundel County Commissioners in 1934. The loop, which extended along Farragut Road to Bay Drive, up to the dogleg at Lawrence and Barry avenues, to Decatur Avenue, with Decatur to East Lake Drive and Sands Avenue and back along East Lake Drive to Upshur Avenue, was given a tarred hard surface by the county. The rest of the roads remained oyster shell.

Bond's financial status did not improve, and in June 1936 Bay Ridge again came on the auction block. This time the property and stock went to outside interests. Thomas Bond died on December 12, 1936. By 1941 the Bay Ridge land had become the property

Fig. 39. 71 Bay Drive c. 1933, one of the earliest year-around homes

of the county commissioners for nonpayment of property taxes. Kass Realty Corporation of Delaware agreed to pay the taxes owed and took over the county's interest in 1941. Three years later a formal deed from everyone involved conveyed the fee simple title and all rights and interest in the unsold property to Kass Realty. Garfield I. Kass, president of Kass Realty, became the sole owner in 1946. Upon his death in 1975, his Bay Ridge property descended to his heirs.

Throughout the 1930s home and lot owners in Bay Ridge received little support from the various troubled developers. Whatever benefits were lacking had to be supplied or obtained or lobbied for by the residents themselves, usually through the Bay Ridge Civic Association (BRCA). Mosquito and erosion control, police protection, road signs, garbage pickup, entertainment, and all forms of community improvement became the responsibility of part-time volunteers.

As maintenance of vacation homes became less feasible during the Depression years, an increasing number of families chose to live in Bay Ridge all year around. Among the first year-around

Fig. 40. The Reesers' garage/apartment on Mayo Avenue with gasoline pumps and kerosene tanks c. 1935

Fig. 41. For many years during the 1930s and early 1940s the Reeser family operated a summertime grocery store in the lower floor of their home at 71 Bay Drive and, later, in the garage behind it. The summer poinsettias along the porch were Mrs. Reeser's special pride.

Fig. 42. Ready to go to the beach, David (Dusty) Rhodes and ladies loaded the car at Bancroft Avenue, 1931.

residents were Marjorie Gloth and her mother on Sands Avenue, the Abbotts on East Lake Drive, and J. B. and Eldeane Wilson on Farragut Road. Another was William Earl Reeser, who moved to Bay Ridge with his wife and son in 1929 to build houses. Between 1930 and 1950, he built more than twenty of them, mostly on Mayo Avenue, Bancroft Avenue, and Bay Drive. His son Marvin tells of their weekly winter shopping excursions to Annapolis, where dinner and a movie made these trips an important change from the remoteness of rural living. By the late 1930s there were eight or nine Bay Ridge children attending the high school in Annapolis, and the county provided a school bus, with one stop at Farragut Road and Mayo Avenue.

Summers were a different story, however. As soon as the weather warmed and the trees began to bud, the city folk unboarded their houses and began to prepare for vacation living. When school was out, they moved down for good. For a year or two in the early 1930s, a Greyhound bus brought working fathers to Bay Ridge from Washington on Friday nights and picked them up again on Sunday.

Summer rentals, either while the homeowners were elsewhere or in houses built especially for that purpose, were common. Having tasted the advantages of Bay Ridge beaches and atmosphere, the renters of one summer frequently became the homeowners of succeeding years. What Bay Ridge Realty's imaginative advertising had accomplished in the 1920s, word of mouth and on-site experience continued in the 1930s. Neighbors and friends from the city and relatives from as far away as Pittsburgh became part of the Bay Ridge community.

Softball games in front of Dr. Barnhart's on River Drive, parades, picnics, and fireworks on the Fourth of July, Bay Ridge Civic Association–sponsored dinners and dances, as well as the tedious community chores of mosquito control and beach cleanup brought the residents together for both pleasure and work. On the other hand, by the late 1930s there was dissension within the community between residents of liberal, aggressive views and those with a more conservative financial outlook.

Fig. 43. "Would Be's" vs "Had Been's"—traditional Fourth of July softball game on River Drive beach c. 1926

Fig. 44. Fourth of July parade along an unpaved River Drive, c. 1931, included a junior bride and groom and sea-nettles, the swimmers' nemesis—even then.

Fig. 45. Lake Ogleton dock, 1931, with a variety of motorboats and the original Bay Ridge clubhouse in the right background

Figs. 46–51. (top to bottom, left to right) Everbody's doing it! Crabbing in Lake Ogleton from the dock at the end of Bancroft Avenue, early 1930s

Fig. 52. Summer fun. Clowning around on Bancroft Avenue, 1931

Fig. 53. Dolly Sharp in beach pajamas beside a tranquil Chesapeake c. 1931

Fig. 54. Launching the "BRYSC" into the lake at the foot of Sands Avenue c. 1945. The heavy wooden catboat, built by the Leatherburys in Galesville, belonged to Margaret and Rolf Paulson and the other members of the "Bay Ridge Yacht and Sailing Club."

Fig. 55. Rolf Paulson as a young boy, with a good catch, beside the Peter Paulson summer home, 7 East Lake Drive, c. 1927

Fig. 56. "Lercrett and Louie," 1931

Fig. 57. Hurricane Hazel, October 1954, battered the Mayo Avenue beach and the Campbell and McDowell piers.

The first serious disagreement arose over which parts of Bay Ridge should be included in the special taxing district set up to pay for erosion control. The problem of erosion had become acute in 1933. That year for three days in late August, a northeaster battered Maryland's coast with gale-force winds and heavy rains; more than four inches fell in the Annapolis area. Then, on Wednesday, August 23, a hurricane plowed in from Bermuda. Winds along the bay coast were estimated at less than fifty miles per hour, but that was enough to push the already swollen waters of the bay and rivers into crashing waves that ravaged the sodden banks. Tides as high as eight feet above normal flooded the Annapolis harbor and spread up Prince George Street to Randall Street. Bembe Beach was abandoned as waters piled boats seventy-five feet inland. Fifty feet of land at the end of Severn Avenue in Eastport was carried away, along with a two-story stucco house.

Fig. 58. Bayfront under siege, looking south from McDowell's pier in front of 63 Bay Drive, early 1940s

Fig. 59. Cliff in front of 51–53 Bay Drive after a storm in the 1940s, when undercutting caused the lawn at the top of the bank to slide. Braces attempted to hold back the slide.

In Bay Ridge, where spray from the Mayo Avenue beach was blown as far as Farragut Road, the damage was disastrous, as the Annapolis *Evening Capital* reported the next day.

> Bay Ridge suffered heavily from the storm, and the Bay Drive [probably referring to River Drive as well] today was impassable due to high water, fallen trees, and washouts. A considerable portion of the cliff overlooking the Bay was washed away and is decorated with a fringe of fallen trees. Several houses were flooded and the porches of others today were covered with stormdrift and debris. The piers in Ogleton Lake were destroyed. Cars were blocked in at summer houses by the fallen trees and limbs.
>
> At the Baur House the loss was estimated at $10,000. The long pier was badly damaged and several pavilions were blown down. The water covered the floor of the Baur Club more than a foot deep, leaving the dance floor covered with silt.

Fig. 60. A familiar sight at the Mayo Avenue beach, 1938

Fig. 61. Bayfront panorama north from McDowell's pier c. 1940. The bulkheads and groins installed in 1934–1935 protected the toe of the bank north of Mayo beach; the rest of the bank was shelved as sand and soil eroded.

When the waters receded and people could walk around Tolly Point again, it was that "fringe of fallen trees" that shocked them, for those trees had, two days before, been as much as fifty feet inland.

Bay Ridge Realty immediately requested a meeting with the county commissioners, followed by a petition from property owners asking for aid. After a report by the State Waterfront Commission called the storm "the most severe hurricane in the history of the state," the Maryland General Assembly in special session passed a law allowing special taxing districts to be created within Anne Arundel County to provide funds to pay the interest and principal on bonds that would finance erosion prevention structures and the cost of repairs to those structures. The Anne Arundel County Commissioners, acting as a District Council, would levy a tax against the assessable property in each district sufficient to pay the debts or, after the bonds were paid off, to keep the works in repair. In January 1934 Bay Ridge was one of six county communities to request erosion protection under the 1933 law, but it was the fall of that year before bids were received for the project. The Bay Ridge Shore Erosion Control District, which would pay off the necessary bonds, included only that part

of the community north and west of Farragut Road, at that time the most populous part of Bay Ridge.

During 1934 and 1935, 2,025 feet of timber bulkhead, with groins every sixteen feet, were constructed between Mayo Avenue and Tolly Point, and 1,303 feet of stone wall extended the works around the point on River Drive. The total cost was $75,000, $32,000 of which was paid by the federal government and $43,000 by special county bonds.

Within only a few years after the construction of the bulkhead, it was obvious that it would soon be undermined and that the rest of River Drive needed bulkheads and jetties as well. Horace J. Donnelly, Jr., then BRCA president, was not pleased to learn in 1940 that out of more than $1,000 levied for erosion repairs and maintenance during the preceding five years, almost one-half had been paid to county commissioners sitting as the Bay Ridge Shore Erosion District Council. Since both Bay and River drives were then county roads, Mr. Donnelly suggested an amendment to the 1933 law to have the county take over the maintenance and extension of erosion projects along the bay- and riverfronts. Although this amendment did not pass the legislature, the county did credit the community for monies expended on council activities.

139

Property owners in the section of Bay Ridge south and east of Farragut Road were interviewed by committees of the BRCA in 1941, and again in 1955, with the hope that they would agree to become part of the erosion control district. Each time they refused. Instead, individual owners of property along Bay Drive experimented with their own erosion control methods. The Maloney family placed a tier of cement blocks at the toe of the cliff in front of 51–53 Bay Drive. Charles P. Maloney, owner of the Maloney Concrete Company in Washington, had cubic forms made and, when his trucks returned from a job, the leftover concrete was poured into the forms and a ring was placed in the top of each cube for easy transport and placement. The Maloney project has been remarkably successful; others have not fared as well. A walk along the Bay Drive beach will reveal a variety of stones, concrete shapes, and rusted pipes, which attest to someone's hard work and largely futile hopes.

The BRCA minutes throughout the 1940s and 1950s are littered with complaints about undermined bulkheads and backwashed jetties. Part of River Drive west of Barry Avenue was washed out and impassable for more than a year in 1945–46, and a series of bad storms in the mid-1950s almost completely destroyed the bulkhead along the Bay Drive cliffs. The Bay Drive bank south of Mayo Avenue was noted as being seriously undercut as early as 1941, and Hurricane Hazel in 1954 cut further inroads of ten to twenty feet in some places.

Thus Bay Ridge's official fight to save its land from the inexorable forces of nature has been going on for more than fifty years. Occasional battles have been won, a larger number lost, and the war continues to this day. Over the years there have been studies and recommendations by both private and public agencies; but, as the county Board of Public Works stated in 1956, "Due to the high cost involved, the residents of that community have been unable to finance these projects and very few of the recommendations were carried out." The same problems still trouble Bay Ridge residents.

A second controversy plaguing early residents of Bay Ridge centered on the question of incorporation, which was presented as a solution to several problems of general concern. Foremost among those problems was the question of zoning. The covenants established by the deeds from Bay Ridge Realty expired in 1935, and the community wanted to continue to protect its character with similar restrictions. In those days the county government left zoning pretty much up to the developer, and Bay Ridge's relationship with the successors to Thomas Bond was questionable at best. In addition, noncounty roads were poorly maintained and county-owned ones fared only slightly better. Finally, in March 1938 the county withdrew watchman Theodore Christenson from Bay Ridge against his wishes and stationed him in Eastport. Bay Ridgers protested vigorously, but in vain. Mr. Christenson's death on April 20, 1938, was mourned by the entire community.

Feeling frustrated and very much on their own, a group of property owners led by Bay Ridge Civic Association president, Herbert S. Ward, met in January 1939 at 73 Bay Drive and decided that if Bay Ridge were an incorporated town it would have more clout with the county and more control over its own welfare. The group prevailed upon State Senator Louis N. Phipps to introduce a bill into the General Assembly establishing the "Town of Bay Ridge." The bill passed the Senate, but when it reached the House of Delegates other Bay Ridgers protested, sure that incorporation would raise taxes. Meetings were held, position papers distributed, and angry charges leveled back and forth between the two factions. An informal vote showed the opposition to incorporation to have mustered greater numbers, if not greater aggregate property value. Eventually the legislature adjourned with the bill still in House committee, and the issue died. Bay Ridge would have to cope with its problems in other ways.

In an attempt to improve fire-fighting capabilities, Mr. Ward installed two cast-iron pipes out into the water on the bayfront at Mayo and Upshur avenues to allow fire trucks to pump seawater directly onto a fire. They were tested successfully during the summer of 1940 but received little if any use before clogging up and rusting away. (In the late 1970s this idea was tried again with similar results.)

Police protection continued to concern the community. In its early years, the BRCA had worked out an agreement with the county to have Officer Christenson paid as a watchman. But when the county exercised its right to remove Officer Christenson, the community looked for another method of payment that would ensure greater control over its police protection. For a few months the civic association tried hiring a watchman and relying on voluntary donations to pay his salary, but the experiment was not successful. In January 1939 the community, with the consent of the county commissioners, employed an "Inspector of Garbage Collection" whose salary and expenses would be included in the fee assessed by the county for garbage service. Joseph W. Hopkins, Sr., thus became, technically, the garbage inspector; but during his twenty years of service in Bay Ridge, he was far more than that. He ticketed speeders, checked locks on unoccupied homes, caught stray dogs, and managed to maintain a working relationship with the BRCA Police Committee, which was responsible for his activities. He kept a roster of everyone in the community, logged his daily observations in the "incident book," delivered newspapers from time to time, and drove around Bay Ridge more often than anyone could ever want to. Officer Hopkins became a tradition—he knew everyone, knew their daily habits, knew their children, knew their dogs. The Hopkins family lived in the old Buffham house for the first three or four years of his duty and then moved to the house built by Earl Reeser at 28 Upshur Avenue.

By 1941 Bay Ridge was a settled summer community with enough permanent residents to maintain continuity. Almost all the roads had been taken over by the county, and many had been

Fig. 62. Officer Joseph W. Hopkins, Sr., in full uniform c. 1940. The siren and light on his Chevy's left fender, removed from a Rescue Hose firetruck that wrecked c. 1928 in Arundel-on-the-Bay, was used as an air raid siren during World War II.

given a stone and tar surface—a pleasure for drivers, but a sticky pain for barefooted walkers on hot summer days. The houses had been numbered, new wooden street signs installed by the BRCA, and regular year-around mail service instituted. The problems of mosquito and erosion control remained, as did the annoyances of roadside parking, traffic, loose-running dogs, and general community upkeep. Committees investigating the proposed opening of the Lake Ogleton channel and the building of a community center on the lake were encouraged by the interest of Kass Realty Corporation. Of the 141 homeowners in 1941, almost half belonged to the BRCA.

With the reality of war in December 1941, the community was drawn into a larger effort from which neither it nor the country would emerge unchanged. One change was dramatic for a family that had owned and operated a part of Bay Ridge as a private business for more than a decade. At the beginning of the Depression, Andrew and Elsa Loffler of Washington, D.C., owners of a meat packing business and purveyors of "Loffler's Skinless Franks," came to Bay Ridge with their family and purchased a lot on Bay Drive and Hull Avenue. Jane Anderson O'Meara recalls that Mr. Loffler so liked her father's Spanish house down the street that he asked Col. Anderson to design one for his family in a similar style.

The Lofflers also purchased the Bay Ridge Inn. Their daughter, Helene, and her husband, Raymond Baur, turned the quiet boarding hotel into a full-fledged beach resort that flourished all during the

Fig. 63. Gloryanne Baur in her white terry beachrobe stood next to the "razzledazzle" at the Baur's Beach playground c. 1939.

Fig. 64. The entrance to the Bathers' Grill, Baur's Beach, 1935

Fig. 65. Tahiti on the Chesapeake, Bay Ridge Beach c. 1950

Fig. 66. Baur's Beach c. 1935, taken from the swimming and diving platform that remained after the long pier was destroyed in the 1933 hurricane. At the far left, beyond the cabanas, is the inlet to Black Walnut Creek and Highland Beach.

Depression. The Baurs' daughter, Gloryanne Baur Sandrey, writes of her parents and those years with fond memories.

> Mama had a special dream during those trying depression years. Why not turn Baur's Beach into a South Seas Island–type resort, instead of another Coney Island–type of commercialized resort? Give the working people (those lucky enough to have jobs) from Washington and Baltimore a tropical dreamlike place to escape to from their dull work-a-day worlds. And so the dream became a reality. During the off-season, when the family wintered in Coral Gables, Florida, Papa gathered up palmetto fronds, tiki statues and coconuts and sent them north each Spring. The beaches and grounds became a veritable "Tahiti Beach North." Unique? Yes. And the people loved it. Palm-frond huts and buildings dotted the wide expanse of golden sands. Even the Life Guard station for our full staff of life guards (our "babysitters") was thatched like a Tahitian hut. Name any kind of playground or water sports equipment, including surf boards, and we had it. Besides our big diving and sliding board station, there were all kinds of specially designed water sports and floats that Papa built himself; the "Sea Biscuit," a large doughnut shaped float, was popular, but the famous "Beer Barreled Polka Float" was the hit of 1939, 1940 and 1941.

Raymond Baur added bathhouses, a dance pavilion where the Rivers Chambers Band held forth on long summer nights, and a row of cabanas where families "could spend the whole day at the beach with some of the comforts of home." There were tennis courts, ping-pong tables, a bowling alley, a baseball diamond, and picnic grounds under the trees.

The resort, known informally as "Baur's Beach," was a popular place for company picnics or the lavish outings of groups such as the Washington Board of Trade. Celebrities were frequent guests: Mrs. Sandrey remembers Babe Ruth, Lou Gehrig, Jack Dempsey, Ethel Barrymore, Joel McCrae, and Dick Powell.

Elsa Loffler presided over the main dining room of the hotel, and Mrs. Sandrey writes:

I can still see her now, greeting us (like she used to greet visiting ambassadors of state), fly-swatter in hand (she detested flies). The big lobby of the old Tudor-style Inn was a veritable museum of highly carved Ching Dynasty Chinese furniture. She reigned supreme in this highly unlikely setting of beachside oriental splendor. How she loved to take guests on tours of her Chinese Museum, explaining how she and my grandfather had collected most of these priceless antiques when they lived and entertained at their large Washington, D.C. home.

Those happy days were coming to a close however, and by the summer of 1941, the Loffler and Baur families began to talk of selling.

My brother, Ray, and I, young as we were, can still remember the hushed but foreboding conversations between our parents—way into the wee hours of the night. Talks of gas rationing, cut-backs on pleasure travel, food shortages—all these voices of impending "War doom," really put a damper on our late summer fun. But like most kids our age, we would try real hard to ignore the bitter news—dig our toes deeper into the warm, golden sand, and with a quick shiver, dive right back into the cool refreshing Chesapeake Bay for another swim out to the big diving and sliding board station, or dream about making one more rowboat trip out to our little private island (which, strange to say, seemed to grow smaller and smaller each year).

If someone ever asked me when the end of my childhood came, I would have to admit that it was that late autumn day in 1941. I remember it so well. We were all down at the big main bathhouse that day. In Uncle Al's "Bathers' Grill," our overworked juke box was grinding out Glenn Miller's "Sunrise Serenade" for the umpteenth time. Two National Guard soldiers from Ft. Meade, Md., were sitting at the bar, hungrily devouring Papa's world famous deviled crabs, along with Uncle Al's frothy draught beer. It was a dismal day outside. Papa had closed up the beach cabanas for the season, put away all the umbrellas, summer sports equipment, and beach furniture. The huge dance pavilion, which used to host . . . the Annapolis June Week Banquets and Papa's famous planked shad bakes, was all shut down. There was a decided chill in the air. Rows upon rows of tables were stacked with upturned chairs like dead soldiers awaiting resurrection. Back in the bathhouse, Mama was sitting behind the cash register at the enclosed ticket office (she used to teasingly call it her "cage"). She was sadly adding up the past Labor Day receipts, and the expression on her face told us all that summer was definitely over. . . . When we gathered for lunch that late Autumn day, our family all hovered around the big native stone fireplace in the main lobby—right in the shadow of "Oscar," the big carved ebony dragon that was the official greeter in the Chinese lobby. I remember it so well. Grandmother Elsa had thrown some driftwood logs on the fireplace and the effervescent glow somehow had taken the chill out of the air. But it didn't soften the impact of the words that were to follow. The family decision was firm. The clouds of war were growing darker and the ensuing economics were getting graver. The family had finally agreed that it would be on the part of wisdom to sell the place to Mr. Wills and his family.

B. B. Wills was no stranger to the resort business. He had owned steamship lines in Maryland, New York, and Massachusetts, and most recently had bought the Tolchester resort across the bay. During the war Mr. Wills rented the Bay Ridge Inn to the federal government as a rest home for wounded Merchant Marine seamen. Often shell-shocked and in need of a quiet, safe place to recuperate, these men could relax on the beach or putter in the workshop on the front porch of the hotel.

In 1945 the Soviet Government Purchasing Commission rented the other part of the resort, with the casino, bathhouses, and cabanas. A summer camp was established there for the children of the commission and Soviet Embassy staff. Parents and other adults came down on weekends. The venture was considered successful by both the Russians and the Bay Ridge community, even though the guests' fondness for cucumbers without the peels made cleaning the beaches a chore for the staff.

Following the war, the resort was reopened to the public. Company outings were again popular, as was Navy Day for the U.S. Naval Academy graduating class and their parents. The Wills family kept much of the Baur's South Seas Island decor, although some of the buildings have changed over the years. Ben Wills, Jr., the present owner, came to Bay Ridge Beach as manager for his father in 1957, the same summer the swimming pool was built and a disastrous fire destroyed the old bathhouse.

A part of Bay Ridge and yet not a part, Bay Ridge Beach has, over the years, been cheerful host to BRCA socials and employed generations of Bay Ridge children on its summer staff.

Fig. 67. Even on chilly days, Bay Ridge children preferred to go barefoot—Mayo Avenue beach c. 1943.

Fig. 68. Bay Ridge redheads' mothers made them wear beach hats and cover-ups when they played on the riverfront beach—Marcia McLaine c. 1945.

Fig. 69. Warren McLaine, Jr., and Edwin Fowler enjoyed a sunny day at the Fowler residence on Decatur Avenue, 1939.

World War II affected the rest of the community as well. Immediately after war was declared, local citizens met with the Civil Defense officer of Anne Arundel County, the elderly Col. John Douw, who told them that an air raid warden would be appointed for the Bay Ridge District and instructors would show people how to meet emergency conditions, but the problems of local defense were up to the community. Herbert Ward became chairman of the Bay Ridge Civilian Defense Council, with Philip Alter vice-chairman in charge of emergency police, Paul Raymond air raid warden, Miss Mary Irene Roeth Red Cross chairman, Earl Reeser fire protection chairman, and Officer Hopkins, the policeman. Joseph B. Trew donated a half-ton paneled Dodge truck for defense use, and Fred Smith provided his enlarged garage on Mayo Avenue for truck storage and the Red Cross "Canteen."

Though they probably did not realize it, Bay Ridgers in 1941 were reacting to the same fears that had brought out coast watchers during the Revolution and the War of 1812. Tolly Point was still a major landmark and the naval radio complex on Greenbury Point a potential target for sabotage. Again there was the possibility that the enemy would intrude upon Bay Ridge soil, and the Defense Council even considered placing barbed wire on the beaches. While this idea was scrapped early on, the council did set up night-time patrols. Wearing hard hats and armbands and armed with flashlight and note pad, the men of Bay Ridge walked their territory. They checked to be sure that blackout shades were drawn in every house, that automobile headlights were properly shielded, and, perhaps nervously, that the beaches were quiet.

Through private contributions, the civil defense truck was stocked with stretchers, blankets, first-aid supplies, pumps, sand, ladders, rope, shovels, and other fire-fighting equipment. The women of the Bay Ridge Red Cross Branch gathered survival supplies in Mr. Smith's garage—dishes, silverware, water, peanut butter. "They told us you can survive on water and peanut butter," remembers Ella Paulson. In addition to their other Red Cross duties in Annapolis, the women met in Smith's garage to make bandages while their preschoolers played around them.

Gas and rubber rationing made trips to town a less frequent event, and the Reesers continued their summertime store in their garage on Mayo Avenue. But once, when someone said there was sugar for sale, Helen Shores walked the five miles into Annapolis to get it. Ships from Baltimore often met U.S. Navy minesweepers off Tolly Point; Miss Roeth watched the loaded transports as they gathered in convoys for dawn trips down the bay.

During the war many former summer residents, confined to the city by rationing and other concerns, gave their houses a rudimentary winterizing and rented them to navy families. The Post Graduate School at the Naval Academy brought young officers to Annapolis, and they and their instructors were in desperate need of housing. Often, when the men went overseas, their wives and children remained in Bay Ridge. It was a safe place in troubled times. By early 1945 thirty-five Navy families and academy bandsmen were renting in Bay Ridge; but most left that summer when the Post Graduate School moved to Harvard University.

Toward the end of the war the community gradually returned to normal and began looking ahead. Zoning restrictions proposed by the BRCA in 1944 were adopted by the county commissioners the following January. Requiring that Bay Ridge be "strictly residential," with only single-family homes, the restrictions no longer prevented minority ownership, but otherwise set standards similar to those of the pre-1935 deeds—regulating house size and cost, requiring indoor plumbing, prohibiting hunting, and allowing no animals except dogs and cats, neither of which was to run loose. Rabies had recently been found in nearby areas, and there was apprehension that the large population of Bay Ridge rabbits, squirrels, and foxes would become infected and pass the disease to family pets.

On the other hand, the mosquito control problem appeared to be solved. In its August 1945 issue the short-lived *Bay Ridge Review* heralded the benefits of a new insecticide, DDT. Quoting a Baltimore entomologist as saying the powdered form "is quite harmless," the *Review* suggested that screens could be painted with DDT, dogs and cats powdered with DDT for flea control, and the whole community fogged with the liquid version as protection against mosquitoes. In short, DDT "should revolutionize the extermination of objectionable insects." Bay Ridge could not wait for the substance to be released for civilian use. For more than twenty years community mosquito control had relied on methods used by Americans in the tropics. With the leadership of Henry Porter, who had seen firsthand the effects of malaria in the Panama Canal Zone, Bay Ridgers poured oil and kerosene on marshes and stagnant ponds, placed oil-soaked cotton waste in the upper marshes, and checked their lots to be sure that no standing water was allowed to breed mosquito larvae. "Let's make each Saturday 'Mosquito Day,'" wrote Mr. Porter in 1938, as he advocated sending servants and children out to dump any rainwater that had collected around their yards. The BRCA spent hundreds of dollars each summer on sprayers, oil, and laborers to open ditches and cut down brush in order to curtail the accumulation of standing water. The whole business was regarded as a nasty but necessary chore. DDT was first used in Bay Ridge in the spring of 1947 as a spray, and that summer it was also sprinkled in dry form on the beaches to control flies.

For the year-around families, still in the minority in the community, winter at Bay Ridge continued to have a special charm and camaraderie. It always seemed so quiet then, as the geese honked their way south and the days grew short. There were long visits over a cup of tea on cold, rainy afternoons and rambling walks in the woods on Hull and Herndon avenues to gather bittersweet and running cedar. The beaches were deserted; the water rimmed with ice. Soon it was time to find and cut the perfect pine for Christmas. As the bitter northwest winds blew across the River Drive beachfront, Miss Roeth and her friend Jessie

Fig. 70. Henry G. Porter filled his backyard on Decatur Avenue with purple martin birdhouses in his ceaseless war against the mosquito.

Fig. 71. Mary Irene Roeth (1882–1985) in the garden behind her house at 90 River Drive, late 1930s.

Fig. 72. "The Jolly Old Gent himself—looking kinda cagey (or has he just sighted a bathing beauty on the beach?) May 13, 1945"

Watson would light a fire in the fireplace, bring out the afghans, and settle in for winter projects with the radio or Miss Watson's talking books for company. Christmas at their house was always a special treat, with the large dining room table covered with a lace cloth and cut-glass dishes piled high with holiday cakes and cookies. The quiet child could stuff herself by the fire, unnoticed, while her elders talked.

The first snow meant safe sledding on deserted roads—the Bay Drive hills were best—and as the weather grew colder, the children would vie to see who was brave enough to try out the ice on the lake. Perhaps because there were so few children here in the winter, they all knew each other and looked out for each other, at least against strangers, no matter where they lived in Bay Ridge. There was a proprietary sense among them, not shared with the "tenderfoots" who went back to city homes in the fall. Bay Ridge children rode the school bus together with youngsters from Arundel-on-the-Bay, Annapolis Roads, and Bay Ridge Avenue to Eastport Elementary, where the older children caught another bus to junior high and high schools. For years the only Bay Ridge school bus stop had been at Farragut Road and Mayo Avenue. By 1945 the route was extended to Lawrence Avenue and Bay Drive, but not until 1948 could mothers persuade the county to send the bus as far as East Lake Drive and Decatur Avenue.

Local dairies and the Jewell Tea man delivered milk and bread and other staples every few days; laundry was picked up and delivered; and the bookmobile, with its horn that played "Mary Had a Little Lamb," brought the county library to Bay Ridge every other week. For brief periods of time nursery and Sunday schools operated within the community. There were Scout troops, a football team and other loosely organized sports, and a 4-H club that met at George and Jean Hebbard's on River Drive. Major shopping was saved for trips to Baltimore or Washington, but groceries were bought in Annapolis or picked up on the way home at LaChappelle's Grocery, now C&C Liquors, on Bay Ridge Road.

In the summer the Good Humor truck made its daily rounds, offering ice cream and popsicles—just before dinner. After dinner there was the ritual walk to the beach. Grown-ups would sit on benches or fallen logs while little children played "catch the wave" until the Norfolk boat went down the bay and it was time to go home to bed. Older youngsters played hide and seek and caught fireflies after dusk, and teenagers spent carefree evenings in backyard summer houses listening to Frank Sinatra and flirting just a bit. Adults read on quiet porches, enjoying the cool breezes of evening that brought with them the scent of honeysuckle and roses.

Still primarily a summer community at the beginning of the 1950s, by the end of the decade Bay Ridge was well on its way to becoming a part of American suburbia. The problems faced by the community during this period reflect its changing nature.

The position of Officer Hopkins illustrates these changes. For more than ten years he had been, ostensibly, the "Inspector of Garbage Collection," with additional police duties as directed by the BRCA. But by 1954 the real scope of his activities and the need for their definitive enforcement were recognized by the county commissioners. At that time Mr. Hopkins was made a "Special Officer" with the authority of a regular county policeman within Bay Ridge to enforce the laws of the state and county and the regulations of the BRCA. An assessment for the Special Officer was thereafter included in the Bay Ridge property taxes.

Also by the mid-1950s the community saw a need for lighting at the entrance gates. In December 1954 homeward-bound Bay Ridgers were greeted by temporary Christmas lights, and the following summer permanent service was installed under the direction of J. B. Wilson.

Fig. 73. Bay Ridge Bulldogs Championship Team, 1951. Left to right, row 1: Jackie Runyon, Steve Martin; row 2: Eddie Erdelatz, Ernie Hall, Dave Paulson, Bob Callahan, Ernie Clark, Bill Harmon, Wayne Dickson, Ralph Campbell, Bill Campbell; row 3: Jim Dollar, Tom Schley, Don Holland, Dave Brashears

Fig. 74. Hi-jinks on River Drive beach, 1942—Mary Ann Hollander (second row left) and friends

Fig. 75. Thomas R. Bond in front of the first Bay Ridge clubhouse. This picture appeared on a Christmas card sent by Mr. Bond c. 1929.

Another sign of the emergence of Bay Ridge as a year-around community was the completion, finally, of a permanent clubhouse. The need for a community center had been perceived since the early days of the summer colony, and the first clubhouse was built in 1927 by Thomas Bond. Less grand than the one proposed in early Bay Ridge Realty brochures, it was a two-story white clapboard building with a red roof situated on the southwest shore of Lake Ogleton. Virtually inaccessible except by water, it was nevertheless used for dances, games, and parties. Damage sustained in the 1933 hurricane and subsequent vandalism rendered it useless by the middle of the decade.

In 1939 the need for some sort of community center was voiced in BRCA meetings. With the uncertain status of the developer, the citizens of Bay Ridge figured to build something themselves. War intervened, but in 1944 the idea was again brought forth as an appropriate tribute to Bay Ridge men and women in the armed services.

Plans for a lakeside community center were predicated on opening the channel into Lake Ogleton. Although the lake had been accessible to good-sized vessels in the nineteenth and early twentieth centuries, the entrance had closed up by the time Bay Ridge was developed as a summer colony. Apparently a three-foot-deep channel had been dug about 1923, but that, too, had closed by the late 1930s. As is the case now with Black Walnut Creek, the entrance to Lake Ogleton was barred by a narrow strip of sand across which a shallow inlet meandered, its depth and location determined by wind and tides. The landward ends of the sandbar supported grasses, bushes, and, as the ground rose toward Annapolis Roads on one end and Bay Ridge on the other, a few tenacious trees.

151

Fig. 76. Lake Ogleton c. 1927

In 1941 Kass Realty Company offered to give three lots on Lake Ogleton to the BRCA if it had the channel opened. The Anne Arundel County Engineer drew up plans for a six-foot-deep channel protected by jetties, and the community of Annapolis Roads offered to share the cost of construction. As with the plans for a community center, however, the war postponed channel activities until 1944.

With the revival of interest in both the clubhouse and channel in 1944, negotiations for suitable lots were resumed with Kass Realty by Earl Reeser, then president of the BRCA and a vigorous supporter of the community center.

Since the channel opening had not been accomplished and Mr. Kass was no longer willing to donate land outright, the BRCA agreed to purchase lots for its community center. On September 27, 1944, the association received title to Lots 34 and 35, Section 7, for $800. Most of the purchase money had been raised by benefit dinners given that summer by the women of Bay Ridge.

Fund raising continued the following summer with card parties and the first Bay Ridge Jamboree held at the home of George Huguely, 17 Bay Drive, on September 1, 1945, which netted more than $1,100 for the proposed center. Mr. Reeser drew up preliminary plans for a 60-by-100-foot building, and financing was arranged for construction of the clubhouse and a pier.

In June 1945 property owners from Bay Ridge and Annapolis Roads met at Bay Ridge Beach with representatives of the U.S. Army Corps of Engineers to ask for federal support in opening the channel. Their arguments centered on the need for a safe harbor for oyster boats and other commercial fishermen as well as for recreational boaters. Without such a harbor, they said, storm-threatened boats were often run ashore at Bay Ridge to save the lives of the watermen. The Federal Rivers and Harbors Act of 1945 authorized a study of the need for opening both Lake Ogleton and Black Walnut Creek.

Formal architect's drawings for the community center were reviewed in the spring of 1946. They proposed a 40-foot-square, two-story structure with porches and a dining room on the upper floor. Almost immediately, however, construction was postponed until building conditions were "more favorable," and the money raised by private subscription was returned. Residents were disappointed but continued to work on clearing and grading the community lots, hoping that at least the land could be used for tennis courts and picnic tables. A small shed for storage was built, and electrical service installed.

Finally the Bay Ridge teenagers accomplished what adults had only discussed and hoped for. During the summer of 1947 teens organized by Mr. and Mrs. Waldo Tastet drew up plans for a concrete-floored, screened-in pavilion, 26 by 40 feet, to be built on the south corner of the community lots "leaving room for the eventual Community House." Clarence Kettler, president of the Junior Association, presented the plans to the BRCA in July, and the association agreed to drill a well and put in sanitary facilities. Construction began at once, with residents supplying most of the materials and labor. The $4,000 cost was financed by a mortgage held by residents George Huguely, Waldo Tastet, and Earl Reeser. The mortgage was released in 1958.

As originally built, the Bay Ridge Clubhouse perched uneasily at the edge of a swamp and included only the main meeting room of the present building with screened-in sides above the block

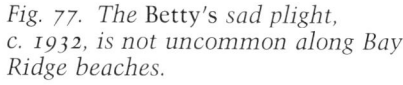

Fig. 77. The Betty's *sad plight, c. 1932, is not uncommon along Bay Ridge beaches.*

half-walls. A separate building housed bathrooms and other utilities. The clubhouse was dedicated at a Halloween party in October 1947 and was an immediate success with the entire community. Although ostensibly a summer meeting place for teenagers, it was used for BRCA meetings, Homemakers Club meetings, and Wednesday night socials.

Meanwhile enterprising youths had also solved the channel problem. Sands Avenue boys Glenn Alter, Earl Chambers, and Buddy Gates simply went out behind the Alter's house on Sands and dug a trench across the sandbar. Given the opportunity of easy flow, the water itself enlarged their efforts and, with some maintenance by other children and adults, small boats again had access to the lake. Had not local efforts carried the day, Bay Ridge might never have had a channel: the federal government's study resulted in an unfavorable report in 1948, was reauthorized in 1950, and dragged on until the early 1960s.

In the late 1940s many Bay Ridge youngsters were obsessed with small boats. During the summer of 1949, the Bay Ridge Boating Squadron, sponsored by parents, offered a course in seamanship to children aged eleven through fifteen. Taught by fathers and their friends, all members or instructors in the U.S. Power Squadron, the course encouraged safe handling of small craft and was well received. The children spent the winter months building and repairing boats and dreaming about summers on the water. But, unlike the light-weight fiberglass boats of today, their tiny wooden vessels were too heavy to keep on the beach. In the summer of 1950, these children asked the BRCA to build a pier in front of the clubhouse. The next year the association authorized $500 for the construction of the first community pier.

Improvements to both the clubhouse and pier began in 1952 and became continuing projects of the BRCA. Apparently giving up its plans for a more elaborate clubhouse, the community accepted the existing building and made major renovations in 1952. The interior was completed, and tile floors and windows were installed with funding from Homemakers Club benefit dinners, an oyster roast, stag parties, and private donations as well as BRCA contributions. A kerosene space heater allowed limited winter use, but since the bathrooms and kitchen facilities remained in other, uninsulated buildings, clubhouse activities ceased in freezing weather.

With improvements to the channel in the early 1960s, larger boats could be moored in the lake. The small community piers that had grown like Topsy over the years were renovated and a new 100-foot pier built. Slowly Bay Ridge was gaining the facilities it needed as an evolving year-around community.

As the permanent population increased, so did concern for clear directives on the use of the areas that are now called Bay Ridge Commons, that is, the land set aside by the first developers for the use of all property owners and residents. In 1951 the BRCA voted to retain counsel to ensure common access to, and use of, the common areas. A few years later a serious test case arose. The

Fig. 78. Designed to resemble the certificates of the adult U.S. Power Squadron, these diplomas were coveted rewards for a summer of diligent study.

owner of land at the end of West Lake Drive attempted to close off the end of that street, including Worden Path. His claim that the street end and turnaround were used only by parking lovers was probably correct, but the BRCA saw the move as a dangerous precedent for private control of platted public land and in 1954 took the case to court. The court's decision confirmed the right of Bay Ridge property owners to these common lands and directed the owner of Oak Point to remove his barriers.

Another incident in 1954 was not so directly solved. In the spring of that year John J. McKenna, a local resident and D.C. realtor, rented three houses to the Soviet Embassy for the summer. This action would not, in itself, have necessarily presented a problem. Soviet Embassy personnel had summered here in the 1930s at Col. Anderson's house on Bay Drive and in 1945 at the Bay Ridge Beach; the Colombian ambassador had spent at least one summer here with his family in the 1940s; and many other foreign visitors had been welcomed over the years as guests of Bay Ridge families. In this time of McCarthyism and the Cold War, however, the situation threatened to become an international incident. In May the Soviet Embassy notified Officer Hopkins of its rentals and the plan to lodge adults at 89 Bay Drive and 16 Bancroft Avenue and to use 11 Bancroft as a summer camp for children of embassy personnel. Viewing the latter as a violation of the single-family-per-house zoning regulation, the BRCA sent protest letters to Mr. McKenna and the Anne Arundel County Zoning Department. Shortly after the fourteen or so children and their four counselors arrived, one of their new neighbors began a letter-writing campaign to his representatives in Congress. The congressmen referred the matter to Secretary of State John Foster Dulles.

By the time the septic system at 11 Bancroft Avenue overflowed in early July, county, state, and federal agencies were involved and the incident was being reported on television and in the metropolitan newspapers. Headlines such as "Bay Ridge Appeals to Law

Fig. 79. 89 Bay Drive c. 1930

to Ward off Red 'Invasion' " in the *Baltimore Sun* on July 7 and "Red Smallfry Hold a Beachhead Here" in the *Washington Daily News* on July 14 did nothing to calm tension in the neighborhood. The Russians swam and sunbathed and played; the locals stared and kept their distance. Those who met the Russian ambassador, Giorgi N. Zaroubin, and his wife found them to be "as nice as they could be," says Mattie Gates. Her uncle, Albert Z. Wilson, allowed the Russians the use of his pier on the bayfront and was surprised and delighted with the gifts of caviar and other Russian delicacies that followed. But the community in general remained suspicious.

Fearing repercussions against U.S. Embassy personnel in Moscow, the State Department was reluctant to approach the Soviet Embassy on the matter and obviously hoped the whole business would blow over before congressional pressure forced some action. Meanwhile the county zoning officer verified the violation and asked the state's attorney to prosecute Mr. McKenna, the Russians being protected by diplomatic immunity. The end of summer and the Russians' return to Washington relieved the State Department's headache, but Mr. McKenna was called before the county court for deliberately disregarding the restrictions of his community.

In 1952 the BRCA requested that the county designate Bay Ridge as a "manor-type" development—that is, allowing only two houses per acre. Shortly thereafter Kass Realty filed a plat with the county for fifty-six half-acre lots in the area of Herndon Avenue and Black

Fig. 80. Mayo Avenue and Bay Drive from the air, 1952. Materials for the long jetty were stacked by the beach path.

Fig. 81. Stephen Josey, not quite tall enough, 1950

Walnut Creek and opened Walnut Drive off Herndon. For the third time in the postwar period, Bay Ridge residents thought they would see the end of their deeply wooded areas. First there had been the proposal for a large number of small houses on the north side of Farragut Road. Three were built between Perry and Upshur avenues before the idea died. Later the curious toured the new, all-metal Lustron house at 64 Farragut Road, a sample of the many slated to be built on undeveloped Hull and Herndon avenues. The deal for Lustron houses did not go through, nor did the lots along Walnut Drive sell, and the woods remained undisturbed. Eventually Walnut Drive was closed, at the association's request, to prevent parking there.

Community activities during the 1950s continued into the winter with dances, carol sings, and George Fulton's popular Las Vegas nights. The first newcomers' reception was held in October 1955. By 1957 there were almost three hundred homes in Bay Ridge, and in April of the following year a special meeting of the civic association was held to amend the by-laws in order to provide for year-around meetings. The U.S. Post Office Department stamped Bay Ridge's new status as a permanent community in 1962 when it changed its mail service from rural to city delivery. The small development that had begun forty years before as a remote summer colony was now a popular suburban residential community.

Boats moored at BRCA piers, 1986

4. The Suburban Community

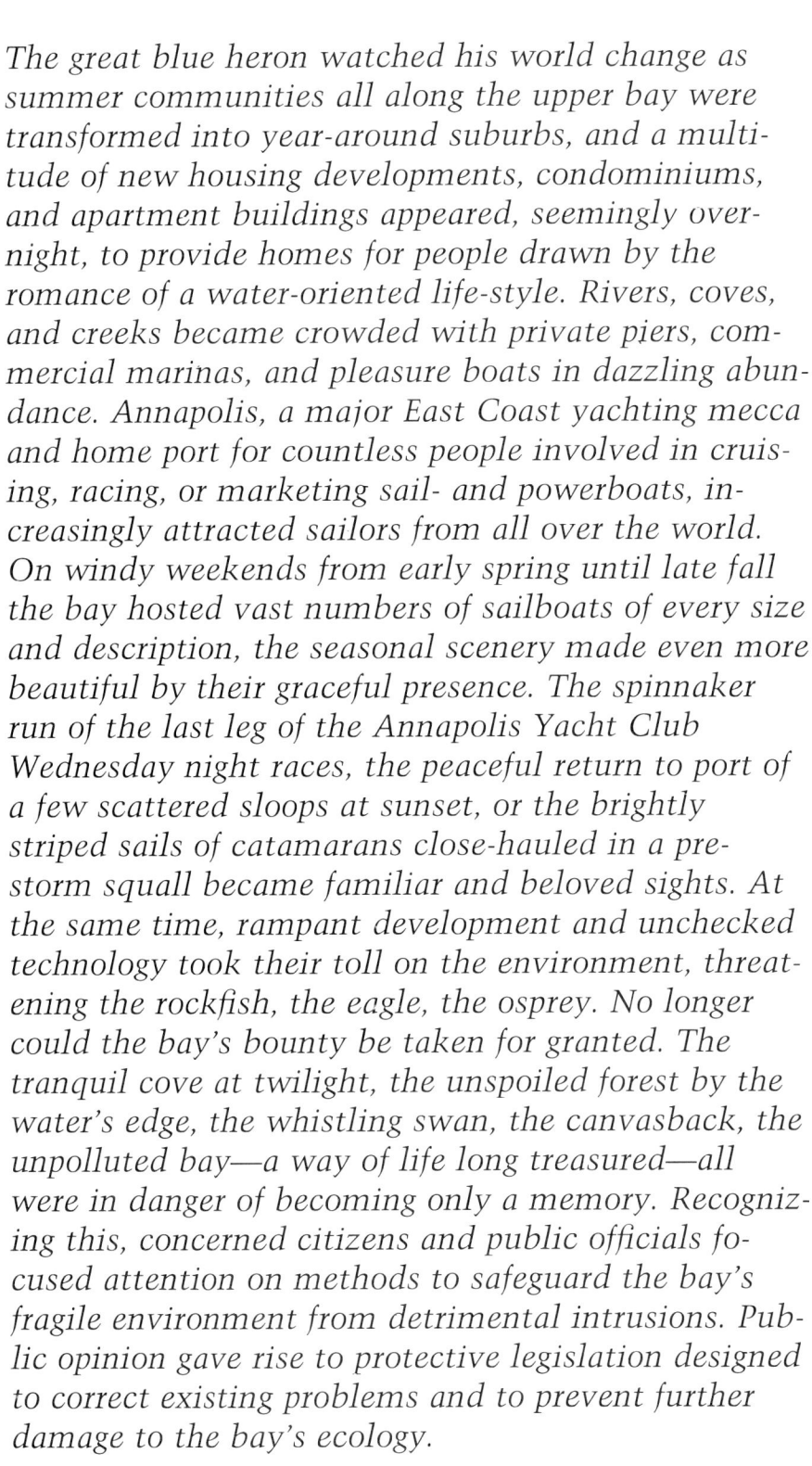

The great blue heron watched his world change as summer communities all along the upper bay were transformed into year-around suburbs, and a multitude of new housing developments, condominiums, and apartment buildings appeared, seemingly overnight, to provide homes for people drawn by the romance of a water-oriented life-style. Rivers, coves, and creeks became crowded with private piers, commercial marinas, and pleasure boats in dazzling abundance. Annapolis, a major East Coast yachting mecca and home port for countless people involved in cruising, racing, or marketing sail- and powerboats, increasingly attracted sailors from all over the world. On windy weekends from early spring until late fall the bay hosted vast numbers of sailboats of every size and description, the seasonal scenery made even more beautiful by their graceful presence. The spinnaker run of the last leg of the Annapolis Yacht Club Wednesday night races, the peaceful return to port of a few scattered sloops at sunset, or the brightly striped sails of catamarans close-hauled in a pre-storm squall became familiar and beloved sights. At the same time, rampant development and unchecked technology took their toll on the environment, threatening the rockfish, the eagle, the osprey. No longer could the bay's bounty be taken for granted. The tranquil cove at twilight, the unspoiled forest by the water's edge, the whistling swan, the canvasback, the unpolluted bay—a way of life long treasured—all were in danger of becoming only a memory. Recognizing this, concerned citizens and public officials focused attention on methods to safeguard the bay's fragile environment from detrimental intrusions. Public opinion gave rise to protective legislation designed to correct existing problems and to prevent further damage to the bay's ecology.

CHAPTER 4

The Suburban Community

CAROL CUSHARD PATTERSON

During the 1960s Bay Ridge shifted from summer colony to suburban community, and today only a handful of its 375 homes are maintained strictly for summer living. As new highways constructed for fast travel brought the Annapolis area within commuting distance of Baltimore and Washington, all of Anne Arundel County developed at an unparalleled rate. It is an interesting testimony to the pleasures of life in Bay Ridge that at this time so many Bay Ridge children and even grandchildren, all with happy memories of summers spent "at the beach," began to return as adults to restore, remodel, and winterize the old cottages as permanent homes for their own growing families. They have always known what newer residents are quick to learn; that Bay Ridge is special.

With deep roots for neighborly cooperation already laid down in an active civic association, and with a strong legacy of holiday *joie de vivre* carried over from a long history of summers past, Bay Ridge was soon well-established as a thriving permanent community with its own customs and traditions, many of which have been maintained to the present day.

Fig. 1. September, 1980

Because Bay Ridge is bordered by open water and is, therefore, especially vulnerable to the onslaught of storms, a definite spirit of "roughing it" is also present. Neighbors, thoroughly accustomed to electricity and telephone outages during seasonal tropical storms, gales, blizzards, and tail ends of hurricanes, simply seek out their emergency candles, help one another secure the boats, and then batten down "for the blow," knowing full well that in the aftermath they will meet again to survey the damage and clear beaches, roadways, and yards of storm debris. Also present is the generally held feeling of always "being on vacation," a feeling which many claim has never left them even after several decades of year-around Bay Ridge living.

For many reasons, then, people have chosen to live in Bay Ridge. Some value the water sports—the sailing, swimming, waterskiing, or an afternoon of fishing for "blues" off Tolly Point or trotlining for crabs in the lake. For some it is the quiet atmosphere, the lack of pretension, the relaxed sociability that comes from a lifetime or even a year of shared experiences with neighbors and friends. Or perhaps it is the feeling of closeness to nature, the simple beauty of a moonlit bay when the fresh scent of wild honeysuckle and rambling roses growing in profusion on the bayside cliffs are dispersed by salt breezes.

Whatever the reason, Bay Ridge, with its sandy beaches, sheltered harbor, deep woods, shaded roads, and incomparable views of the Chesapeake, leaves an unforgettable imprint on mind and heart. This is clearly reflected in the college application of a third generation resident who, when asked to discuss significant non-academic experiences shaping his life, described growing up in Bay Ridge as follows:

Fig. 2. Crab catch, Lake Ogleton, 1986

> Like Huckleberry Finn, my friends and I were free to explore and enjoy the bay, every nook and cranny we could reach by small boat, every mood, every season. We spent the long days of our childhood joyously living out invented adventures. We were Columbus and Balboa discovering new lands, Tarzans swinging high out across Lake Ogleton from thick vines, or narcotics agents spying from a tree fort for evidence of drug smuggling on the bay. We flew our kites and played lacrosse in gusty March winds high up on Tolly Point. And in summer, in addition to our chores, we built rafts and clubhouses, swam, sailed and waterskied. We spent winters after school ice skating on our lake and feeding waterfowl on the ice-bound Bay. There was not a hunter among us. We treated our feeding winter visitors with all the respect of foreign dignitaries, even rescuing and caring for those in distress. We lived close to nature in all her moods. Through the violent, icy storms of winter; the bright, windswept, white-capped days of spring; the sun-soaked, sultry days of summer; and the glorious ripe-apple autumn days; and from each magnificent sunrise to each breathtaking sunset, we were absolutely free to explore the limits of our imagination.

The all-important, time-proven guardian of this very quality of life is the Bay Ridge Civic Association, which, in a mingling of continued traditions and greatly expanded functions, provides special annual events and pleasurable social activities for residents of all ages; arranges for police protection and erosion control; encourages burglar protection through an ongoing Operation Identification program; serves, as the 1986 *Bay Ridge Directory* explains, as "a watchdog and liaison for county and state actions affecting Bay Ridge;" maintains surveillance for zoning violations and supports county zoning regulations; sponsors informational programs, youth activities, and cleanup projects; produces and distributes a monthly newsletter, pertinent informative flyers, and a community directory; maintains a community clubhouse, basketball court, grounds, adjoining piers and launching ramp for the use of its members; and provides a forum at regular meetings for discussion of concerns and the presentation of new ideas. Governed by its members through an elected volunteer board of directors, served by a host of actively involved committee chairmen, and well supported by a high resident membership, this association has, over the years, worked diligently in many ways for the community welfare.

But never before had outside forces so threatened Bay Ridge with adverse change as in the late 1960s and in the 1970s. Many of the challenges of those years were challenges facing the nation at large—modern-day problems of overpopulation and unplanned overdevelopment of rural areas, of increased crime, of mishandling and pollution of the environment, of discontented youth in the heyday of the "drug culture." The BRCA met these challenges head on under the leadership of its president, Charles Stanley Hollander (August 1967–August 1969, August 1970–May 1972, May 1973–May 1974, May 1985–May 1986), the proverbial right man in the right place at the right time. The measures taken then to safeguard Bay Ridge were largely accomplished in four action-packed years, and were achieved with the greatest possible participation and support of vitally concerned Bay Ridge residents.

The first alarm was sounded during a complete revising of county zoning restrictions in September 1971. Bay Ridge, then a community of only 298 homes with a total of 509 unimproved lots (largely undeveloped woodlands) was suddenly faced with the prospect of high-density housing. Residents were advised of this situation in the October 1971 issue of the *Bay Ridge Newsletter*.

Fig. 3. Delivering the Bay Ridge Newsletter *on River Drive, 1983*

> Probably, the most important single safeguard for any community is its zoning restrictions. . . . Within recent months the 2nd Election District, which includes Bay Ridge, has been embroiled in a complete revamping of zoning. . . . Bay Ridge has been designated R-5 . . . in which five single family dwellings per acre can be built. These homes can be detached, semi-detached or duplex.

At a County Planning and Zoning hearing on September 17, Bay Ridge residents had protested the R-5 designation. In response, the Planning and Zoning Department had recommended only that townhouses be deleted from Bay Ridge's R-5 category.

But that was not sufficient to preserve the characteristics of Bay Ridge. At a County Council hearing on October 20, BRCA president, Stan Hollander, had made this request:

> Bay Ridge is an old established community which contains 298 homes encompassing approximately 50% of all platted lots. . . . It is our contention that the residents who have lived in this community, shared in its building and contributed so much to the Annapolis area have a right to expect that their community retain its present characteristics. Those characteristics are, in our opinion, well described by our present manor-type zoning, i.e., a minimum of 15,000 sq. ft. and single family detached homes. However, there is no present zoning category that resembles manor-type. Therefore, we request that an R-3 category be added to the list of 24 existing zoning categories and that townhouses, duplexes and semi-detached dwellings be excluded.
>
> Please note that we are not requesting any change in the zoning that has been in effect since 1957 but are pleading that the characteristics of that zoning be retained.

The newsletter urged residents to speak out as individual property owners at an additional hearing scheduled for November.

> It will be important to have good representation at that meeting because one or more representatives of the developer will be speaking *for* R-5 and probably for reinstatement of townhouses.
>
> Attendance at the November 3rd zoning meeting is one way to help protect the interests of our community. Another way to help would be to write to our county councilman, Warren Duckett, and to the Council Chairman, Phillip Scheibe.

Resident turnout at the November meeting was overwhelmingly supportive. Good news was announced in the newsletter for February/March when the Planning and Zoning Department more than satisfied the Bay Ridge request by limiting development to two homes per acre.

> On 7 March the County Council approved our requested change of zoning from R-5 to R-2! This action culminates five months of meetings, discussions, waiting and "fingernail biting." . . . On behalf of the community, Stan, many thanks!
>
> Our thanks also go to Mrs. Marion McCoy, County Planning and Zoning Officer, and to Councilman Warren Duckett, both of whom were extremely helpful.

Taking a different tack, but not unexpectedly, the developer, Bay Ridge Properties, Inc., a subdivision corporation for the development of 350 Kass-owned lots in Bay Ridge—next appealed for a waiver of county subdivision regulations requiring the developer to submit detailed plans relating to road improvements, storm drains, lot size, and recreational area set-asides, among others. Again, in hearing after hearing, residents doggedly persisted in their support of the county regulations designed to protect community integrity. In December 1973 the *Bay Ridge Newsletter* reported:

> The hearings were well attended by Bay Ridgers, several of whom spoke strongly in support of the county's stand to maintain R-2 zoning regulations in Bay Ridge. Mrs. Thomas Outerbridge, Mrs. Eugene Cronin, Mr. Charles Garrish, and Mr. Harry Ritterbush were among those who spoke as private citizens, while Mrs. Walton Grubbs spoke on behalf of the Bay Ridge Garden Club.

Eventually the Bay Ridge Properties, Inc. (BRPI) appeal was denied by the county's Board of Appeals. The importance of this decision was detailed in the January 1974 newsletter:

> As a test case in which the new zoning regulations were upheld, this is a landmark decision for the people of this county as it directly affects their community welfare and their tax dollar. At issue was the 1969 subdivision regulations law by which the developer is responsible for installation of public improvements. Prior to this, a developer could sell off the lots and rely upon the county to make the necessary improvements. But under the new law, *before* the developer can sell any lots, he must show the county exactly what improvements he intends to make and sign an agreement promising to do them. . . . Marion McCoy, the county's planning and zoning officer, told the board that her office "had no clear idea of what [the developer] wanted to do except develop without doing anything." The Board of Appeals warned that a blanket waiver of regulations "would create a large precedent and affect thousands of lots in the county." . . . In the meantime, until plans are submitted and approved, building permits for property sold by BRPI will continue to be withheld.

As an added protective measure, the BRCA Zoning Committee began its own surveillance of property sales and building permits. There was concern in June 1975 that with the coming of sewerage there would be more and more pressure to change the characteristics of the area by developers, builders, and speculators. In an effort to keep residents knowledgeable and to keep rumors to the minimum, the newsletter began a monthly listing of building permits and sales in property. Today Bay Ridge continues to support strict enforcement of its zoning laws and regulations on the premise, stated in the *Bay Ridge Newsletter* for Summer 1977, that:

> A community with few or no violations is in the best defensive position when hard-won protective zoning laws are threatened. . . .
> A future change to an undesirable zoning designation can occur whenever community apathy towards zoning violations exists and whenever requests for precedent-establishing zoning exceptions are permitted to go unchallenged.

Fig. 4. A view of Lake Ogleton from the air showing the mouth of the Severn River (top) and Chesapeake Bay (right), 1982

Concurrent with the struggle to safeguard the undeveloped community platted lots, Bay Ridgers also became seriously concerned about the fate of their beaches, the open spaces between Bay Drive, River Drive, and the water. This concern prompted resident Marcia Outerbridge to ask, at the zoning hearing on September 15, 1971, if that portion of Bay Ridge land might qualify for the new zoning classification called "open-space districts," which, if granted, would assure the perpetuation of that land in its present "parklike setting." Mrs. Outerbridge, acting on a twenty-four hour notice on behalf of the BRCA, then composed the required petition and with the help of Caroline Josey, collected the necessary deeds and signatures. As a result, the open-space designation was granted and still remains effective, having successfully survived an attack upon the open-space category itself, in January 1974, by developers and speculators with financial interests in county open-space lands.

In yet another bold but successful action, the BRCA, with Stan Hollander as president, retained a lawyer, William Kirk, in June 1971 to initiate a declaratory judgment suit [Bay Ridge vs. Kass Realty Company, Inc.] to clarify the extent of property owners' beach use rights. This was the final step in the legal determination of residents' present rights to land now known as the Bay Ridge Commons. A previous judgment in 1954, the Worden Path case, secured the community's rights to platted paths. In the 1970s, rights to the property on the water sides of River and Bay drives were in need of clarification. Although Kass Realty had been paying taxes on the land and claimed ownership of it, Bay Ridge residents contended that the developer had clearly specified in early plats and deeds that this land be reserved for the exclusive use of Bay Ridge property owners and residents.

After more than three years of preparation and waiting, the suit was argued in the Circuit Court for Anne Arundel County on April 9–10, 1974, with Judge Ridgely P. Melvin presiding. The suit would determine once and for all the residents' exclusive rights to the platted community land, including the right to improve and protect the beaches. The majority of the time during the two-day session was devoted to three specific instances in which individual residents claimed ownership of beach property due to adverse possession. The favorable results of this suit were announced in the June 1975 *Bay Ridge Newsletter*.

> The declaratory decree of the Circuit Court for Anne Arundel County was issued on May 29, 1975. The ruling is as follows:
> 1. Lot owners, their guests and tenants have the *exclusive* right to use the waterfront area shown on the plats of Bay Ridge between Bay Drive and River Drive and Chesapeake Bay for bathing, boating, fishing, sunbathing and other water related activities customarily engaged in by those who "go to the beach." This includes the right to use *any* walkways, steps, or stairs located thereon for access to the water. This exclusive right of use by Bay Ridgers collectively extends to all waterfront areas except that:
> (a) Ralph E. Campbell and Helen Campbell, their guests and tenants have the present right to maintain and use the pier and pavilion located opposite their property [73 Bay Drive] to the exclusion of other lot owners. The "Pavilion" is at the bottom of the stairs. The covered gateway, stairs, and upper terrace can be used by all residents.
> (b) Mrs. Florence Greenfield has the right at the present time to maintain and use the 8 x 10 foot cabana on the beach near Herndon and Bay to the exclusion of other lot owners.
> (c) Thomas Shull, at the present time has the right to maintain and use the pier located opposite lots Nos. 3 and 4, Block 19 to the exclusion of other lot owners. The fenced in upper terrace and the stairs can be used by all residents.
> 2. Judge Melvin states, in regard to residents' rights to repair or restore the beach, "It seems well settled that in general the holder of an easement has the right to repair or restore the subject of that easement." In this case Bay Ridge property owners hold the easement.

The newsletter emphasized the importance of this ruling for all Bay Ridge residents.

> In summary, it is now known that Bay Ridge property owners do have the exclusive rights to the beaches. The beaches, for all practical purposes, belong to us collectively.
> One very important lesson learned from the suit is that adverse possession is a problem that cannot be ignored. It is now clearly

understood that land regularly ventured upon by community residents cannot readily be claimed for individual ownership due to adverse possession. It has been proposed by Stan Hollander that a specific day of the year be designated "Land Use Day," a day on which one or more groups appointed by the Association walk over each piece of property to which all residents have rights based on the ruling of the court. This, together with a recorded open letter of intent to all residents, should minimize future serious claims to adverse possession.

Fig. 5. Gathering at Tolly Point on Land Use Day, 1974

Land Use Day has, since then, developed into a pleasant community event with residents meeting annually on the designated November morning at Tolly Point for coffee and donuts before walking the Bay Ridge Commons, which include, in addition to the beaches, the special walking paths (Bagley, Porter, Clark, and Worden) and the ends of Mayo, Bainbridge, Sands, and Parker avenues. These areas are maintained, mowed, and protected by Bay Ridge residents, as is Kass Park, the ball field off West Lake Drive, use of which has been made available through the generosity of the family of Garfield I. Kass, the owners.

In response to problems engendered by rapid development of land on the peninsula, the Annapolis Neck Peninsula Federation (ANPF) was organized in 1971, with Stan Hollander as one of the founding officers representing the BRCA. As described in the July 1971 *Bay Ridge Newsletter*, the ANPF originated as a federation of communities "banded together by a mutual interest in an orderly development of the 'Forest Drive Corridor' and in the general well-being of its citizens ... [in the hopes that] by thus uniting, we will have sufficient numerical strength, both in city and county, to effectively obtain governmental attention whenever problems affecting our communities are to be solved." By January 1975 it was possible to state in the newsletter:

> The positive results of citizen support have been demonstrated time and again during the past several years, particularly when it has

been in response to ANPF drives to stop the numerous attempts to increase zoning density in this area. ANPF will continue to need your support whenever the interests of speculators and developers, heedless of the detrimental effects of overbuilding in the peninsula area, are at variance with the good of the community. Detrimental effects of overbuilding include a continued population explosion, increased traffic problems, sewerage overload, crowded educational facilities, environmental pollution and ecological damage.

For similar reasons the BRCA is actively affiliated with the Severn River Association, a coalition of civic and public interest groups focusing on like concerns along the Severn River; and the Black Walnut Creek Commission, an association of the communities located around the creek at the south end of Bay Ridge, devoted to the preservation of the creek in good health, with a special interest in sediment control and storm water management at construction sites.

Equally interested in preserving the natural beauty of Black Walnut Creek is Ben Wills, Bay Ridge resident and owner-operator of the Bay Ridge Inn and Beach, now in his family for nearly half a century. The last large—thirty-three acres—privately owned public beach resort in Anne Arundel County, the Beach is operated in somewhat the same tradition as its turn-of-the-century predecessor on Tolly Point. Bay Ridge Beach, with its wide expanse of sand, its wooden palm-thatched cabanas, its pool and poolside Sadie Thompson Pago Pago Bar, and its acres of tall-wooded picnic groves along Black Walnut Creek, still attracts large beach crowds from Memorial Day to Labor Day. In 1969, with taxes on com-

Fig. 6. Black Walnut Creek facing south from Bay Ridge, 1985

Fig. 7. Whistling swans glide past riverside jetty, 1985

mercial waterfront property sky high, this establishment handily survived by initiating a year-around program of catering for banquets, meetings, parties, and balls, all held in the inn's luxurious dining and dancing facilities. Mr. Wills, as a Bay Ridge resident and as a businessman with commercial property located in a setting of extreme natural beauty, shares the community concern about any possibly detrimental development of area land, particularly on Black Walnut Creek.

A wetlands victory was won on August 14, 1985, when the Maryland Board of Public Works, in full accord with the Black Walnut Creek Commission, led by Bill Hatchl, denied a Wetlands Application (No. 85–014) for new development in this sensitive area because the plans did not then include provisions for storm water management needed to protect the pristine ecological condition of this small but lovely tributary of the bay.

In light of united concern with the effects of overdevelopment on the peninsula, Bay Ridge and other ANPF communities have consistently opposed the annexation of additional land by the city of Annapolis. In March 1974, for example, Bay Ridgers led by official spokesperson, Mrs. Outerbridge, attended a State Judicial Proceedings Committee hearing to support a bill designed to ensure that all residents of an area, affected directly or indirectly by a proposed city annexation, have the privilege of voting for or against annexation. The newsletter of that month stressed the importance of this privilege.

> The importance of safeguarding this privilege should not be underestimated, particularly if at some future date the city might be in the position (by annexation) to create a high density zoning area in

> the immediate vicinity of Bay Ridge. . . . The results of such an annexation could also place Bay Ridge in an enclave, cut off from present or future county facilities and services.

This bill was subsequently signed into law in late spring 1974, but was declared null and void by the Circuit Court for Anne Arundel County on November 20, 1981. It has not been reintroduced, and the annexation threat continues to cause concern, as excerpts from a letter from Tom White, BRCA president, dated November 14, 1983, illustrate.

> The Bay Ridge Civic Association feels strongly that a limit has been reached on the amount of land on the Annapolis Neck that should be annexed. . . . As we already have sewer lines in place that we are currently paying for, and have no desire for public water in our community, we are happy with the services that the county provides us, and feel it can provide services more efficiently and cost effectively than the city. We have a county library and county park to serve us, and the county has purchased land for a fire station in the Neck area. There is no way the city could purchase these resources from the county government without taxing us all over again to pay for this purchase.
>
> Under the county we have control over our future. The set-up of county government actually gives us more independence than we would have under the city. We tax ourselves under a special taxing district to provide erosion protection and control, as do a number of waterfront communities on the Neck, and also to provide additional police protection. There is no provision for a Special Taxing District in the city. . . . The city of Annapolis has shown itself more eager to put in hotels and higher density housing, and we prefer to keep this area residential as much as possible.

The BRCA also preferred to keep the area crime free. The quality of life in Bay Ridge in the 1960s had been as near to idyllic as is possible in any small community; but with the unprecedented population increase in the surrounding area coupled with the widespread drug and alcohol abuse of the 1970s, it was inevitable that crime-related problems would develop. Bay Ridge, too, received its share of trouble. Residents for the first time felt a need to lock doors and to worry about prowlers at night. The scenic drives along the bay, river, and lake encompassing the community became after-dark raceways on weekends, as tire-squealing, often inebriated speeders even careened, at times, across lawns and beaches, leaving behind a trail of deep ruts, tilting mailboxes, flattened bushes, and beer cans. Removal of roadside and beach litter became a Sunday morning chore, both time consuming and necessary, as the broken glass from bottles flung out car windows was particularly hazardous to barefoot children on the beaches. Boats, boathouses, the community piers, and at least ten homes were robbed and/or vandalized. Bicycles were stolen all too often, stripped, and the parts sold; while gasoline was siphoned from cars, once resulting in a fire.

Isolated incidents stand out. In broad daylight, from his car on River Drive, a drunk man shot and killed a whistling swan floating in a flock offshore, never noticing the children at play on the same beach. One Sunday morning a young boy found his small but prized rowboat garishly painted with obscene words, brutally axed, and sinking beneath the water. A family returned home at 9:00 P.M. to find that not only had they been robbed of all their jewelry and valuables, but that a large number of matches had been lighted and dropped on rugs throughout the house.

Clearly, it was time for BRCA leaders to mobilize defensive efforts in yet another direction. Excerpts from the newsletter, special fliers and BRCA minutes tell the story.

> June 1971 newsletter: During the coming weeks a petition will be circulated ... which will lead to a change in a county provision that restricts our community to one special police officer ... to permit us to hire a qualified officer on summer weekends during hours when Mr. Johnson is not patrolling.
>
> April 1973 flier: Bay Ridge is now in the midst of a small community crime wave. What was once a community virtually free of vandalism and crime has become a high crime area. In the past two months ten homes have been burglarized. ... If you notice a strange automobile parked in your area, jot down the tag number. In the event an incident occurs that particular day/night just call Mr. Johnson and give him the number.
>
> May 1973 newsletter: Detective Jay B. Craig of the Annapolis Police force will be assisting Officer Johnson in the control of traffic and maintenance of order.
>
> January 1974 newsletter: Bay Ridge has hired a second special policeman to patrol on a part-time basis ... during night hours.

At the January 1974 BRCA meeting the citizens voted to hire an additional police officer. Next, they launched Operation Identification, a citizen-police program offering each resident an opportunity to protect valuables with an engraving pencil supplied free of cost. Door stickers warned potential intruders: "We have joined Operation Identification. All items of value on these premises have been marked for ready identification by law enforcement agencies." In the winter 1976 issue of the newsletter, Wayne Tarun, Operation Identification chairman, urged all residents who had not yet joined this program to do so, reminding them that it "is a nationally recognized campaign to curb burglary, theft and vandalism. . . . A high percentage of community participation gives Bay Ridge the right to post the Operation Identification warning sign at the community entrance."

In June 1975 Bay Ridge initiated another program of community action. Led by president, Beverly Jack, and board members Dan McNew and Frank Ervin, the BRCA worked with county police chief Ashley Vick to arrange for a county policeman to patrol in Bay Ridge for his full tour of forty hours per week in addition to the regular protection given by the county. The officer's salary, patrol car, uniforms, and equipment were to be paid for by Bay Ridge property owners, who, at a special meeting held May 19, voted to approve the assessment of an additional 29 cents on their tax rate to raise the $21,000 necessary. The county council approved the special community benefit district tax increase for Bay Ridge on June 16.

In December 1976 the BRCA was awarded the Anne Arundel County Certificate of Appreciation for "generous and public-spirited contribution to the Anne Arundel Crime Prevention Program and for displaying the leadership that will help to make our county a safer place in which to live." The certificate was signed by Ashley Vick, chief of police, George Bachman, chairman of the County Council, and Robert Pascal, county executive.

With increased police protection and community awareness, acts of crime were eventually brought under control. Acts of nature, however, are another matter altogether. The April 1974 low tide is a fascinating case in point. As recounted here from the summer issue of the 1974 newsletter:

> Strong and persistent northwest winds pushed weekend (April 4–6) tides on the western shore of the bay to their lowest levels since 1908. The winds that began Thursday, April 3rd and reached sustained speeds as high as sixty miles an hour, stemmed normal incoming tides and pushed the water towards the Eastern Shore and into the Atlantic Ocean.
>
> Boats were left absolutely high and dry at all Bay Ridge piers. Residents turned out in droves to stroll, dig clams, remove litter, or hunt for artifacts on the Bay floor, exposed far beyond the longest piers on the Bay side and the jetties on the River side. Our thanks go especially to the many residents who took advantage of the low tide to clear swimming and pier areas of harmful debris.
>
> Needless to say, local history buffs had a field day. Pictures were taken of the exposed stub ends of the old steamship landing where guests arrived by water to stay at the Bay Ridge grand hotel on

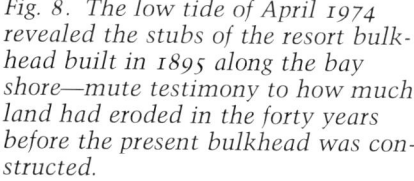

Fig. 8. The low tide of April 1974 revealed the stubs of the resort bulkhead built in 1895 along the bay shore—mute testimony to how much land had eroded in the forty years before the present bulkhead was constructed.

Tolly Point. Many thick blue-glass pop and beer bottles dating back to the late 1880s were found in the area near the hotel pier, thereby proving the ancient lineage of the "litter-bug." Large pieces of thick hotel china with "Bay Ridge" clearly inscribed were also found.

As winds gradually subsided on Sunday, tides slowly returned to normal, thus closing a curtain, briefly opened, on days past.

Unfortunately not all acts of nature are so benign. The winter blizzards of 1965 and 1979, buried the community in exceptionally deep snow drifts, crippled telephone and electrical service, and left residents snowed in for several days. Subzero weather in January 1977 sustained frozen conditions on the bay and lake for most of the month, with resulting widespread ice damage to jetties and piers. The February 7, 1977, BRCA Board of Directors minutes reported that at BRCA piers "forty mooring pilings have been torn out due to the ice and probably more will go."

Most damaging however, have been recent major tropical storms. Tropical Storm David undermined the Bay Drive cliff bulkhead in 1979 and Tropical Storm Agnes, seven years earlier, brought extremely high tides and problems with storm debris, an account of which was recorded in the July 1972 issue of the *Bay Ridge Newsletter*:

> *Tropical Storm Agnes* came to Bay Ridge the night of June 21st, bringing in her wake unusually high tides which covered the community pier by 11:00 P.M. At 7:30 the next morning, persons checking their mooring lines at the pier reported strong winds with gusts in which it was difficult to stand. A few trees blew down. And that was about it, for us—until the aftermath, when we learned that the Bay was temporarily polluted, prohibiting swimming, and too debris-strewn for safe boating. And, whereas Bay Ridge was relatively untouched by the storm itself, proof of disaster elsewhere, finally came floating down the Bay en masse to our shores!
>
> A drowned doe was discovered among the litter of logs and junk on Bay Drive beach. On River Drive beach the litter included a dead chicken, a badger, the headboard of a bed, and broken kitchen cabinets. Unbelievable amounts of logs and fallen trees of all shapes and sizes constituted the bulk of the debris. Many residents recognized a good opportunity to store up firewood for an entire winter. In fact, those living near the waterfront are to be commended for promptly tackling the monumental job of cleaning the mess from the beaches. Even so, parents should still be on the alert for the broken bottles, spray cans of possibly poisonous substances, and jagged metal containers, etc. that remain—some half buried under sand, potentially hazardous under the feet and in the hands of small children.

Storms such as these have had a cumulative effect on the Bay Ridge shoreline. Through the years erosion control measures established after the hurricane of 1933 served to curb, but not to stop, the gradual eroding away of beaches during severe storms when pounding waves took their annual toll. By the early 1970s shoreline erosion in Bay Ridge had reached the critical point. The Bay Drive cliff bulkhead, severely damaged by Tropical Storm David in 1979, was in disrepair and no longer capable of retaining the eroding land, especially in an area between Lawrence and

Fig. 9. Pounding waves of Tropical Storm Juan, October 1985, raced across riverside beaches, submerging jetties and beach furniture, while unusually high tides brought waters close to the road.

Fig. 10. Beach boats and storm debris lay scattered on beaches in the aftermath of Juan, 1985

Bancroft avenues. The beaches along River Drive, barely held in place by damaged and broken wooden jetties, had all but disappeared in many sections. During the storms of late autumn and winter, portions of the road were regularly flooded as waves breaking and crashing across them created a temporary shoreline in front yards. The road itself, in front of 56 River Drive, was undermined and weakened as water action removed supporting soil beneath the blacktop.

Happily for now, these problems within the Bay Ridge Shore Erosion Control District have been successfully remedied, largely due to the efforts of Emerson E. Deale, BRCA Erosion Committee chairman, who, working through the Maryland Department of Natural Resources, initiated action, obtained all necessary permits, and arranged for the two major erosion control projects of 1973 and 1980–81, and to the efforts of his successor, Henry T. Meneely, Jr., who similarly expedited the second phase of the Bay Drive project in 1985.

The first project rendered the jetties more efficient and made possible the later rebuilding of the River Drive beaches. At this time every other jetty was repaired, rebolted, and supported with large deposits of stone riprap. Thus fortified, these jetties were able to provide sturdy support for sand retention when, in the summer of 1983, the final step was taken—a momentous project accomplished by the Dredging Section of the Department of Natural Resources, involving the replenishment of the badly eroded River Drive beaches with sand pumped from the Lake Ogleton entrance channel, where too much sand had become a problem.

Fig. 11. Erosion of Mayo Avenue beach bank exposed a drainage pipe c. 1976

Fig. 12. Rock jetties help hold the shoreline near the riverside nettlenets, and seagulls congregate, one to a post, 1985.

As a result, owners of deep-water keel boats moored in the lake no longer have to wait for high tide to enter the bay, and, simultaneously, the River Drive beaches are at last restored to much of their former usefulness. The widened beaches have once again come into their own, playing host to crowds of happy children and sunbathing adults, to beach parties marked by bright umbrellas and volleyball nets, and to sailors whose beach boats—catamarans, catboats, and sailboards with gaily striped and patterned sails—brighten the summer scene with colorful activity.

The first phase of the second project, completed in November 1981, also with erosion fund monies, resulted in the repair of approximately 110 feet of storm-damaged timber bulkhead along the Bay Drive shoreline in an area between Bancroft and Lawrence avenues and included the terracing of the cliff to curtail land erosion in the same place. The second phase in 1985 has resulted in the restoration of the remaining storm and erosion-damaged bulkhead along Bay Drive from Tolly Point to Mayo Avenue and its reinforcement with stone riprap.

Erosion projects outside the Bay Ridge Shore Erosion Control District continue to be undertaken on an ad hoc basis, with guidance from the BRCA Environmental Committee.

As neighbors worked together to solve community-wide problems, they increasingly came together, too, for community-wide entertainment and recreation. The Bay Ridge Clubhouse was often a focus of such activities. A new addition to the clubhouse was

Fig. 13. Bay Ridge Civic Association clubhouse and piers seen from the basketball court, 1985

completed in September 1968 to satisfy the needs of winter use. James M. Jones, resident and builder, enlarged and winterized this building complete with kitchen, bathrooms, hot and cold running water, and electricity. Storm windows were installed the following December. Storms and weather had their way, and the clubhouse underwent a "facelifting" in 1973, and renovation in 1977, accomplished by clubhouse chairman and builder, Frank D. Ervin. The kitchen was given a new roof and the old outhouse was refurbished; roofs on both buildings were reshingled. New interior paneling, lights, a heating system, and storm doors at the lake entrance were installed.

Today, the clubhouse is a comfortable center for social events, meetings, club programs, members' rental group functions, and special classes or courses such as yoga, slimnastics, aerobics, and CPR. It has also been used for a police project for fingerprinting children and for lectures on such timely topics as pollution, drug awareness, the energy crisis, and the Chesapeake Bay environment—the latter by resident Dr. L. Eugene Cronin.

A basketball court was completed in December 1969, funded by residents' donations. By 1981 the grounds had been graded and seeded; trees had been planted; sidewalks and bulkhead had been completed; and an outdoor underground wiring system for lights, plus overhead lights for the basketball court, had been installed. In addition the oyster shell base of the boat launching ramp was replaced with reinforced concrete. A new pier was constructed in 1974, and, after ice had damaged the two existing piers in 1977, they were redesigned and reconstructed in a project that involved dredging the lake near the piers to create additional deep-water slips.

Today the piers are equipped with water, light, and electrical facilities. The BRCA pier complex is the only authorized marina in Bay Ridge and is restricted to the rental use of BRCA members. This regulation, designed to prevent any commercialization of Lake Ogleton, was upheld in court on May 12, 1980: Circuit Court Judge Raymond G. Thieme ruled, as the *Bay Ridge Newsletter* for June 1980 reported, "that only boats belonging to residents of a residental property or their guests may be docked at private piers."

The Garden Club, founded in 1967 with twenty-nine charter members, increased to an approximate membership of ninety in the late 1970s. These ladies have provided Bay Ridge with landscaping, plantings, and erosion-reduction projects that have beautified the community—the clubhouse grounds, Bay Ridge entrance areas, and roadways—and have helped preserve the Bay Drive cliffs. They have held May basket and plant sales in spring, bulb sales in fall, and have sponsored community tree spraying programs. They are responsible for the beautiful floral basket displays that seasonally grace the brick entrance walls and for elegant tablesettings and centerpieces at community and Garden Club welcoming teas, luncheons, and social functions held at the clubhouse. They offer special programs with guest speakers at

Fig. 14. BRCA piers and clubhouse (right) seen from Lake Ogleton, 1985

monthly meetings, arrange field trips to famous gardens, sponsor contests for Christmas decorations and May baskets and have produced major Bay Ridge holiday functions, notably, the Christmas House Tours. In Annapolis, they help decorate Hammond-Harwood House and make wreaths for State Circle at Christmas time.

During the 1960s and 1970s a host of social and recreational activities abounded for all. Because of the efforts of the BRCA, the Garden Club, and individual residents, the community could boast a swim program featuring a swim team (1957–74), swim lessons, and life-saving courses held at the Bay Ridge pool and, afterwards, swim lessons at the nettle nets; youth baseball teams in Farm League, Little League, and Pony League competition, with home

Fig. 15. Little Leaguers found a novel way to thank BRCA for sponsorship—Fourth of July parade, 1976

field at Kass Park; a Recreational League basketball team, Girl Scouts, Brownie Scouts, Cub Scouts, and a drama troupe known as the Bay Ridge Junior Players (1965–75) that rehearsed and performed in a tree-shaded clearing on the clubhouse grounds known as the Sylvan Theater. A Teen Club held its regular dances in the clubhouse and took beginner bridge and chess lessons at the home of the BRCA president. In the mid-1970s a Teen Outing Club was formed, and Sunday father/son and Wednesday night mother/daughter softball games became popular. Poker nights and regularly scheduled bingo gatherings with donated desserts, popcorn, and soft drinks were well attended. Formal and semiformal BRCA dinner dances were held at the Bay Ridge Inn, while family covered-dish suppers, oyster roasts, crab feasts, teas, and welcoming receptions were held at the clubhouse. Daytime and evening bimonthly bridge clubs met in private homes, as did a mothers' twice-weekly cooperative playgroup for two- and three-year-olds. The youth activities, in particular, involved an army of volunteer parents in addition to standing committee chairmen and included

Fig. 16. BRCA flyer, 1985

Fig. 17. A 1979 Fourth of July parade float—a popular sentiment

scout leaders, den mothers, badge and cookie campaign mothers, chaperones, coaches, assistant coaches, carpool parents, swim team timers, record keepers and ribbon writers, costume makers, and sailing and waterskiing instructors.

Organized youth sports were gradually discontinued in Bay Ridge in the late 1970s as the Peninsula Athletic League (PAL), with support and active participation of BRCA leaders, took over this function. By the 1980s some of the other activities enjoyed previously were decreased in scope and new activities were introduced to accommodate changing interests and the decline of weekday volunteerism with the advent of the two income family. Nevertheless, certain special events held annually over the years, and handed down virtually intact, still receive full support and have now become cherished traditions. These include the major community fund raiser, the Jamboree, the Fourth of July Parade and Beach Events, the Christmas Dinner Dance, the Twelfth Night Potluck Supper, the Garden Club Christmas Tea, the October Wine and Cheese Party for newcomers, the Spring Community Cleanup, Spring Dinner Dance, and Land Use Day.

A Bay Ridge Journal
In Four Seasons

Looking back through newsletters of the past twenty-five years, it seems that Bay Ridge life could be measured in seasons, each marked by special events involving residents of all ages. These first decades of Bay Ridge as a suburban community, compressed into a seasonal composite of memories, might read as follows:

Winter

Boats are hauled in time for early season storms and thoughts turn to the holidays. Reservations are taken for the annual BRCA Christmas Dinner Dance at the Bay Ridge Inn. The Garden Club, in its busiest season, welcomes newcomers to an elegant Christmas Tea. Branches and boughs of boxwood, pine, spruce, and holly are brought to the clubhouse along with pruning shears, wreath frames, and bright ribbon for the Christmas Greens Workshop. The date is set for a Christmas Decorations Contest and, after many weeks of preparation, the specially decorated homes of the Garden Club's Christmas House Tour (1969–73) are finally ready for viewing. Each home is decorated according to a specific theme evocative of the Christmas spirit, each transformed by the magic scent of bayberry and pine, the glow of an oak fire, the ingenious use of natural materials, by candles, bright polished silver, and red ribbon, into a Victorian Christmas, a Colonial Christmas, a Contemporary Christmas—all as a Garden Club present to residents young and old who by day or starry cold night tour the festive sites in merry groups. An on-going Christmas buffet featuring homemade Christmas delicacies and holiday cheer is served at one of the houses.

Bay Ridge teenagers convert the clubhouse into a fairy-tale Gingerbread House for a children's Christmas party and provide a horse-drawn surrey, complete with jinglebells, to take the children in turns for a day of old-fashioned hayrides and carol singing through the streets of the community (1976). Santa and his elves

Fig. 18. *An ice-covered riverside jetty held its own against the winter elements, 1977. The curve in its spine reveals the effort.*

Fig. 19. Winter snowfall at 126 River Drive, 1979

visit the community by car delivering candy and listening to Christmas wishes. Girl Scouts provide Christmas presents for the elderly at nursing homes, and Cub Scouts celebrate with a progressive dinner and carol sing. The Christmas season, with holiday parties and New Year's Eve celebrations, concludes with the traditional Twelfth Night Potluck Supper at the clubhouse.

Ducks and whistling swans now grace the waterfront in profusion. Hunters' guns heard afar bring to mind an oft-remembered winter's tale of Vincent Engels and the swan.

> November 1971: In the fall of 1969, a whistling swan, wounded in the neck by a hunter's bullet, flew in from the Eastern Shore to our River Drive beach. The injury to his long drooping neck was such that it was virtually an impossibility for the bird to lower his head and raise it again to obtain underwater food; and then, only with great difficulty could he swallow. Mr. Vincent Engels of River Drive daily fed the swan by hand from the jetty all through the long winter months. By Spring migration time, with a very visible kink, the neck had healed and the swan began his long journey north with the others. Interested residents wondered if "Old Crooked Neck" (as he had been dubbed) would manage to survive on his own. The answer came when he returned in the fall to winter again in front of Mr. Engels' home. Yesterday, he flew in for the third winter. Mr. Engels met him at the jetty with a bag of cracked corn.

Heavy snow begins to fall in late afternoon and older boys, now sated with years of sledding down Bagley Path, band together in prearranged work crews and rise at dawn to meet—snow shovels in hand—ready to tackle the standing jobs and to canvass the community to corner the remaining snow removal market in keen competition with rival groups of friends. By noon most residents are on the road. The cold snap settles in and ice soon follows snow.

> November 1973: During the recent freeze, delighted residents flocked to the lake to ice skate both day and night. Container fires warmed hands on shore and pier lights were turned on to illuminate the lake! Currier and Ives could not have painted a cheerier scene.

> Winter 1977: Winter 1977 can rival any in history for sub-zero weather and frozen conditions on the bay. Lake Ogleton, solidly frozen day after day, has been a skater's heaven, with children from Bay Ridge, Anchorage, and Annapolis Roads meeting on the ice after school and on weekends for skating, ice hockey and evening parties. And at one point in the freeze, with the Bay frozen as far as the eye could see, several adventurous Bay Ridgers experienced what may well prove to be a "once in a lifetime" ice skating journey from Lake Ogleton to Spa Creek in Annapolis.

The February thaw finds canvasbacks wending towards shore, in long curving lines between ice flows, for handouts of corn. The impatient ones fly in for "no brakes" crash landings on the ice, come to prolonged skidding stops and, with only momentary loss of dignity, arrive first at the corn.

Fig. 20. Skaters of all ages found conventional and unconventional ways to enjoy the ice on Lake Ogleton, 1973.

Spring

Fig. 21. Rounding Tolly Point—cyclists and joggers by land and sailors by water. The Chesapeake Bay Bridge is seen in the distance, 1985.

Robins and laughing gulls return along with kites, lacrosse sticks, and children in shorts. Gentle breezes mingle with the scents of varnish and creosote from boats and piers. Ospreys build their big stick nests atop tall lake channel markers. Spring peepers warble in the swampy woodlands, in low places near the old railroad bed. May baskets with fluttering pastel ribbons soften entrance doors. Forsythia is everywhere, and dogwood and daffodils line Farragut Road. Crowds gather at the flagpole for the annual Garden Club Plant Sale, where pots of red and pink geraniums vie with bright marigolds, petunias, and impatiens, with vegetable seedlings and perennials dug from mature Bay Ridge gardens; here too, cookies, cupcakes, and Helen Mack's lemon bars attract a young clientele.

The annual Spring Cleanup of roadside and beach litter brings young and old trashbag-toting neighbors outdoors to prove that work can be play. The Thursday evening bridge club prepares a surprise baby shower. Pier slips are rented, and the county mosquito truck begins its Wednesday rounds. Girl Scouts hold a tea for their mothers, and Brownies receive their Fly-up wings as they cross the bridge from Brownies to Girl Scouts (1969). The cliffs are

185

planted with daylilies and wild roses by the Garden Club, Girl Scouts, and Cub Scouts to hold the land, and, walking through the woods near the clubhouse, one might come across many hidden bouquets planted by the Girl Scouts and the Brownies under the direction of Mrs. James Stephens (1970). Ice-damaged nettle-net posts are straightened and the nets installed. The election of new BRCA board members is held, as is the luncheon for the installation of Garden Club officers. Boats are launched, and the musical tinkling of stays on metal masts increases and diminishes with each gust of wind at the piers. A Bike-a-thon benefits the Cystic Fibrosis Foundation, and Little League batting practice begins. The Spring Dinner Dance is held beside a moonlit bay.

Fig. 22. Signs of warm weather—catboats and catamarans on Bay Ridge beaches, 1986

Fig. 23. Sailboat snugly moored at BRCA pier in Lake Ogleton, 1985

Summer

The bay is once again a sailor's paradise, and beaches are alive with people, boats, umbrellas, sand toys, inner tubes, and floats. Teenage slalom skiers convert the lake into a miniature Cypress Gardens. Special T-shirts are designed for runners attending the First Annual Bay Ridge Blue Heron Run (1985), and June weather inspires a mammoth community yard sale. Bay Ridge Bulldog baseball uniforms hang to dry on backyard clotheslines next to Bay Ridge Marlin sweatshirts and red racing swimsuits emblazoned with the coveted team patch. Honking, open convertibles return on summer evenings laden with cheering, dusty, grass-stained Little Leaguers with Slurpees in hand or with wet-headed swimmers holding soggy towels, Visine, and half-used boxes of Jell-O. The *Bay Ridge Newsletter* faithfully reports all game and meet results and team statistics.

Bay Ridge Junior Players hold tryouts and begin rehearsals for "Sleeping Beauty," "Rumplestiltskin," "Another Cinderella," or "Five Chinese Brothers," themselves in charge of script adaptation, songs, choreography, direction, and production for the two performances, which annually prove a highlight of the summer

Jamboree. Teenagers and children complete the Upshur Avenue steps down the cliffside to the beach. Girl Scouts, busy with a Paper-Pickup Project, collect thirty-thousand pounds of paper for recycling between March and July 1971.

As Fourth of July approaches, floats are constructed, costumes prepared, and bikes decorated, just as in years past:

> August 1973: The 1973 Fourth of July Celebration ... was held on a typically hot, sunny day, with just the hint of an off-shore breeze to wave the flags lining the Parade route.
>
> The festivities began with the morning softball games. The Mother and Daughter game, with Pat Dove in charge, was won this year by the daughters. The mothers were so badly beaten that the score could not be mentioned. Skeeter Deale ran the Father and Son ball game, with the fathers winning and the sons complaining.
>
> The highlight of the day is, of course, the Parade—this year coordinated by Jane and Bill Hoveland. The decorated cars, bikes, trikes, wagons, floats, skits, and musical units assembled at 1:00 at Maggio's corner to proceed down Bay Drive to River Drive Beach where the Beach Events were subsequently held. Here, too, is the site of the Bake Sale, and food and coke stands, the proceeds of which go to support the Swim Program.
>
> Many thanks to the Parade Judges . . . . Miss Marlin of 1973 is Beth Shrader.
>
> Bells, in support of the national project, "Let Freedom Ring," were rung for the specified 5 minutes at 2:00 under the direction of Cecil Martin!
>
> Following the Parade, refreshments and socializing, the Beach Events began. . . . Those with energy left to expend competed in running, swimming, sailing, 3-legged and sack races; not to mention the hilarious greased watermelon/water competition and the Egg-Toss.

The blue crab becomes plentiful in August and chicken-neckers crab from the piers, jetties, and boats while others run trotlines

Fig. 24. "Spirit of '76" unit with fife, drum, and flag in parade, July 4, 1971

Fig. 25. Crab-catching cooperation, 1972

with salted eel for bait. It is no trick at all to scoop crabs by the dozens from jetty pilings—if one gets there first. By evening the scent of Old Bay Seasoning wafts from open kitchen windows, followed by the tapping of crab mallets, punctuating front porch crab feasts. At the community crab feast of August 1979, "ninety-one dozen delicious crabs" are consumed.

Summer winds down with end-of-season events. The Bulldogs celebrate the conclusion of another exciting season of baseball with a swim party and barbecue supper at the home of their coach and:

> August 1973: The swim team finished the racing year with a beach party! Coach Maxine Orndorff, was greeted on her arrival with a spontaneous rousing cheer and was then promptly tossed in the Bay. . . . Swimmers selected their team pictures, enjoyed a hot-dog roast, were presented with a special Bay Ridge Marlin cake, and left with the happy prospect of sleeping late in the mornings for the rest of the summer.

The Jamboree, featuring play performances, a raffle, rides, bingo, dancing, and booths for baked goods, white elephants, garden items, stuffed animals, dippy duck, ball toss, Bay Ridge T-shirts and bags, candy, and various foods and beverages, proves to be another success.

> Autumn 1975: A large crowd was present from the arrival of the ponies and the fire engine to the last spin of the Big Six Wheel! To those who assisted in the planning, repairing, cake baking, booth-manning and general operation of the JAMBOREE, the association thanks you! It is well-worth mentioning that once again many teenagers and older children enthusiastically participated in the hard work involved.

Fig. 26. Summer, 1974

Fig. 27. A gusty wind for sailboarding—popular watersport of the eighties, 1980

All in all, 44 families contributed time and help. Hundreds of others helped by attending. The Results?! A truly good time was had by all! Marcia Outerbridge reports a net profit of $2,783.62!

The summer closes with a potluck picnic and country music concert.

Autumn 1975: Picnic baskets and bright checkered tablecloths were spread on the Club House lawn at sunset. . . . Bay Ridge families listened to, sang along with, and thoroughly enjoyed the music of a blue-grass group as well as the tender songs (many of them original) of Michael Kinder of Bay Drive. No one enjoyed the concert more than the young children who kept time with the music, dancing beside the lake with balloons held high in the evening breeze.

Fig. 28. The fishing lesson. The freighter in the background lay at anchor awaiting dockage in Baltimore harbor, 1985.

Fig. 29. The great blue heron, a fishing expert in his own right, poised for action on a tall piling, 1984

Fig. 30. Overleaf, Aerial view of Bay Ridge facing south, June 1980

Autumn

Fishermen return to Tolly Point for rockfish (until 1985) and "blues." The Brownie Scouts plant a bushel of daffodils at the corner of East Lake Drive and Farragut Road, and young boys in shoulder pads and helmets bike to PAL Park for afternoon football practice. The Neighbor-to-Neighbor Aid Group plans ways and means of providing transportation and help for the sick and housebound. The annual oyster roast is held on clubhouse grounds, with oysters steamed and fried, Chincoteagues on the halfshell, fried clams, homemade potato salad, and coleslaw. The Garden Club plants Cherokee Princess and Cloud Nine dogwood along Farragut Road and sets a formal table, under the direction of Catherine Faulds, for the October Wine and Cheese Party to welcome new and old residents.

For Halloween, teenagers transform the clubhouse into an intricately designed Haunted House.

> Winter 1977: The idea was the brainchild of artistically talented David Feiten, teenager [now with Walt Disney Productions], who, with help from members of the Outing Club, created, constructed, and operated his fantastic monsters, all molded from clay and plaster. The Clubhouse was a maze of scary witches, spiders, ghosts and lizards! Through word-of-mouth advertising alone, more than 750 children and adults paid to visit the Haunted House in three nights of operation!

In other years Girl Scouts or parents hold Halloween costume parties for young children at the clubhouse, complete with pumpkin-carving contest, ghost stories, songs, and refreshments.

On a November Saturday, residents meet at Tolly Point to walk the Bay Ridge Commons and record the event for Land Use Day. The year comes full circle with these words from the "History Corner" of the Autumn 1976 newsletter:

> Bay Ridge 1976 ... in autumn ... white clouds, white sails against a blue bay, a blue sky ... sparkling blue on blue ... rich harvest moon or chill starlight ... far off geese honking ... the welcome return of canvasbacks, mallards, whistling swans to eel-grass wetlands, to our very shores ... crisp breezes heavily scented ... clematis vines and late honeysuckle on River Drive rocks, on Tolly Point cliffs ... bright red firethorn and golden trees ... return of the oyster tongers ... November skipjacks at dusk ... cattails by Lake Ogleton ... Indian summer haze and apples ... dark clouds, the sudden squall ... red and yellow leaf-strewn lawns ... chimney smoke at twilight ... and winter ... Few Bay Ridgers this autumn would disagree with Capt. John Smith's description of the Chesapeake written three centuries ago: "a faire Bay compassed but for the mouth with fruitful and delightsome land."

And so, too, this book has come full circle. Through all the seasons of the three hundred and eighty years since Capt. John Smith first explored the Chesapeake, as people past and present have lived beside her shores—in towns, on farms, or in small communities such as Bay Ridge—Smith's opinion of the bay country has held true:

a country that may have the prerogative over the most pleasant places knowne for large and pleasant navigable Rivers. Heaven and earth never agreed better to frame a place for man's habitation.

SOURCES

The authors' notes and materials used in the preparation of *Bay Ridge on the Chesapeake* have been placed in the Bay Ridge Collection, MdHR D 1710, in the Maryland State Archives and are available at the Maryland Hall of Records, Annapolis, Maryland.

The quotations from Capt. John Smith at the beginning and end of the book are from "The Sixt Voyage, 1606," *Travels and Works of Captain John Smith,* ed. Edward Arber, 2 vols. (Edinburgh: John Grant, 1910), 2:344, 359.

CHAPTER 1:

Chapter 1 is based on a title search of the Bay Ridge land, using land, court, and tax records at the Maryland State Archives and the Anne Arundel County Courthouse. Biographical information was obtained from the research files of the Legislative History Project at the Maryland Hall of Records, census records at the Hall of Records and the Maryland State Library, various court records at the Maryland Hall of Records and the Anne Arundel County Courthouse, the *Maryland Gazette,* and secondary sources listed below. The notes on Thomas Tolly's estate value are from the research files of Dr. Jean Russo, Research Director of Historic Annapolis, Inc.

Citations for quoted material are as follows: Thomas Tolly's title: Patents, Liber SD#A, folio 319; Tolly's inventory: Testamentary Papers, Box 2, folder 11; John Andrews' title: Anne Arundel County Land Records, Liber RD#2, folio 425; Henry Margaret Ogle's opinion of Lafayette: McWilliams and Radoff, "Annapolis Meets the Crisis" (see below), page 423; Benjamin Ogle's comment on intruders: Shirley Baltz, *A Chronicle of Belair* (see below), page 56; description of houses on Tolly Point, 1798: 1798 Federal Direct Tax, Anne Arundel County, (MdHR M423); resurvey of Ogleton: Patents, Liber IB&GGB#H, folio 516; Benjamin Ogle's obituary: *Maryland Gazette,* July 21, 1809; sale of Ogleton: *Maryland Gazette,* September 21, 1815; Anna Key Steele's reminiscences: Anna Key Bartow Cumyn, *The Bartow Family: A Genealogy* (see below), pages 148–50. All sources cited are located at the Maryland Hall of Records.

The following books and articles contain helpful information on families, events, or the general history of the period:

Baldwin, Jane, ed. *The Maryland Calendar of Wills.* 8 vols. Baltimore: Wm. J. C. Dulany Co., 1901, Kohn and Pollock, 1906–28.

Baltz, Shirley V. *A Chronicle of Belair.* Bowie, Md.: Bowie Heritage Committee, 1984.

———."The Chronicle of Belair." In *Belle Air in Bowie.* Bowie, Md.: Bowie American Revolution Bicentennial Committee, 1977.

Barnes, Robert, comp. *Maryland Marriages, 1634–1777.* Baltimore: Genealogical Publishing Co., 1978.

Browne, William Hand, ed. *Archives of Maryland.* Vol. 1. Baltimore: Maryland Historical Society, 1883.

Cordell, Eugene Fauntleroy. *The Medical Annals of Maryland.* Baltimore: Medical and Chirurgical Faculty of the State of Maryland, 1903.

Cumyn, Anna Key Bartow, comp. *The Bartow Family: A Genealogy.* Montreal: Privately printed, 1984.

Duncan, Louis C. *Medical Men in the American Revolution, 1775–1783.* Carlisle, Pa: Medical Field Service School, 1931.

McIntire, Robert Harry. *Annapolis Maryland Families.* Baltimore: Gateway Press, 1980.

McWilliams, Jane W. and Morris L. Radoff. "Annapolis Meets the Crisis." In *Chesapeake Bay in the American Revolution,* edited by Ernest M. Eller. Centreville, Md.: Tidewater Publishers, 1981.

Moss, James E. *Providence, Ye Lost Towne at Severn in Mary Land.* Washington, D.C.: Privately printed, 1976.

Papenfuse, Edward C., and Joseph M. Coale III. *The Hammond-Harwood House Atlas of Historical Maps of Maryland, 1608–1908.* Baltimore: Johns Hopkins University Press, 1982.

Papenfuse, Edward C.; Alan F. Day; David W. Jordan; and Gregory A. Stiverson, eds. *A Biographical Dictionary of the Maryland Legislature, 1635–1789.* 2 vols. Baltimore: Johns Hopkins University Press, 1979, 1985.

Ridgely, Helen W. *Historic Graves of Maryland and the District of Columbia.* New York: Grafton Press, 1908.

Scharf, J. Thomas. *History of Maryland.* 3 vols. 1897. Reprint. Hatboro, Pa.: Tradition Press, 1967.

Shomette, Donald G. *Pirates on the Chesapeake.* Centreville, Md.: Tidewater Publishers, 1985.

Skordas, Gust, ed. *The Early Settlers of Maryland.* Baltimore: Genealogical Publishing Co., 1968.

CHAPTER 2

Chapter 2 is based on land, court, assessment, and corporation records at the Maryland Hall of Records and the Anne Arundel County Courthouse. Specific quoted material may be found in John E. Merriken, "This Was Bay Ridge" (see below), pages 30–36; and in the Annapolis *Evening Capital,* May 14, 1886–March 4, 1918, and the Annapolis *Maryland Republican,* January 4, 1879–September 8, 1883, for the dates given in the text. Both newspapers are available on microfilm at the Maryland Hall of Records.

Other helpful sources include:

Burgess, Robert H., and H. Graham Wood. *Steamboats out of Baltimore.* Cambridge, Md.: Tidewater Publishers, 1968.

"Chesapeake Chautauqua." *Book of the Royal Blue* 3, no. 9 (June 1900).

McIntire, Robert Harry. *Annapolis Maryland Families.* Baltimore: Gateway Press, 1980.

Merriken, John E. "Annapolis and Elkridge." *National Railway Historical Society Bulletin* 38, no. 6 (1973): 16–25.

———. "This Was Bay Ridge." *The Bulletin, National Railway Historical Society* 46, no. 5 (1981):30–36.

White, Clarence Marbury, Sr., and Evangeline Kaiser White. *The Years Between.* New York: Exposition Press, 1957.

CHAPTER 3

Most of the information in Chapter 3 is from the authors' interviews with persons already acknowledged, from personal knowledge, or from the minutes, papers, and correspondence of the Bay Ridge Civic Association, 1927–65. The reminiscences of Gloryanne Baur Sandrey and Jane Anderson O'Meara are extracted from their unpublished manuscripts in the authors' possession. Other quotations are from the *Washington Herald,* May 25, 1910 (courtesy John E. Merriken); the Annapolis *Evening Capital,* August 24, 1933; Turbit H. Slaughter, "Shore Erosion Control in Tidewater Maryland," *Journal of the Washington Academy of Sciences* May 1967, page 117; *Bay Ridge Review,* August 1945; the Bay Ridge *Observer,* March 1938.

Additional manuscript sources include the papers of the U.S. Department of State, May–September 1954, at the National Archives, Washington, D.C.; land and court records of Anne Arundel County at the Anne Arundel County Courthouse; Sanborn Map Company, Fire Insurance Maps, Bay Ridge, 1930, 1959, at the Maryland Hall of Records; and the private papers of James B. Wilson in the authors' possession.

Published materials consulted for this chapter include the Annapolis *Evening Capital,* 1918, 1927, 1933; Baltimore *Sunday Sun Magazine,* May 24, 1953; *Bay Ridge Review,* June–Christmas 1945; the Bay Ridge *Observer,* November 1937, March 1938; and Joseph Browne, *From Sotweed to Suburbia* (Baltimore: Gateway Press, 1985).

CHAPTER 4

Again, much information in Chapter 4 comes from interviews and the authors' personal knowledge as well as the minutes, papers, and correspondence of the Bay Ridge Civic Association, 1960–85. Quoted material is from the *Bay Ridge Newsletter,* 1967–85, for the dates given in the text; from the personal papers of L. Noel Patterson, Jr.; from the *Bay Ridge Directory,* 1985; and from Kathy Schmick, "Bay Ridge to Follow Building Rules," Annapolis *Evening Capital,* December 28, 1973, Anne Arundel Report section.

PHOTOGRAPH AND ILLUSTRATION CREDITS

Unless otherwise noted all photograph reproductions in this book and in the Bay Ridge Collection are the work of Paul Houston.

Figure numbers relate to the text. MdHR D 1710 numbers relate to the Bay Ridge Collection, Patterson & McWilliams, 1985, in the Maryland State Archives at the Maryland Hall of Records.

NON-CHAPTER PHOTOGRAPHS

Location	MdHR D 1710 No.	Source	Courtesy
cover front	284	MdHR G 82–375	Maryland State Archives, Special Collections
cover back			Capital Gazette Newspapers, Inc.
pages 2–3	411		Marion E. Warren
page 4	23	Family Album—Waddy-Rhodes	Jean Rhodes
page 9	380	Bay Ridge Realty Company poster, c. 1932	Joseph W. Hopkins, Jr.
page 11	381	Bay Ridge Realty Company poster, c. 1932	Joseph W. Hopkins, Jr.
page 16			Alex Castro
pages 20–21	183	Frank Leslie's *Illustrated Weekly*, February 8, 1879	Benjamin B. Wills, Jr.
pages 36–37	278	MdHR G 182–1092	Maryland State Archives, Special Collections
pages 104–105	329	Family Album—Roeth	Raymond Hayden
pages 158–159	400		Carol C. Patterson
page 202	412		Polli Barker Rodriguez
pages 206–207	185	Frank Leslie's *Illustrated Weekly*, February 8, 1879	Benjamin B. Wills, Jr.
page 208	173		Steamship Historical Society of America Collection, University of Baltimore

Photographers:
(Photographer's name given when known; figure numbers follow.)

Alex Castro 16
Keith Harvey cover back
Carol C. Patterson 158–159
Marion E. Warren 2–3

CHAPTER 1

Figure No.	MdHR D 1710 No.	Source	Courtesy
1	160	Patents, Liber 5, folio 266	Patricia C. Guida
2	158	Patents, Liber SD No. A, folio 319	Patricia C. Guida
3	317	Patents, Liber SD No. A, folio 319	Maryland State Archives
4	316	Patented Certificate #1104, Anne Arundel County	Maryland State Archives
5	253	U.S. Coast and Geodetic Survey Chart #385, 1884 (see also MdHR D 1710–348,1846)	National Archives
6	308		Philip Cumyn
7	249	MdHR G 1427–187	Maryland State Archives, Special Collections
8	309		Philip Cumyn
9	248	MdHR G 1427–297	Maryland State Archives, Special Collections
10	171	Anne Arundel County Land Records, Liber SH 28, folio 105	E. Aubrey Collison, Clerk of the Circuit Court, Anne Arundel County

Photographer:
Brian Merritt 6,8 (reproductions)

CHAPTER 2

Figure No.	MdHR D 1710 No.	Source	Courtesy
1	349		William P. Barnhart
2	104	Family Album—Vansant	James S. Vansant
3	39	Family Album—Barker	Charles Barker
4	254		National Archives
5	282	MdHR G 182–1087	Maryland State Archives, Special Collections
		See also MdHR D 1710–4 Family Album—Randall-Worthington	Margaret and Virginia Worthington
6	207		Maryland Historical Society
7	300		Benjamin B. Wills, Jr.
8	78	Smithsonian Institution Photo No. [41–553B]	Smithsonian Institution
9	87		Benjamin B. Wills, Jr.
10	236	*Evening Capital*, June 17, 1890	Maryland State Archives
11	235	*Evening Capital*, June 25, 1889	Maryland State Archives
12	227	*Evening Capital*, August 5, 1891	Maryland State Archives
13	234	*Evening Capital*, June 20, 1894	Maryland State Archives
14	237	*Evening Capital*, June 9, 1891	Maryland State Archives
15	240	*Evening Capital*, July 25, 1893	Maryland State Archives
16	107	Family Album—Vansant	James S. Vansant
17	19	Family Album—Brooks	Sandy Brooks Newark
18	238	*Evening Capital*, May 26, 1893	Maryland State Archives
19	12	Family Album—Brooks	Sandy Brooks Newark
20	65	Family Album—Randall-Worthington	Margaret and Virginia Worthington
21	64	Family Album—Randall-Worthington	Margaret and Virginia Worthington
22	179		Steamship Historical Society of America Collection, University of Baltimore
23	181		Steamship Historical Society of America Collection, University of Baltimore
24	288	MdHR G 1477–5847	Maryland State Archives, Special Collections
25	177		Steamship Historical Society of America Collection, University of Baltimore
26	180		Steamship Historical Society of America Collection, University of Baltimore
27	182		Steamship Historical Society of America Collection, University of Baltimore
28	192	Corneal J. Mack Private Collection	C. John Mack and Marie Leffingwell
29	283	MdHR G 182–1087	Maryland State Archives, Special Collections
30	286	MdHR G 182–777	Maryland State Archives, Special Collections
31	218		Eugene H. Sloane
32	265	Anne Arundel County Plat Book A, n.p.	E. Aubrey Collison, Clerk of the Circuit Court, Anne Arundel County
33	280	MdHR G 182–1091	Maryland State Archives, Special Collections
34	279	MdHR G 182–109	Maryland State Archives, Special Collections
35	224	*Book of the Royal Blue*, June 1900	Enoch Pratt Free Library and Chessie System Railroads
36	242	*Evening Capital*, June 4, 1896	Maryland State Archives
37	223	*Book of the Royal Blue*, June 1900	Enoch Pratt Free Library and Chessie System Railroads
38	246	*Evening Capital*, June 27, 1901	Maryland State Archives
39	245	*Evening Capital*, June 27, 1901	Maryland State Archives
40	206		L. Noel Patterson
41	105	Family Album—Vansant	James S. Vansant

42	86	J. E. Merriken Private Collection	John E. Merriken
43	84	J. E. Merriken Private Collection	John E. Merriken
44	83	J. E. Merriken Private Collection	John E. Merriken
45	89		Vesta Tombaugh
46	231	*Evening Capital*, July 17, 1885	Maryland State Archives
47	225	*The Baltimore Sun*, March 8, 1937	Enoch Pratt Free Library and *The Baltimore Sun*
48	228	*Evening Capital*, August 27, 1889	Maryland State Archives
49	269		James C. Schryver
50	267		L. Noel Patterson
51	277	MdHR G 182–1086	Maryland State Archives, Special Collections
52	90		Vesta Tombaugh
53	81	Family Album—Riley	Annie Riley Smith
54	289	Found offshore in low tide of 1974 and in excavations at foot of Mayo Avenue, Fall, 1975	L. Noel Patterson and Strohecker Corporation.
55	106	Family Album—Vansant	James S. Vansant
56	25	Family Album—Brooks	Sandy Brooks Newark
57	226		Steamship Historical Society of America Collection, University of Baltimore
58	233	*Evening Capital*, July 2, 1885	Maryland State Archives
59	287	MdHR G 1477–5848	Maryland State Archives, Special Collections
60	176		Steamship Historical Society of America Collection, University of Baltimore
61	175		Steamship Historical Society of America Collection, University of Baltimore
62	85	J. E. Merriken Private Collection	John E. Merriken
63	285	MdHR G 182–782	Maryland State Archives, Special Collections
64	178		Steamship Historical Society of America Collection, University of Baltimore
65	174		Steamship Historical Society of America Collection, University of Baltimore
66	229	*Evening Capital*, August 27, 1889	Maryland State Archives
67	232	*Evening Capital*, July 11, 1888	Maryland State Archives
68	37	Family Album—Brooks	Sandy Brooks Newark
69	88	J. E. Merriken Private Collection	John E. Merriken
70	359	Bay Ridge Realty Company poster, reprint	Rhonda H. Robins
71	239	*Evening Capital*, July 21, 1893	Maryland State Archives
72	78	Family Album—Riley	Annie Riley Smith
73	3	Family Album—Randall-Worthington	Margaret and Virginia Worthington
74	10	Family Album—Brooks	Sandy Brooks Newark
75	244	*Evening Capital*, June 6, 1899	Maryland State Archives
76	79	(See also MdHR D 1710–80) Family Album—Riley	Annie Riley Smith
77	230	*Evening Capital*, June 19, 1899	Maryland State Archives
78	247	*Evening Capital*, June 27, 1901	Maryland State Archives
79	268		L. Noel Patterson
80	243	*Evening Capital*, June 22, 1903	Maryland State Archives
81	156	Bay Ridge *Observer*, 1937	Dorothea Kelly and Carola Grubbs

Photographers:
George R. Buffham 2
Howard Handford Hopkins 24, 59
L. Noel Patterson 40, 54
Perkins Photography, Baltimore, Md. 55
Margaret Taylor Randall 5, 20, 73
George W. Riley 53, 72, 76
Eugene H. Sloane 31
Marion E. Warren (reproduction) 48

CHAPTER 3

Figure No.	MdHR D 1710 No.	Source	Courtesy
1	62	Family Album—Brooks	Sandy Brooks Newark
2	26	Family Album—Brooks	Sandy Brooks Newark
3	312	Bay Ridge Realty Company business card	Bonnie Stumpf Belch, grandniece of Thomas R. Bond
4	310	Bay Ridge Realty Company business card	Bonnie Stumpf Belch
5	164	Bay Ridge Realty Company brochure	Sandy Brooks Newark
6	33	Family Album—Brooks	Sandy Brooks Newark
7	392		Polli Barker Rodriguez
8	60	Family Album—Abbott	Ed and Margaret Mason
9	61	Family Album—Abbott	Ed and Margaret Mason
10	366	Bay Ridge Realty Company poster, reprint	Rhonda H. Robins
11	2	Bay Ridge Realty Company plat	Jane W. McWilliams
12	1	Bay Ridge Improvement Company of Anne Arundel County plat	Judith C. Housley
13	9	Family Album—Brooks	Sandy Brooks Newark
14	163	Bay Ridge Realty Company brochure	Sandy Brooks Newark
15	169	Bay Ridge Realty Company brochure	Sandy Brooks Newark
16	315	Bay Ridge Realty Company print	Bonnie Stumpf Belch
17	153	Bay Ridge Realty Company poster	Harvey R. Butt, Sr.
18	172	H.G. Porter Private Collection	Christopher and Charlotte Rhines
19	324	Family Album—Roeth	Raymond Hayden
20	40	Family Album—Porter	Christopher and Charlotte Rhines
21	46	Family Album—Brooks	Sandy Brooks Newark
22	35	Family Album—Porter	Christopher and Charlotte Rhines
23	41	Family Album—Porter	Christopher and Charlotte Rhines
24	49	Family Album—Porter	Christopher and Charlotte Rhines
25	32	Family Album—Brooks	Sandy Brooks Newark
26	53	Family Album—Porter	Christopher and Charlotte Rhines
27	57	Family Album—Ervin	Adelaide Ervin
28	52	Family Album—Porter	Christopher and Charlotte Rhines
29	92	Family Album—Hollander	Richard A. Hollander
30	75	Family Album—Ervin	Caroline Ervin Josey
31	56	Family Album—Ervin	Adelaide Ervin
32	344	Family Album—Hollander	Stanley Hollander
33	383	Bay Ridge Realty Company poster	Joseph W. Hopkins, Jr.
34	211	Family Album—Baur	Gloryanne Baur Sandrey
35	365	Bay Ridge Realty Company poster, reprint	Rhonda H. Robins
36	361	Bay Ridge Realty Company poster, reprint	Rhonda H. Robins
37	326	Family Album—Roeth	Raymond Hayden
38	321 322	(composite) Family Album—Roeth	Raymond Hayden
39	126	Family Album—Reeser	Marvin Reeser
40	138	Family Album—Reeser	Marvin Reeser
41	141	Family Album—Reeser	Marvin Reeser
42	17	Family Album—Waddy-Rhodes	Jean Rhodes
43	325	Family Album—Roeth	Raymond Hayden
44	124	Family Album—Paulson	Margaret Paulson
45	22	Family Album—Waddy-Rhodes	Jean Rhodes
46	6	Family Album—Waddy-Rhodes	Jean Rhodes
47	29	Family Album—Waddy-Rhodes	Jean Rhodes
48	7	Family Album—Waddy-Rhodes	Jean Rhodes
49	20	Family Album—Waddy-Rhodes	Jean Rhodes
50	30	Family Album—Waddy-Rhodes	Jean Rhodes
51	24	Family Album—Waddy-Rhodes	Jean Rhodes
52	18	Family Album—Waddy-Rhodes	Jean Rhodes
53	5	Family Album—Waddy-Rhodes	Jean Rhodes

54	112	Family Album—Paulson	Margaret Paulson
55	116	Family Album—Paulson	Margaret Paulson
56	21	Family Album—Waddy-Rhodes	Jean Rhodes
57	263	Family Album—Hopkins	Joseph W. Hopkins, Jr.
58	131	Family Album—Reeser	Marvin Reeser
59	137	Family Album—Reeser	Marvin Reeser
60	140	Family Album—Reeser	Marvin Reeser
61	135, 136	(composite) Family Album—Reeser	Marvin Reeser
62	259	Family Album—Hopkins	Joseph W. Hopkins, Jr.
63	213	Family Album—Baur	Gloryanne Baur Sandrey
64	216	Family Album—Baur	Gloryanne Baur Sandrey
65	191	Bay Ridge Beach Collection	Benjamin B. Wills, Jr.
66	379	Hopkins Family Collection	Joseph W. Hopkins, Jr.
67	146	Family Album—Seaman	Jane W. McWilliams
68	369	Family Album—McLaine	Ruth McLaine
69	372	Family Album—McLaine	Ruth McLaine
70	307	Baltimore *Sunday Sun*, May 24, 1953, H.G. Porter Private Collection	Christopher and Charlotte Rhines
71	332	Family Album—Roeth	Raymond Hayden
72	142	Family Album—Seaman	Jane W. McWilliams
73	334	Family Album—Campbell	Bill Campbell
74	66	Family Album—Hollander	Mary Ann Hollander Wilson
75	193	Bay Ridge Realty Company Christmas card	Jean Rhodes
76	320	Family Album—Roeth	Raymond Hayden
77	121	Family Album—Paulson	Margaret Paulson
78	306	Bay Ridge Boating Squadron Certificate, Outerbridge Private Collection	Marcia McLaine Outerbridge
79	194	Bay Ridge Realty Company brochure	Jean Rhodes
80	339	Family Album—Campbell	Bill Campbell
81	74	Family Album—Josey	Caroline Ervin Josey

Photographers:

Landon Brooks 6
Atlantic Foto (copyright 1925) 18
Victoria Hollander 29
Joseph W. Hopkins, Jr. 57
Marvin Reeser 58, 59, 60, 61
Hayman Studio 66
Guy L. Seaman 67
Stu Whelan 73

CHAPTER 4

Figure No.	MdHR D 1710 No.	Courtesy
1	96	L. Noel Patterson
2	397	Carol C. Patterson
3	100	L. Noel Patterson
4	296	Steve Mason
5	195	L. Noel Patterson
6	378	L. Noel Patterson
7	355	L. Noel Patterson
8	217	Eugene H. Sloane
9	276	L. Noel Patterson
10	274	L. Noel Patterson
11	149	Jane W. McWilliams
12	292	L. Noel Patterson
13	295	L. Noel Patterson
14	290	L. Noel Patterson
15	199	Carol C. Patterson
16	301	Bay Ridge Civic Association
17	71	Caroline E. Josey
18	201	L. Noel Patterson
19	203	L. Noel Patterson
20	197	L. Noel Patterson
21	291	L. Noel Patterson
22	407	Carol C. Patterson
23	400	Carol C. Patterson
24	202	Judith C. Housley
25	93	L. Noel Patterson
26	101	Carol J. Hutchinson
27	97	L. Noel Patterson
28	250	Capital Gazette Newspapers, Inc.
29	251	Capital Gazette Newspapers, Inc.
30	297	Steve Mason

Photographers:

Keith Harvey 28, 29
Judith C. Housley 24
Carol J. Hutchinson 26
Steve Mason 4, 30

Jane W. McWilliams 11
Carol C. Patterson 2, 15, 22, 23
L. Noel Patterson 1, 3, 5, 6, 7, 9, 10, 12, 13, 14, 18, 19, 20, 21, 25, 27
Eugene H. Sloane 8

BAY RIDGE TODAY

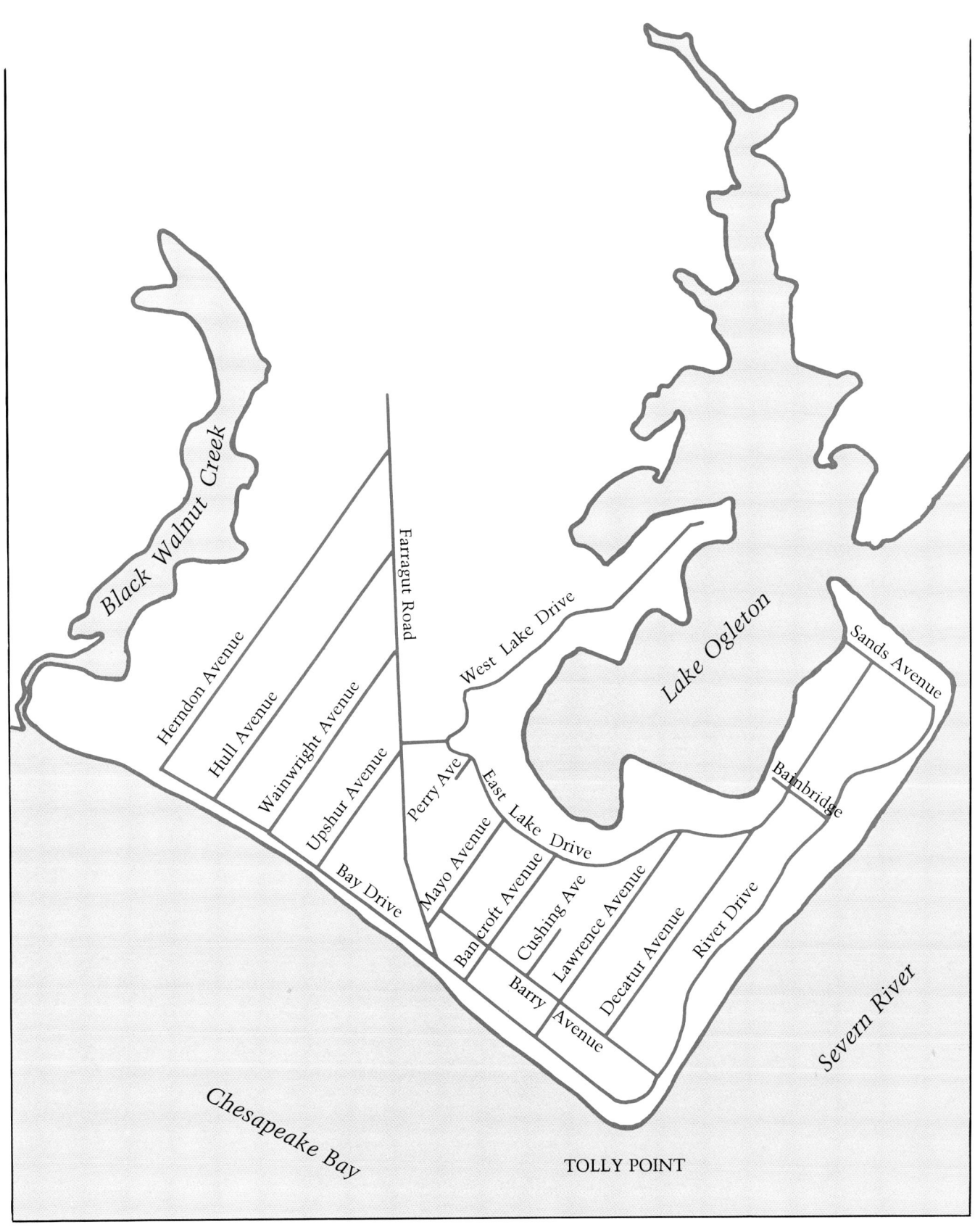

INDEX

Abbott, Edward, 81
Abbott, Pearl, 111
Abbott, Reese, 111, 112, 131
Agreement (patent), 30
Alma, Mike, 71
Alter, Glenn, 154
Alter, Philip, 147
Anchorage, 184
Anchors Aweigh, 61
Ancient Order of Foresters, 95
Ancient Order of Hibernians, 92
Ancker, Walter, 91
Anderson, John F., 76
Anderson, Katie, 91
Anderson, Col. Peter M., 125, 142
Anderson, William, 71
Andrews, John, 27, 28
Annapolis and Elkridge Railroad, 75
Annapolis-Bay Ridge Hiring and Livery Stables, 40
Annapolis Bicycle Agency, 100
Annapolis Cove, 28
Annapolis Day, 98
Annapolis Gun Club, 86
Annapolis Local Improvement Association, 80, 82
Annapolis Neck peninsula, 28, 31, 40, 171
Annapolis Neck Peninsula Federation, 168
Annapolis Presbyterian Sunday School picnic, 99
Annapolis Roads, 28, 119, 149, 152, 184
Annapolis Yacht Club, 160
Anne Arundel County Certificate of Appreciation, 173
Anne Arundel County Crime Prevention Program, 173
Anne Arundel County Fair, 65, 66, 80, 82, 83, 84, 85, 86
Anne Arundel County Grange, 82
Annexation issue, 170–171
Anti-Saloon League, 100
Ariel Boat Club, 92
Arundel-on-the-Bay, 28, 52, 98, 141, 92, 94, 100, 101, 149
Arundel-on-the-Bay Railroad, see Chesapeake and Columbia Street Railway
Association of Amateur Oarsmen, 67
Auer, Professor, 62, 87, 88
Austrian Military Band, 77, 79
Avery and Larus, 71

Bachman, George, 173
Back Creek, 41, 72
Back Creek Bridge, 42, 81
Bagley Path, 168
Baker, Miss, 94
Baker, Mr. (manager), 94, 95
Bainbridge Avenue, 168
Baldwin, Edward, 32
Baltimore and Annapolis Short Line Railroad, 42, 44, 76, 78
Baltimore and Eastern Shore Railroad, 50, 54
Baltimore and Eastern Shore Railroad Terminal, Bay Ridge, 50–54
Baltimore and Ohio Pattern-makers, 91
Baltimore and Ohio Railroad, 40, 80, 90, 96, 97, 103
Baltimore and Washington horticulturalists, 88
Baltimore Oddfellows, 92
Baltimore Wheelmen, 90
Bancroft Avenue, 111, 131
Bancroft Avenue (11), 155

Bancroft Avenue (16), 155
Barber, John T., 101
Barnhart, Dr. Grant S., 125, 127, 128, 131
Barry Avenue, 111, 129, 140
Barry Avenue (1), 117
Barry Avenue (11), 62–63, 102, 111, 128
Bartlett, Major George, 89
Bartow, Jacob Field, 33
Baseball, resort era, 65, 80
Basil, J. S. M., 83
Bateau races, 84
Baur, Gloryanne, see Sandrey, Gloryanne Baur
Baur, Helene Loffler, 142, 146
Baur House, 137
Baur, Ray, 145
Baur, Raymond, 142, 144, 145, 146
Baur's Beach, 142, 144
Bay City, 49
Bay Drive, 115, 129, 131, 137, 140, 149
Bay Drive (17), 126, 142, 152
Bay Drive (33), 126, 155
Bay Drive (43), 117
Bay Drive (51–53), 137, 140
Bay Drive (63), 136
Bay Drive (71), 130, 131
Bay Drive (73), 141, 167
Bay Drive (81), 111, 113
Bay Drive (83), 127
Bay Drive (87), 117
Bay Drive (89), 155
Bay Drive beach, 175
Bay Ridge, 48, 76, 77, 78, 79
Bay Ridge and Annapolis Railroad, 40, 44, 48, 72, 73, 76, 78, 79, 80, 107, 111, 119, 129
Bay Ridge Beach, 122, 137, 142–146, 152
Bay Ridge Boating Squadron, 154
Bay Ridge Bulldogs, 150, 180, 187, 189
Bay Ridge Civic Association (BRCA), 128, 130, 131, 140, 141, 142, 148, 150, 152, 153, 154, 155, 156, 157, 161–182, 162, 178, 179, 180, 181
Bay Ridge Civilian Defense Council, 147
Bay Ridge Clubhouse, 142, 151, 177, 178
Bay Ridge Commons, 154, 166, 168, 191
Bay Ridge community piers, 154
Bay Ridge Company, 34, 48, 67, 80, 85, 87
Bay Ridge Electric Company, 63
Bay Ridge Electric Park and Steamboat Company, 67, 96, 97
Bay Ridge Electric Railway, 64, 84, 97
Bay Ridge Estates, 117
Bay Ridge Hotel (modern), 110, 137, 142, 145
Bay Ridge Hotel (Victorian), 42, 44, 52, 54–60, 67, 75, 76, 94, 100, 102, 103, 111, china, 175
Bay Ridge Improvement and Transportation Company, 67, 73
Bay Ridge Improvement Company, 91, 97, 114
Bay Ridge Inn, 42, 110, 142, 146, 169, 180; see also Bay Ridge Hotel (modern)
Bay Ridge Jamboree, 126, 152, 181, 189
Bay Ridge Junior Players, 180, 187
Bay Ridge Marlins, 187, 189
Bay Ridge Musical Day, 96

Bay Ridge Properties, Inc., 164, 165
Bay Ridge Realty Company, 108, 109, 110, 113, 114, 115, 117, 126, 129, 131, 138
Bay Ridge Re-Organization Committee, 91
Bay Ridge Shore Erosion Control District, 138, 176, 177
Bay Ridge Steamship Pier, 48, 49, 74, 78
Bay Shore Drive, 41, 42, 45, 66, 72, 80, 81, 87, 93, 95
Beach rights and land use, 166–168
Belair, 28, 29
Belvoir, 31
Bembe Beach, 136
Bergen Point, 48, 65, 72, 74, 75
Betty, 153
Bicycling, Victorian craze, 66, 92, 96
Bijou Opera Company, 63, 80
Bike-a-thon, 186
Black Walnut Creek, 24, 29, 30, 34, 55, 110, 144, 153, 157, 169, 170; see also Saughier's Creek
Black Walnut Creek Commission, 169, 170
Bladen, William, 27, 28
Bladen Street depot, 42
Blue Heron Run, Annual, 187
'Bombardment of Fort Sumter,' 85
Bond, B. F., 91
Bond, H. S., Jr., 91
Bond, Hugh L., 87
Bond, Thomas R., 113, 115, 117, 151
Bond, Prof. William, 71, 76, 81
Boswell, Thomas T., 113, 115
Brady, Martin, 81
Brandt, Jacob, Jr., 33, 34
Brashears, Dave, 150
Brighton and Bay Ridge Electric Railway, 93
Brighton Beach, 98, 112, 113, 114
Brighton Villa, 92, 101, 112
Britten, George H., 45
Brooks family, 107
Brooks, Landon, 30, 112, 115
Broomall, Clarence, W., 99
Brothers Weston, 88
Brown, Jas. H., 44, 73
Brown, William, 71
Brownie Scouts, 185, 186, 191
Brown-stocking Nine of Bay Ridge, 80
Buffham brothers, 91
Buffham, Ethel, 68, 102, 103, 111
Buffham, George R., 40, 61, 62, 63, 67, 100, 101, 102, 103, 111
Bugeye races, 84
Burtis, Capt. William H., 45, 46
Burton, W., 91

C & C Liquors, 149
Cake Walk, 90
Calef, Jennie, 73
Callahan, Bob, 150
Camden Station, 42
Camp Arnold, 75
Campbell, Mr., 40
Campbell, Mrs., 40
Campbell, Bill, 150
Campbell, Helen, 167
Campbell, Ralph, 150, 167
Campbell's pier, 136
Camp LeCompte, 83
Camp Parole camp-meeting, 94
Cape May and Delaware Navigation Company, 97
Carey, Mrs. George, 103
Carr, Katie, 94

Carvel Cottage, 62, 103, 110, 111, 117
Cat-hole Creek, 29, 30, 33, 97
Catholic Literary Society, 92
Cedar Crest Farm, 102
Cedar Grove (patent), 31
Celtic Club of Baltimore, 92
Chambers, Earl, 154
Chambers, Prof. 90
Championship Tub Race, 81
Chaney, R. G., 71
Chautauqua Beach, 98, 99, 100
Chautauqua Literary and Scientific Circle, 62, 98
Chelsie (patent), 30
Chesapeake and Columbia Street Railway, 54, 90
Chesapeake Chautauqua, 67, 98
Chesapeake Resort Company, 91
Chinck Point, 72
Christenson, Theodore, 128, 129, 140
Christian Endeavor Society, 100
Christmas activities, 148–149, 181–182
Civil War, 33
Civil War veterans, 65
Claiborne, see Bay City
Clan-na-Gael excursion, 96
Clark, Ernie, 150
Clark Path, 125, 168
Climate, 17
Columbia, 44, 48, 50, 52, 55, 82, 84, 88, 90, 93, 94, 96, 97; displayed in flowers, 90; post season hop, 89
Columbian ambassador, 155
Colvin, J. L., 80
Congress of Nations, 94
Corbessier, Prof. A. J., 81
Coulter, Ruth Violet, 98
Craig, Det. Jay B., 172
Crane, J. G., 91
Crime, 171–173
Cronin, Dr. L. Eugene, 165, 178
Crosby, O. T., 86
Crystal Social Club, 100, 101
Cub Scouts, 183, 186
Cummings, J., 100
Curry, J. H., 45
Cushard, Dr. William G., Sr., 125

Daisy Anchor, 89
Dancing pavilion, 62, 82, 98
Davis, Mary, 45
Daw, George, 115, 117, 127
DDT, 148
Deale, Emerson E., 176
Decatur Avenue, 125, 129, 149
Declaratory Judgement suit, 166; decree, 167
Defence, 29
DeKalb statue unveiling, 80
Dewey, Admiral George, 44
Dewey Drive, 34
Dickson, Wayne, 150
Disston, Hamilton, 71
District of Columbia National Guard, 88, 90; Sixth Battalion, 89
Dollar, Jim, 150
Donnelly, Horace J., Jr., 139
Dorsey, Mr., 94
Douw, Col. John, 147
Druid Hill Park mansion house, 71
Duckett, Warren, 164
Dulles, John Foster, 155
Durand, Elizabeth, 24
Durand, William, 23, 24, 25
Durham, Jerome, 72
Duvall, Louis, 30, 31
Earle, George T., 83
Earstan, W. H., 91

203

East Lake Drive, 125, 129, 131, 149
East Lake Drive (7), 135
East Lake Drive (136), 112
Eastport, 28, 136
Eastport peninsula, 29
Eden, Robert, 29
Eline, J. Frank, 88
Elks, Baltimore Lodge No. 7, 90
Elliott, Mrs., 45
Emerich, Professor, 71
Emma Giles, 48, 50, 98
Empire State, 48, 50, 76, 78
Engle, George, 115
Engles, Vincent, 183
Erdelatz, Eddie, 150
Erosion, 30, 136–140, 175–177, 186
Ervin, Adelaide D. (Mrs. Edward J.), 119, 122, 127, 128
Ervin, Edward J., 127
Ervin, Frank, 172, 178
Ervin family, 125
Evans, George F., 127
Excelsior, 48

Farragut Road, 111, 115, 129, 131, 139, 140, 157
Farragut Road (64), 157
Fashions, 72, 74, 74, 91, 119, 127
Faulds, Catherine, 191
Fauna, see wildlife
Federal Rivers and Harbors Act of 1945, 153
Feiten, David, 191
Fifth Regiment Band, 71, 90
Finkle, Blanch, 69, 97
Fires, major, 67, 79, 102–103, 111
Fireworks, see Pyrotechnical displays and dramas
Flora, 17
Football, 150
Fort, Samuel, 88
Fourth Battalion Infantry Field Band, 88
Fourth of July events, modern, 131–132, 181, 182; resort, 72, 93, 96–77
Fourth Regiment Band and Field Music, 90
Fourth Regiment Maryland National Guard, 90
Fowey, 29
Fowler, Edwin, 147
Fowler, Sinclair, 125
Fowler family, 125
Frazier, Officer, 79
Frederick Rifles, 83, 92, 94, 95
Fulton, George, 157

Gable, Mr., 77
Gadd, Mr., 93
Garden Club, 179–182, 185
Gardiner, Lottie, 99
Garrett, Robert, 80
Garrish, Charles, 165
Gates, Buddy, 154
Gates, Mattie, 110, 156
Gauder and Hamm (scullers), 77
Gay Nineties, 39
Geographical data, 17
Geraci, Frank, 81
German Village, 96, 98
Gillis, Ezekial, 28
Girl Scouts, 149, 183, 185, 186, 187, 191
Glavis, Dr. G. O., 71
Gloth, Marjorie, 131
Godfried, Mr., 40
Goodman, Bessie, 45
Goodman, Robert, 45
Goodman, Roy, 45
Goodwin, Bertha, 91
Goodwin, John, 76
Governor's Guards, 83
Grand Army Day, 72, 95
Grand Army of the Republic, 65–66, 75, 95
Grand Jubilee Concert, 85
Grant, U. S., commemoration, 75

Great Music Festival, 83
Great Southern Band, 90
Great United German Saengerfest Association of Baltimore, 83
Greenbury Point, 23, 29, 147; lighthouse, 94
Greenfield, Mrs. Florence, 167
Grollman, Arthur, 94
Grubbs, Carola (Mrs. Walton), 165

Hackett's Point, 29
Hall, Ernie, 150
Hardesty, Phoebe, 69, 97
Harmon, Bill, 150
Harris, Elizabeth, 24
Hartge, Capt. Emil, 89
Hatchl, Bill, 170
Hebbard, George, 149
Hebbard, Jean, 149
Heptosophs, 95
Herndon Avenue, 148, 156, 157
Hewett, James C., 71
Higgins, Julia, 45
Highland Beach, 55, 144
Hill, Henrietta Margaret, see Ogle, Henrietta Margaret Hill
Hill, Henry, 27
Hill, J. M., 77
Hill, Joseph, 27, 28
Hill, Richard, 24, 25, 26, 27, 28
Hillsmere, 28
Hite, D. M., 71
H. L. Baya, 48
Holland, Don, 150
Hollander, Charles Stanley, 122, 163, 164, 168
Hollander, Mary Ann, see Wilson, Mary Ann Hollander
Hollander, Richard A., 122
Hollander, Ronnie, 125
Hollander, Victoria, 125
Holliday, Thos., 79
Homemakers Club, 154
Hooper, M. E. S., 91
Hopeland Band, 95
Hopkins, G. M. (atlas), 34
Hopkins, Joseph W., Jr., 107
Hopkins, Joseph W., Sr., 141, 147, 150, 155
Horn Point, 29, 30, 31
Horse races, 84
Hoveland, Bill, 188
Hoveland, Jane, 188
Howard Zouaves, 79, 83
Howe, Adm. Richard, 29
Howell's Creek, 24, 25, 26, 27, 29, 30; see also Lake Ogleton
Huguely, George, 152, 153
Hull Avenue, 148, 157
Hurley, Thomas J., 73
Hurricane Hazel, 136, 140
Hurricane of 1933, 136–138, 144, 151

Iceboats, 73
Ida, 48, 74
Improved Order of B'Nai B'rith, 92
Incorporation, 140–141
Indian Landing, 98
Indians, 23
Innes, Frederick N., 81, 83, 85
Ireland, John, 73
Iroquois Cycle Club of Baltimore, 90
Isabella's Farm (patent), 27, 28, 29, 30
Italian cruisers off Bay Ridge, 92
Jack, Beverly, 172
James's Cove, 29
James's Hill (patent), 27, 28, 30
Jane Moseley, 48, 73, 74, 80
Jenkins, Ellen, 46, 93
Jickling, C., 81
John A. Bemis, 48
Johnson, Mr., 172
Jolly's Waxworks, 61

Jones, George W., 83
Jones, James M., 178
Josey, Caroline Ervin, 119, 166
Josey, Stephen, 157
Jousting tournaments, 71, 81
Judson, H., 87
Juvenile Corps de Ballet of Baltimore, 85, 87

Kahl, George, 115, 117, 128
Kass, Garfield I., 130, 152, 168
Kass Park, 34, 168
Kass Realty Corporation, 130, 152, 156, 167
Kelly, Capt. R. T., 73
Kettler, Clarence, Jr., 44, 153
Kettler, Clarence, Sr., 122
Kettler, Clifford E., 115
Key, Elizabeth, see Maynadier, Elizabeth Key
Key, Francis Scott, 32
Key, Maria Lloyd, see Steele, Maria Lloyd Key
Keyes, Herbert A., 102, 103, 119
Kidd, Capt., 113
Kinder, Michael, 190
Kirby, Capt. Isaac, 97
Kirk, William, 166

LaChappelle's Grocery, 149
Lagen, C. A., 91
Lake Drive, 27
Lake Ogleton, 24, 34, 41, 63–65, 67, 68, 90, 91, 94, 97, 132, 134, 137, 142, 151–154, 166, 176, 179, 184, 187; see also Cat-Hole Creek; Howell's Creek
Lake Ogleton Bridge, 42
Lamont, Midshipman W. D., 110
Land Use Day, 168, 181, 191
Laurel Guards, 92
Lawrence Avenue, 111, 129, 149
League of American Wheelman, 66, 91
Leatherburys (Galesville boatbuilders), 135
LeBron, Mollie, 71
Levy, Jules, 71, 72, 84
Loffler, Andrew, 142
Loffler, Elsa, 129, 145, 146
Loffler family, 126
Lord, C. K., 91
Lord Baltimore Society, 81
Louise, 45
Lowe, Prof. Marshall, 99
Low tide, April 1974, 54, 173
Lustron house, 157
Lutheran Day, 99

Mack, Helen, 185
Maffail, 87
Maloney, Charles P., 140
Maple Fishing Club, 100
Martenet, Simon J. (map), 32, 34
Martin, C. R., 96
Martin, C. W., 94
Martin, Cecil, 188
Martin, Mamie, 69
Martin, Mary, 97
Martin, Roy, 69
Martin, Steve, 150
Martin, Willie, 97
Martin, William, 97
Mary A. D. Night, 73
Maryland Board of Public Works, 170
Maryland Christian Endeavor Union, 95
Maryland Department of Natural Resources, 176
Maryland Electric Railways Company, 107
Maryland State Teachers Convention, 98
Maryland Steamboat Wharf, 45
May Brown, 100
Maynadier, Elizabeth Key, 31, 32
Maynadier, Henry, 31, 32

Mayo Avenue, 111, 131, 139, 147, 168
Mayo Avenue (15), 115
Mayo Avenue beach, 136, 137, 138, 146, 176
McCoy, Marion, 165
McDowell's pier, 54, 136, 138
McEllin, Dan, 125, 127
McKenna, John J., 155, 156
McKinley, William, 61, 62, 96
McLaine, Marcia, see Outerbridge, Marcia McLaine
McLaine, Ruth, 125
McLaine, Warren, Jr., 147
McLean, Dr. C. C., 98, 99
McNew, Dan, 172
McNulty, Prof. Thomas F., 93
McVay, Lt. Comdr. C. E., 110
Melvin, Mr., 93
Melvin, Judge Ridgely P., 167
Meneely, Henry T., Jr., 176
Merriken, Lt. Col. John E., 44, 50
Merriken, Zach., 97
Merrimac, 83, 84
Methodist Episcopal Day, 99
Mexican Band, 74
Meyer, H. F., 93
Mezzick, Mr., 88
Middle Neck Hundred, 24
Military Congress of All Nations, 83
Military Day, 64, 90
Military encampments, 72, 74, 79, 83, 89, 90
Mischief, 71
Miss Bay Ridge, 119
Mitchell, Annie, 69, 97
Mitchell, William, 69, 97
Monitor, 83, 84
Moore, Alice, 28
Moore, W. G., 75
Mosquito control, 148
Moss, Judge Robert, 117, 125
Murry, H. M., 81
Museum of Natural Sciences and Curiosities, 61
Musgrove, C. G., 93
Musgrove, Col., 98
Musgrove, Thos. G., 91, 93
Musterman, A., 77
Mystery, 98

National Chautauqua Assembly, 64, 98–99
National Rifles, 72
Naval Academy Photography Studio, 62
Naval Association of Amateur Oarsmen, 85
Neal, William, 90
Neighbor-to-Neighbor Aid Group, 191
Neptune Boat Club, 92
Newark, Sandy Brooks, 46, 86
New Worcester (patent), 24

Ocean City, 49, 87
Odenwald, Herman G., 113, 115
Ogle, Benjamin, 28, 29, 30
Ogle, Henrietta 'Henry' Margaret Hill, 28, 29, 30, 31
Ogle, Samuel, 28
Ogleton (patent), 29, 30, 31, 32, 34
Old Crooked Neck, 183
O'Meara, Jane Anderson, 126, 142
Open-space land, 166–167
Opera House, 77, 79, 83, 87
Operation Identification program, 162, 172
Orient Camping Club, 101
Orndorff, Maxine, 189
Orrell, Charles B., 100
Osbourne, M. A., 71
Otter, 29
Outerbridge, Marcia McLaine (Mrs. Thomas), 147, 155, 165, 166, 170, 190

Oyster Fleet, review of, 89
Oyster Navy, 89

Parker Avenue, 168
Pascal, Robert, 173
Patuxent Gun Club, 86
Paul, Henry S., 91
Paulson, Dave, 150
Paulson, Ella, 147
Paulson, Freeman, 125
Paulson, Margaret, 135
Paulson, Peter, 125, 135
Paulson, Rolf, 135
Pawnee Bill's Wild West Show, 86
Pearce, Charles, 71
Pearce, W. B., 71
Peddleford, Miss, 87
Peninsula Athletic League (PAL), 181
Peninsula Athletic League Park, 191
Pennington, Major J. J., 96
Perry Avenue, 157
Philadelphia Yacht Club, 92
Philips, Mrs., 79
Phipps, Hon. Louis N., 141
Pirate treasure, 113–114
Police services, 77, 96, 128, 140, 141, 150, 172–173
Port Deposit, 48, 81
Porter, Henry G., 117, 121, 125, 148
Porter Path, 168
Potomac Steamboat Company, 48
Presbyterian Sunday School, 85
Providence, 23
Pyrotechnical displays, 71, 75, 76, 81, 83, 84, 85, 131
Pyrotechnical dramas, 65, 83–85

Quade, Mr., 64
Quakers, 24, 27
Quill, Thomas, 71
Quill, William, 71

Railroad ferry wharf, 50–54, 87
Ramza and Arnold, 88
Randall, Mr., 82
Randall, Alexander Burton, 93
Randall, Margaret Taylor, see Worthington, Margaret Taylor Randall
Raymond, Paul, 147
Real Estate and Improvement Company of Baltimore City, 114
Red Cross, 147
Redmond, Robert, 81
Red-stocking Nine of Baltimore, 80
Reeser, Marvin, 131
Reeser, William Earl, 131, 141, 147, 152, 153
Reeser family, 147
Reesers' store, 130, 131
Rehn, Mr., 93
Religious dissenters, 23, 24
Rennert, Robert, 101
Resort, balloon ascension, 94; bandstand, 61; baseball, 95; bathhouses, 62, 87; bathing suits, 90; bear pit, 63; boating accidents, 94; boxing exhibition, 92; camera obscura, 61; cycling races, 90, 91; electric lights, 79; exhibition swimming, 91; flying horses, 63; Fourth of July, 93, 96; gravity railroad, 63, 91; gardens, 88; grounds, 72, 74, 90; jousting tournament, 71; mammoth ferris wheel, 93; management companies, 67–68; minstrel entertainment, 94; post office, 96; pyrotechnical displays, 71, 75, 78, 81, 83, 84, 85; pyrotechnical dramas, 65; rowing regattas, 77, 79, 84, 85; special entertainments, 65–66; straw ride, 94; water toboggan slide, 93, 95; wargraph, 61, 96; weather, 92, 99; vaudeville, 64, 88, 96; zoological gardens, 63, 77, 78, 79; see also Bay Ridge Electric Railway; Bay Ridge Hotel (Victorian); Carvel Cottage; Dance Pavilion; Opera House; Restaurant pavilion (cafe)
Restaurant pavilion (cafe), 55–63
Revell, Sheriff, 96
Revolutionary War, 29, 147
Rhodes, David (Dusty), 131
Richardson, C. W., 76
Riley, Alva, 69, 97
Riley, Annie, see Smith, Annie Riley
Riley, Bessie, 69, 97
Riley, George, 69
Riley, George W., 69, 91, 97
Riley, Jennie F., 69, 97
Riley, John W., 69, 97
Ritterbush, Harry, 165
Rivers Chambers Band, 144
River Drive, 113, 115, 119, 122, 137, 138, 140, 149
River Drive (14), 121
River Drive (90), 105, 128, 149
River Drive (100), 149
River Drive (104), 125
River Drive (108), 117
River Drive (114), 117
River Drive (126), 183
River Drive beach, 118, 122, 128, 132, 147, 150, 170, 174, 177
Robinson, Mabel, 94
Rockfish catch, 73
Rodriguez, Polli Barker, 40
Roeth, Mary Irene, 147, 148, 149
Ross, Gen. W. E. W., 75
Round Bay, 98
Rowing regattas, 77, 79, 84, 85
Royal Arcanum Day, 91
Runyon, Jackie, 150
Russians, 145, 146, 155–156

St. Leo's Gymnasium Field Day, 95
St. Vincent's Male Orphan Asylum of Baltimore, 93
Samuel J. Pentz, 48, 74, 75, 77
Sandrey, Gloryanne Baur, 142, 144
Sands Avenue, 113, 129, 131, 154, 168
Saughier's Creek, 24, 25, 27; see also Black Walnut Creek
Saunders, Mr., 93
Savage, Rev. George, 46
Scheibe, Phillip, 164
Schley, Tom, 150
Schrader, Beth, 188
Schryer, Mr., 72
Schultz, Mr., 99
Scott, Elizabeth Ross, 31, 32
Severn, 98
Severn Boat Club, 92
Severn Cycle Club, 95
Severn River Association, 169
Sharp, Dolly, 135
Shores, Helen, 147
Shull, Thomas, 167
'Skull Hall,' 112
Smith, Annie Riley (Mrs. Earl A.), 69, 97
Smith, F. R., 71
Smith, Fred, 115, 147
Smith, Capt. John, 22, 23, 191, 192
Smith, Thomas W., 54, 101
Smouse, F. K., 100
Society of Friends, see Quakers
Sodality of St. Andrew's Church, 81
Sons of Veterans, James A. Garfield Camp No. 1, 75
Sousa, John Philip, 61
Soviet Embassy, 146, 155
Soviet Government Purchasing Commission, 146
Spa Creek, 67
Spa Creek Bridge, 42
Sprague Electric Railway, 86
Sprague system of motors, 63, 64
Steamboats to Bay Ridge, 45–54
Steele, Anna Key, 34
Steele, Frank Key, 34
Steele, Henry Maynadier, 32, 33
Steele mansion, 79
Steele, Maria Lloyd Key, 32, 33, 34
Stephens, Beth (Mrs. James), 186
Stereoptican lecture, 99
Stevens, Ed, 81
Stinchcomb, J., 45
Storms, major, 136–138, 140, 144, 151, 161, 175–176
Stoutenburg, Dr., 105
Strange, Jas., 81
Streets, dedication to county, 129, 141, 142
Sunday law, 88

Tarun, Wayne, 172
Tastet, Mrs. Waldo, 153
Tastet, Waldo, 153
Teemer and Courtney (scullers), 77, 79
Teen Outing Club, 180, 191
Telephones (Victorian), 72
Thames River, 48, 49
Thayer, Prof., 83
Theodore Weems, 40, 45, 48, 71, 80, 87
Thieme, Raymond G., 179
Thirteenth New York Regiment, 83
Thomas, 89
Thomas, Capt. John, 48
Thomas S. Morgan, 97
Thompson, Dennis C., 73
Thompson, Mary, 45
Tipaldi Bros., 81
Tockwogh, 48, 50
Tolly Point, 23, 25, 27, 29, 30, 31, 39, 40, 79, 108, 111, 138, 139, 147, 162, 168, 185, 191
Tolly Point Farm (The Farm), 28, 29, 31, 34
Tolly's Point (patent), 24, 25, 26, 27, 28, 29, 30, 33, 127
Tolly, Thomas, 23, 24, 25, 26
Tolly, Thomas, Jr., 24, 26
Toner, J. C., 71
Toulson, William, 25
Tred Avon, 48
Trew, Joseph B., 147
Tropical Storm Agnes, 175
Tropical Storm David, 175
Tropical Storm Juan, 175
Tryan, Edward K., 77
Turner, Theophilus, 113
Tydings, Thos., 81

Underhill, Col., 76
Union Veterans Corps of D. C., 72, 75
United Baptist Church, 95
United Presbyterian Church, 95
U. S. Army Corps of Engineers, 152
U. S. Department of State, 156
U. S. Merchant Marine, 146
U. S. Naval Academy, 110, 117, Post Graduate School, 147–148
U. S. Naval Academy Band, 61, 71, 72, 76, 77, 78, 79, 80, 85, 87, 88, 90, 97, 98–99
U. S. Post Office, 62
U. S. Power Squadron, 154
Upshur Avenue, 27, 111, 129, 141, 157

Upshur Avenue beach, 121, 122

Vansant, James H., 34, 40, 71, 72, 73, 76, 90, 93
Vansant, Mrs. James H., 72
Vansant, William H., 45
Vaudeville acts, 48, 88
Vick, Ashley, 173
Victor Haven, 119

Wainwright Avenue, 34, 125
Wainwright Avenue (6), 117
Walnut Drive, 157
Walton, Dr. H. R., 95
Ward, Herbert S., 141, 147
Warner, Dr. A. S., 82
War of 1812, 147
Washington, Baltimore and Annapolis Railroad, 42, 44
Washington Light Infantry, 72
Water-toboggan slides, 62
Watkins, Benj., 81
Watkins, G., 45
Watkins, Mrs. Benj., 81
Watson, Jessie, 149
Weaver, Dr. Clarence, 44
Webb, Charles, 82, 83, 84, 87, 88
Webb, Mrs. Charles, 87
Webster, Betsy, 46, 93
Weems Line, 40
Welch, Robert, 94
Welch, Thos., 81
Wellington, Henry, 63, 64, 95
Wells, Elijah, 45
Wesley Chapel M. E. Church, 83
West Lake Drive, 27, 33, 111, 155
White, Clarence M., 128
White, Tom, 171
Wildlife, 17–18, 148, 162, 183
Wiley, R., 71
Wills, B. B., 146
Wills, Benjamin B., Jr., 42, 146, 169, 170
Wilson, Albert Z., 110, 117, 156
Wilson, Eldeane, 131
Wilson, James B., 131, 150
Wilson, Mary Ann Hollander, 150
Withers Durand (patent), 24, 25, 26, 27, 28, 29, 30, 33, 34, 127
Withers, Samuel, 24, 25, 27
Withers, Samuel, Jr., 27, 28
Woman's Home and Foreign Missionary Societies of Washington and Baltimore, 99
Woolford, Mr., (manager), 94, 95
Woolford, W. S., 91
Worden Path, 155, 168
Worden Path case, 166
Workboat sailing races, 86
World War I, 106
World War II, 141, 142, 146, 147, 151, 152
Worthington, Dr. Joseph Muse, 82
Worthington, Margaret, 46
Worthington, Margaret Taylor Randall, 46, 52, 82, 93
Worthington, Virginia, 46
Wright's Band, 90, 92, 94
Wylie, Dr. Hamilton Boyd, 115, 128

Yellow String Band, 95
Young Catholic Friends Society, 95

Zaroubin, Giorgi N., 156
Ziegfield, Oliver C., 96
Zimmerman, Prof. Charles A., 61, 62, 63, 85, 87, 90
Zoning, 115, 140, 148, 155–156, 163–167

205

Oyster buy-boats and skiffs off Tolly Point, 1879

This book was designed by Alex and Caroline Castro, Hollowpress, Baltimore.
The type is set in Trump Medieval with Balmoral Titling, by Monotype Composition Company, Baltimore.
Printed by Collins Printing Company, Baltimore, on 80 lb. Warren's Lustrokote Enamel,
the book is published in 800 copies softcover and 1200 copies hardbound,
October 1986.